# War Crimes



This book is a concise and accessible introduction to the problem of war crimes in modern history, emphasizing the development of laws aimed at regulating the conduct of armed conflict developed from the 19th century to the present.

Bringing together multiple strands of recent research in history, political science, and law, the book starts with an overview of the attempts across the pre-modern world to regulate the initiation, conduct, and outcomes of war. It then presents a survey of the legal revolution of the 19th century when, amidst a global welter of colonial wars, the first body of formal codes and laws relating to distinguishing legal from criminal conduct in war was developed. Further chapters investigate failed but influential attempts to develop the laws of war in the post-World War I period and summarize the major landmarks in international law related to war crimes, such as the Hague conventions and the Nuremberg and Tokyo trials, as well as hundreds of lesser-known post-World War II trials in Europe and Asia. It also looks at the origins and debated significance of the Genocide Convention of 1948 and the 1949 Geneva Conventions, accounts for the acceleration worldwide of war crimes investigations and trials from the 1970s into the 2000s, and summarizes current thinking about international law and the rapidly changing nature of warfare worldwide as well as the memorialization of war crimes.

Including images, documents, a bibliography highlighting the most recent scholarship, a chronology, who's who, and a glossary, this is the perfect introduction for those wishing to understand the complex field or war crimes history and its politics.

**Steven P. Remy** is Professor of History at Brooklyn College and the Graduate Center of the City University of New York. His most recent publications include *The Malmedy Massacre: The War Crimes Trial Controversy* (2017) and *Adolf Hitler: A Reference Guide to His Life and Works* (2022).

## Introduction to the series

Each book in the Seminar Studies series provides a concise and reliable introduction to a wide range of complex historical events and debates, covering topics in British, European, US and world history from the medieval period to present day. Written by acknowledged experts and including supporting material such as extracts from historical documents, chronologies, glossaries, guides to key figures and further reading suggestions, Seminar Studies titles are essential reading for students of history.

Almost half a century after its launch, the series continues to introduce students to the problems involved in explaining the past, giving them the opportunity to grapple with historical documents and encouraging them to reach their own conclusions.

**Series Editors**
Mark Stoyle: mjs@soton.ac.uk
Gordon Martel: Gordon.Martel@unbc.ca

# War Crimes

## Law, Politics, & Armed Conflict in the Modern World

Steven P. Remy

Routledge
Taylor & Francis Group
LONDON AND NEW YORK

Designed cover image: Alamy: Brave Polish Jews stand in quiet defiance as the brutal liquidation of Warsaw Ghetto by Nazi Waffen SS and Wehrmacht troops takes place around them May 1943, P534Y7

First published 2023
by Routledge
4 Park Square, Milton Park, Abingdon, Oxon OX14 4RN

and by Routledge
605 Third Avenue, New York, NY 10158

*Routledge is an imprint of the Taylor & Francis Group, an informa business*



*British Library Cataloguing-in-Publication Data*
A catalogue record for this book is available from the British Library

ISBN: 978-0-367-63293-9 (hbk)
ISBN: 978-0-367-63292-2 (pbk)
ISBN: 978-1-003-11866-4 (ebk)

DOI: 10.4324/9781003118664

Typeset in Sabon
by Apex CoVantage, LLC

# Contents

# Figures

# Chronology

| | |
|---|---|
| **1856** | Paris declaration respecting maritime law |
| **1857** | Indian Mutiny (also known as the Sepoy Mutiny and the First War of Independence) |
| **1863** | "Lieber Code" adopted by the Union Army in the US Civil War; International Committee of the Red Cross founded |
| **1864** | Geneva Convention for the Amelioration of the Condition of the Wounded in Armies in the Field (the first of four Geneva Conventions) |
| **1868** | St. Petersburg Declaration Renouncing the Use in War of Certain Explosive Projectiles |
| **1873** | Institute for International Law founded in Ghent, Belgium |
| **1874** | Brussels Declaration |
| **1899** | Hague Convention adopted |
| **1904–5** | Russo-Japanese War |
| **1904–8** | Fighting between Herero rebels and German forces in German Southwest Africa (today Namibia) produces the 20th century's first genocide |
| **1906** | Convention for the Amelioration of the Condition of the Wounded and Sick in Armies in the Field in Geneva updates provisions of the 1864 Convention |
| **1907** | Second Hague Convention |
| **1914–8** | World War I |
| **1915–23** | Armenian genocide |
| **1917** | |
| *February* | The Russian Revolution begins |
| **1919** | |
| *June* | Versailles Treaty concluded |
| **1921** | War crimes trials in Leipzig, Germany |

| | |
|---|---|
| **1922** | Lausanne Treaty signed between Allies and Turkey; Permanent Court of International Justice founded |
| **1925** | |
| *June* | The **Protocol for the Prohibition of the Use in War of Asphyxiating, Poisonous or Other Gases and of Bacteriological Methods of Warfare signed** |
| *October* | Pact of Locarno signed |
| **1928** | |
| *27 August* | Pact of Paris (Kellogg-Briand Pact) signed |
| **1929** | Provisions of the 1907 Hague Convention regarding the treatment of POWs supplemented at the conference of the ICRC (and updated again in 1939) |
| **1931** | Japan invades Manchuria |
| **1935** | Italy invades Ethiopia |
| **1936–9** | Spanish Civil War |
| **1937** | Japan begins full-scale war against China |
| **1939** | |
| *September* | German and Soviet forces invade Poland |
| **1941** | |
| *June* | German forces invade the Soviet Union |
| *December* | The United States enters the war |
| **1941–5** | The Holocaust |
| **1942** | |
| *January* | The USSR, the UK, the US, and six governments in exile create Inter-Allied Commission on the Punishment of War Crimes |
| **1943** | |
| *October* | United National War Crimes Commission created |
| **1945** | |
| *May* | VE Day |
| *8 August* | London Agreement released |
| *14 August* | VJ Day |
| *October* | United Nations founded in San Francisco |
| *December* | Allied Control Council Law Number 10 promulgated |
| **1946** | |
| *December* | UN General Assembly affirmed provisions of the London Agreement as principles of international law |
| **1948** | |
| *September* | Genocide Convention adopted by the UN |
| *December* | UN adopts Universal Declaration of Human Rights |

| | |
|---|---|
| **1949** | |
| *August* | Geneva Convention adopted by the UN |
| **1945–6** | |
| *20 November–31 August* | IMT in Nuremberg |
| **1945–9** | Period of formal occupation of Germany |
| **1946–8** | |
| *April–November* | International Military Tribunal for the Far East |
| **1946–9** | |
| *December–April* | Nuremberg Military Tribunal |
| **1949** | |
| *December* | Communist forces in China prevail in civil war with nationalists |
| **1945–51** | Military tribunals for Japanese war criminals and collaborators held in Asia and Australia |
| **1950–3** | Korean War |
| **1954** | Hague Convention for the Protection of Cultural Property |
| **1955–75** | Vietnam War (known as the American War in Vietnam) |
| **1961** | |
| *April–December* | Adolf Eichmann tried in Jerusalem |
| *May* | Amnesty International founded in London |
| **1963–5** | |
| *December–August* | Trials of former Auschwitz camp personnel in Frankfurt, West Germany |
| **1972** | Swedish Prime Minister Olof Palme proposes making ecocide an international crime; Biological and Toxin Weapons Convention concluded |
| **1974** | First truth commission established in Uganda |
| **1975–9** | Cambodia ruled by the Khmer Rouge |
| **1977** | Additional Protocols to the 1949 Geneva Convention adopted |
| **1978** | Human Rights Watch founded |
| **1980** | UN Certain Conventional Weapons Convention |
| **1983** | National Commission on the Disappearance of Persons established in Argentina |
| **1991–2001** | Wars in the former Yugoslavia (Slovenia, 1991; Croatia, 1991–5; Bosnia and Herzegovina, 1992–5; Kosovo, 1998–9; Macedonia, 2001) |

| | |
|---|---|
| **1993** | |
| *January* | Convention on the Prohibition of the Development, Production, Stockpiling and Use of Chemical Weapons; |
| *May* | International Criminal Tribunal for the Former Yugoslavia (ICTY) established. Operates until 2017 |
| **1994** | Spring-summer: Rwandan genocide |
| *November* | International Criminal Tribunal for Rwanda (ICTR) established |
| **1995–2002** | Commission of Truth and Reconciliation operates in South Africa |
| **2001–12** | Gacaca courts operate in Rwanda |
| **1998** | |
| *July* | Rome Statute establishing the International Criminal Court (ICC) |
| **2000** | Women's International War Crimes Tribunal held in Tokyo |
| **2003** | |
| *February* | Genocide in Darfur begins; Extraordinary Chambers in the Courts of Cambodia (or the Cambodia Tribunal or Khmer Rouge Tribunal) established; ICC begins operating |
| **2008** | Montreux Document signed |
| **2011** | |
| *March* | Syrian civil war begins |
| *May* | Final conviction of John Demjanjuk in Germany; Commission for International Justice and Accountability (CIJA) founded |
| **2012** | |
| *April* | Charles Taylor convicted by UN Special Court for Sierra Leone |
| **2014** | Bellingcat founded |
| **2015–6** | Hissène Habré tried in Senegal |
| **2017** | African Union resolution urging member states to withdraw from the ICC |
| **2018** | |
| *July* | ICC jurisdiction over crime of aggression activated |
| **2021** | |
| *May* | German government pledges reparations payments to Namibia |
| **2022** | |
| *February* | Russian forces invade Ukraine |

# Who's who

**Akayesu, Jean-Paul (b. 1953):** A former mayor of the Taba commune, Akayesu was accused by the ICTR of doing nothing to protect women being raped by members of Hutu militias (known as "interahamwe") around his office and of ordering fatal attacks on women. Not only was Akayesu, who received a life sentence, the first person to be convicted and sentenced under the terms of the Genocide Convention, but his case also established sexual violence as a crime against humanity and instrument of genocide.

**Alexander II (1818–81):** The Russian Tsar who convened an international conference in 1868 in St. Petersburg to seek international agreement on limiting the use of a highly destructive type of bullet. The resulting declaration – the St. Petersburg Declaration Renouncing the Use in War of Certain Explosive Projectiles – was signed by representatives of 14 European states and the Ottoman Empire, who pledged that their respective armies would not use explosive bullets of a certain size. The declaration was the first international agreement to ban the use of a particular weapon for humanitarian reasons. At the same time, it articulated the principle that there were limits to what actions can be taken by the belligerents in a war and that it was "contrary to the laws of humanity" to deploy weapons that cause excessive and unnecessary suffering.

**Bauer, Fritz (1903–68):** Bauer was a West German state prosecutor and German Jew who had survived the Holocaust. He led the prosecution of 22 former mid-ranking SS officers and capos who served in Auschwitz and had been living freely and openly in West Germany. In what became known as the Frankfurt Auschwitz Trials, the accused were charged not with committing war crimes or crimes against humanity but of violating German law. Eighteen were convicted, with six sentenced to life terms and the others receiving sentences ranging from five to 14 years. Though the trial received extensive coverage by the West German and foreign press, much public opinion in the country was indifferent and even hostile to the proceedings.

**Bernays, Murray (1894–1970)**: A US War Department lawyer who during World War II proposed charging Nazi Party organizations with "conspiracy to commit murder, terrorism, and the destruction of peaceful populations in violations of the laws of War" (Smith, 1982: 51). An individual could thus be found guilty on the basis of membership in a criminal organization, with the extent of his or her knowledge of or participation in its crimes determining the severity of punishment. Bernays had in mind principally the SS, the organization he and many other Allied government officials held most responsible for the Nazi regime's worst crimes. His idea was backed by Secretary of War *Henry L. Stimson* and became one of the main legal bases of the **International Military Tribunals** in Nuremberg and Tokyo.

**Callwell, Charles (1859–1928)**: A British Army officer and veteran of British colonial wars in Afghanistan and South Africa, Callwell wrote one of the most influential books about fighting colonial wars: *Small Wars: Their Principles and Practice* (1899). He intended his book to serve as a guide for what he called disciplined soldiers facing – in his words – "savages and semi-civilized races," who refused to engage with regular armed forces on the open field. For Callwell, small wars were fought for three reasons: to conquer territory, to put down rebellions, or to retaliate for atrocities committed against imperial forces or settlers. He knew that they would often be long wars and that clear-cut victories would be elusive. He also understood that the rules of war that applied in so-called regular wars between civilized states did not apply in small wars.

**Clay, Lucius D. (1898–1978)**: The US Army officer who first served as the Deputy Military Governor of the American occupation zone in Germany from 1945 to 1947 and then commander-in-chief of US forces in Europe and military governor of the US zone, Clay was responsible for overseeing the first crucial stage of recovery and denazification. He successfully navigated two major diplomatic and military crises over the status of Berlin, which was occupied by the four wartime allied states but lay deep inside the Soviet occupation zone. He also reviewed the verdicts and sentences of German war criminals convicted by US Army courts.

**Demjanjuk, John (1920–2012)**: Demjanjuk was a Ukrainian-born Nazi collaborator who served as a guard at the Sobibor death camp during World War II. After the war, he immigrated to the United States and lived freely for decades, though American investigators had known of his past since the 1970s. Demjanjuk was first extradited to Israel, where he was tried and convicted in 1987 as a camp guard at Treblinka, but the verdict was overturned as there was not sufficient evidence proving his service in that camp. He was deported to Germany in 2009, where he was convicted in 2011 of being an accessory to the murder of 28,000 Jews and sentenced to five years' imprisonment. He died in 2012. The trial was important because it set a new standard in German courts: despite the fact that it could not be proven that he killed anyone, Demjanjuk had served at a camp that was designed to murder its prisoners, meaning he – and other former personnel – could be charged as accessories to murder.

**Dunant, Henry J. (1828–1910):** A Swiss businessman who wrote a bestselling book about the suffering of wounded soldiers that he witnessed during a short war fought between Austria and Piedmont in 1859. Dunant's book proposed the creation of a neutral, international organization of volunteer medical professionals dedicated to the care of wounded soldiers in wartime with the idea that belligerents would not interfere with the organization's work in the field. In 1863, Dunant and members of Geneva's elite formed the International Committee for Relief to the Wounded. The Swiss government then offered to host an international conference to promote the new organization's mission. Representatives of 16 states met in Geneva in August 1864 and signed the **Geneva Convention for the Amelioration of the Condition of the Wounded in Armies in the Field**, which aimed to ensure the humane treatment of wounded and sick soldiers and protection for civilians providing treatment. It also established a red cross as the identifying symbol of civilians covered by the convention's terms. In 1875, the International Committee for Relief to the Wounded became the **International Committee of the Red Cross** (ICRC). In 1901, Dunant was the co-recipient of the first Nobel Prize for Peace.

**Adolf, Eichmann (1906–61):** A former SS Lieutenant Colonel, Eichmann was one of the principal architects of the Holocaust. After the war, he escaped from Europe and settled in Argentina, where he lived under a false identity and continued to propagate Nazi anti-Semitism. In 1960, he was captured by the Israeli foreign secret service Mossad and transferred to Israel. Though he never killed anyone personally, Eichmann had combined bureaucratic efficiency with intense ideological commitment to deadly effect. In a widely publicized trial held in Jerusalem, he was convicted of crimes against the Jewish people, sentenced to death, and executed. The publicity generated by the trial raised awareness of the Holocaust and reminded Germans that thousands of perpetrators had gone unpunished. Eichmann's trial was one of the very few involving charges of crimes against humanity held during the Cold War.

**Habré, Hissène (1942–2021):** The dictator of Chad from 1982 to 1990, Habré was ousted in a *coup d'etat* and took refuge in Senegal. A truth commission convened in 1991 and 1992 reported that around 40,000 people had been killed and thousands more tortured by the regime, and revelations by the NGO **Human Rights Watch** revealed a more extensive record of abuses. In 2015, a new Senegalese government, backed by the **African Union**, took the unprecedented step of prosecuting in one of its own courts the former head of another state. In May 2016, the court convicted him of **crimes against humanity**, torture, and sex crimes, and he was sentenced to life in prison. Around the same time, a court in Chad tried and convicted former member of Habré's security services. Human rights activists and advocates of expanding international criminal law hailed the trial in Senegal as a landmark moment for war-related atrocities cases.

**Jackson, Robert L. (1892–1954):** A US Supreme Court Justice, President Harry Truman selected Jackson to serve as the US Chief of Counsel at the IMT in Nuremberg.

**Kambanda, Jean (b. 1955):** A former prime minister of Rwanda, Kambanda was the first head of state to be convicted (by the ICTR) on the charge of perpetrating genocide.

**Lemkin, Raphael (1900–59):** A Polish-born lawyer, Lemkin first proposed and defined the concept of **genocide** in his 1944 book, *Axis Rule in Occupied Europe.* While unable to get it included by name as a charge in the indictments of the Nuremberg or Tokyo IMTs, its essence was incorporated into count 3 (war crimes) of the Nuremberg IMT. Lemkin then worked relentlessly to get the UN to adopt a resolution on genocide, which it did in 1948.

**Lieber, Francis (1800–72):** A German immigrant and legal scholar who wrote codification of the rules of war for use by armies in the field. Issued by the US War Department during the Civil War, it was and remains to be known as the "Lieber Code." President Lincoln ordered the code to be included in the Union Army's General Orders, effective in 1863. The militaries of numerous other nations adopted similar codes, and their articles influenced the language of the **Geneva and Hague Conventions**.

**MacArthur, Douglas (1880–1964):** The US General who served as commander of the Southwest Pacific Theater in World War II and then as Supreme Commander for the Allied Powers in Asia. As the effective ruler of occupied Japan, MacArthur attempted to influence the course of the **International Military Tribunal for the Far East**, most successfully in his steadfast resistance to indicting *Emperor Hirohito*.

**Martens, Fyodor (1845–1909):** A Russian diplomat, jurist, and delegate to the 1899 conference that produced the first Hague Convention. Martens authored a clause affirming that military commanders could not simply do as they wished should they encounter a situation not covered explicitly by the convention's terms.

**McCloy, John J. (1895–1989):** An American lawyer and diplomat who served as the High Commissioner for West Germany from 1949 to 1952. McCloy oversaw the establishment of a stable liberal democratic political system and the early stages of the country's economic recovery. He also dealt extensively with the fate of convicted war criminals, whose continued imprisonment as the Cold War heated up was becoming a major diplomatic problem. McCloy's solution was to create a system for parole and amnesty. By 1958, all German war criminals convicted by the NMT and US Army courts (but not by the IMT) and imprisoned in West Germany had been released.

**Milošovic, Slobodan (1941–2006):** President of Serbia from 1989 to 1997 and President of the Federal Republic of Yugoslavia from 1997 to 2000, Milošovic was determined to create a "greater Serbia," mainly at the expense of Bosnia-Herzegovina, which contained large populations of ethnic Croats and Bosnian Muslims. Milošovic supported Serb separatists in Bosnia and their murderous **ethnic cleansing** operations. He also engaged in a war with separatists in Kosovo. Sanctions and NATO military operations forced him to settle both conflicts. In 1999, he was indicted by the ICTY for crimes committed during the fighting in Kosovo. Following his defeat in presidential elections in 2000, he was arrested by Yugoslav government officials and handed over to ICTY custody to face charges of war crimes, crimes against humanity, and genocide. His trial began in 2002, but he died in 2006.

**Mukwege, Denis (b. 1955):** A Congolese gynecologist and human rights activist, Mukwege pioneered a combined form of physical and psychological treatments for victims of sexual assault during Congo's wars in the 1990s and early 2000s. In 1998, he shared the Nobel Prize for Peace with *Nadia Murad* for their work in calling attention to use of rape and sexual crimes as weapons of war.

**Murad, Nadia (b. 1993):** A Yazidi human rights activist who was kidnapped by **ISIL** and held as a sex slave. She escaped and sought asylum in Germany and in 2016 was named the first Goodwill Ambassador for the Dignity of Survivors of Human Trafficking for the United Nations Office on Drugs and Crime (UNODC). She also published a memoir, *The Last Girl* (2017), and shared the 2018 Nobel Prize for Peace with *Denis Mukwege*.

**Moynier, Gustave (1826–1910):** A Swiss jurist and co-founder of the International Committee for Relief to the Wounded (the forerunner of the International Committee of the Red Cross) and the Institute of International Law.

**Nicholas II (1868–1918):** Russian Tsar who convened the 1899 meeting in The Hague to deal with an accelerating arms race and defuse rising tensions among the European great powers. The delegates, representing 28 nations, considered disarmament, revisited the 1864 Geneva Convention, and otherwise discussed ways to resolve international disputes peacefully. In the end, delegates from 23 states ratified what was the first codification in the form of an international treaty of the laws of war on land and sea. The convention defined belligerents, dealt extensively with the status of prisoners of war and sick and wounded soldiers, and set limits on the "means of injuring the enemy," the status of spies, truces, capitulations, and armistices, and occupations.

**Nyiramasuhuko, Pauline (b. 1946):** A former minister in the Hutu Power government in Rwanda, Nyiramasuhuko was accused by the ICTR of encouraging her son and the group of *genocidaires* he commanded to rape Tutsi women in the town of Butare. In 2011 she was convicted on seven charges and sentenced to life in prison, later reduced to 47 years. She was the first woman to be convicted by an international court for sexual violence committed in connection with genocide.

**Plavšić, Biljana (b. 1930):** One of only two women since the post-World War II trials to have been prosecuted for war crimes by international courts. Plavšić was a former member of the Supreme Command of the Armed Forces of Republika Srpska. She was not a top-level decision maker, but was an enthusiastic supporter of ethnic cleansing. The ICTY indicted her on nine counts, including genocide, but most of the charges were dropped. This was in part because of her subordinate position vis-à-vis the all-male political and military leadership and in part because Plavšić was a cooperative defendant who was able to manipulate assumptions about the supposed impossibility of middle-aged white European women perpetrating war crimes. She pleaded guilty to one count (persecution on political, racial, and religious grounds), was sentenced to 11 years, and released in October 2009. While serving her sentence, however, she published a memoir in which she presents herself as an unapologetic and unrepentant Serb nationalist, even claiming that Bosnian Muslim women were not raped but willingly engaged in a form of prostitution.

**Scott, Winfield (1786–1866):** The commander of US forces in the war with Mexico (1846–8), Scott (who was also a lawyer) created the first modern military commissions. What he called "military commissions" and "councils of war" tried around 400 US soldiers and a small number of Mexican civilians for a variety of offenses that would have been tried by civilian courts had the alleged crimes been committed within the United States.

**Stimson, Henry L. (1867–1950):** An American lawyer, statesman, and two-time Secretary of War (the second time from 1940 to 1945), Stimson was one of the most important American proponents of creating an international tribunal to try high-level Nazi officials.

**Taylor, Charles (b. 1948):** The civil wars in Liberia and Sierra Leone that began in the late 1980s resulted in the creation in 2002 by the UN of the **Special Court for Sierra Leone**. The court, based in Freetown, convicted eight members of three armed factions involved in that country's civil war for war crimes and violations of international humanitarian law. Taylor was the highest-visibility defendant. A former president of Liberia, he supported a rebel faction in Sierra Leone. Taylor was charged with 11 counts related to war crimes and crimes against humanity, convicted on all counts in 2012, and sentenced to 50 years in prison. He became the first head of state to be convicted by an international tribunal.

**Taylor, Telford (1908–98):** An American military officer who served as Counsel for the Prosecution in the **IMT** in Nuremberg and then as Chief Prosecutor for the *NMT*. His 1992 book, *The Anatomy of the Nuremberg Trials: A Personal Memoir*, remains one of the most influential accounts ever written about the IMT and NMT.

**Trainin, Aron (1883–1957):** A Soviet jurist, Trainin made a crucial contribution to the IMT when he proposed including a charge of "crimes against peace" (or "aggressive war") in the indictment. Trainin recognized the charge as a way to indict the leaders of countries, men who might otherwise avoid prosecution for war crimes and other violations of international law. He also hoped that Germany's leading industrialists would be included in the charge. His proposal was taken up with enthusiasm by his American counterparts, who very much wanted to put the highest-ranking Nazi party officials in the dock.

**Yamashita, Tomoyuki (1885–1946):** In late 1944, Japanese General Tomoyuki Yamashita was ordered to defend the Philippines. Though he had ordered nearly all troops to evacuate Manila, thousands remained in the city, where they went on a murderous rampage against American POWs and Filipino civilians. Around 100,000 civilians and 1,000 US soldiers were killed, as were nearly all of the Japanese soldiers, while Manila was devastated. Fighting continued on Luzon for months, with appalling levels of casualties suffered by all sides, combatant and civilian. An outraged General *Douglas MacArthur* convinced President Harry Truman that Yamashita should be tried by a military commission. The single charge leveled against him was that he had failed to control the actions of the men under his command. What made the case distinctive was that it was the first time an officer had been charged with being accountable, indirectly, for war crimes committed by his troops. Moreover, the proceedings were rushed and the court ignored evidence that Yamashita had little to no effective control over the actions of his troops in Manila. He was convicted in December 1945 and sentenced to death. His lawyers appealed the verdict to the US Supreme Court, but the justices upheld Yamashita's conviction with reference to provisions of the Geneva and Hague Conventions. The unfairness of Yamashita's trial notwithstanding, a precedent had been established. **Command responsibility** has since become an important part of IHL, though since 1945 it has been applied selectively.

**von Trotha, Lothar (1848–1920):** Between 1884 and 1890, Imperial Germany took control of what it called German Southwest Africa (today Namibia). Expanding settlements provoked conflict with the Indigenous and pastoral Herero people over scare resources in the largely desert environment. Fighting erupted in January 1904, and a new local military commander, Lieutenant General Lothar von Trotha, who had experience with suppressing revolts in other imperial settings, sought a single decisive battle with Herero forces in which he expressly ordered their annihilation. News of his murderous campaign provoked a rare instance of strong political opposition in Germany to the conduct of colonial forces, and the emperor rescinded von Trotha's extermination order. German forces turned to erecting concentration camps – a practice copied from the British experience in South Africa – in larger towns, in part to suppress the revolt and in part to create a pool of slave labor. Historians consider the campaigns to have constituted the 20th century's first genocide and estimate that around 80,000 Herero and Nama perished between 1904 and 1908, amounting to 75 percent of the Herero population and perhaps half of the Nama.

**Wirz, Henry (1823–65):** A Swiss-born officer of the Confederate army in the US Civil War, Wirz served as the warden of a prisoner of war camp in Andersonville, Georgia, where around 13,000 inmates died as a result of inhumane conditions. Tried and convicted in August 1865 on conspiracy charges and for violating the laws and customs of war, he was hanged. Wirz was the only Confederate officer to be executed following conviction by a **military commission.**

# Acknowledgments

I am most grateful to the scholars, jurists, diplomats, journalists, and activists whose work informed this book. I thank Gordon Martel for the invitation to contribute to this series. It is an honor to be in such distinguished company. I am also grateful to Georgia Lloyd for her close attention and, not least, patience. Miranda Brethour and Robin Tainsh provided invaluable assistance as researchers. As always, my family, friends, and colleagues have been sources of invaluable support and good cheer. Effy and Myshkin brought more love and joy to my life than I thought could be possible. It has been a privilege to have taught at Brooklyn College for more than 20 years. This book is for my students, past, present, and future.

# Introduction

The term "war crime" is of relatively recent origin. Its first appearance in print was in an 1872 book by the liberal Swiss politician and jurist Johann Caspar Bluntschli, who used the term to refer to the operations of French irregulars (known as *franc tireurs*) in the Franco-Prussian War (1870–1). Bluntschli's definition of war crimes was quite narrow: it was limited to attacks by armed civilians against the personnel of occupying forces, actions which he argued could be prosecuted by **courts martial** and result in the execution of the guilty parties. Other jurists soon began using the term in other contexts, reflecting an absence of consensus in that era as to what, in legal terms, "war crimes" were and how their perpetrators should be held accountable.

Bluntschli was one of a small number of men who labored to forge such a consensus, at least among westerners, by establishing the legal and diplomatic foundations for the modern laws of war, now often subsumed under the broader term **international humanitarian law** (IHL). Eight features characterize the laws of war as they have been developed from the late 19th century onward. The first feature is the codification of laws in the codes of national military establishments and in international treaties and conventions. The second is a concern for the justifications for going to war (*ius ad bellum*). The third is about how wars are conducted after they start (*ius in bello*), notably the problem of constraining the conduct of states and armed forces. Fourth is the means of holding those responsible for violating laws and customs accountable for their actions. A fifth is an extensive body of theories, legal commentary, and case law dealing with the above three features. Sixth is the persistent gap between codes and laws and the behavior of belligerents during wartime. Seventh is the relationship between the evolving technologies of war and the law. Finally, there is the selective application of law to certain kinds of armed conflicts and the groups and individuals involved.

Nearly all of these features have deep historical roots. Warfare across the ancient world was characterized by extreme brutality among combatants and non-combatants, with looting, enslavement, rape, the killing of animals, and the destruction of land resources and food stores usually

DOI: 10.4324/9781003118664-1

accompanying the carnage. Yet the world's major ancient civilizations also produced attempts to constrain the initiation and conduct of war. Rulers in ancient Egypt, Mesopotamia, China, India, Israel, Greece, and Rome sought divine justifications for going to war. Once war was decided upon, it would usually be waged with extreme savagery, but there is also abundant evidence that civilizations in Eurasia and the Americas developed elaborate codes of conduct to be observed during armed conflicts. This was also the case in the expanding realms of Islam. By the 11th and 12th centuries, the Catholic Church issued a series of proclamations that sought to impose some restraints on when and how and with what weapons war could be conducted, albeit with very little practical effect. In the early modern period (15th–18th centuries), French and English monarchs produced a series of ordinances and codes to regulate the behavior of soldiers that are strikingly modern in their concern for non-combatants, the protection of property and livestock, and the admonition to spare the lives of surrendering adversaries.

Holding those who violated codes and customs accountable also has a long history. Beginning in the 5th century BCE, pirates operating in the Aegean and Mediterranean were targeted by Greece and Rome on the grounds that pirates committed unjustified acts of violence. The first military courts were created in medieval Europe and England to adjudicate disputes over alleged violations of chivalric codes. Such hearings were originally held before kings and princes and their councils of military advisers, but soon authority to hear cases was transferred to the councils. The emergence of chivalric courts was particularly significant to the later development of the laws of war, as they were the first such entities to establish a judicial procedure for handling violations of codes of conduct.

In the ancient and medieval worlds, scholars, philosophers, and theologians produced a rich body of ideas regarding initiating and waging war. In general, ancient civilizations produced informal laws of war (in that they were not codified in writing or enforced by some kind of judicial structure) that considered when to go to war and what limits combatants should observe. Religious belief systems were the primary inspiration, but a concern for secular, practical matters also begins to appear, as did ideas about a common humanity and the imperative of showing compassion to those outside of one's family and community. That said, humanitarian considerations as conceived of in the 19th and 20th centuries – namely the treatment of captives, the distinction between combatants and non-combatants, and the imperative of limiting the suffering and destruction of war – were almost entirely absent.

Of great significance to the modern era was a body of thought articulated in early modern Europe (15th–18th centuries). The period was marked by spasms of extremely violent rebellions and wars, the latter fueled by intense religious hatreds generated by the Protestant Reformation. A remarkable constellation of mainly Spanish, Italian, French, and Dutch scholars (some of them with military backgrounds) also produced highly detailed treatises on the laws of war, emphasizing proper justifications for going to war and conducting it as humanely as possible. They did not offer radically new visions of the laws of war but provided lengthy elaborations on ideas from ancient Greece and Rome and the Middle Ages. These writings would have little practical effect at the time they were published but would become an essential resource for the modern architects of the laws of war. Of more immediate significance in the early modern era was that decades of highly destructive warfare led individual states to impose more restrictions on their armed forces and, not least, to create professionalized national armies.

In the European context, the late 18th and early 19th centuries witnessed another turning point. Some historians have argued that it was during the wars of the French Revolution and the era of Napoleon Bonaparte that modern "total war" was born, meaning a form of warfare in which entire societies were mobilized for war. States drafted large numbers of soldiers and took control of economic production to an unprecedented degree. The productive capacities of civilians – and not least the power of their affective allegiance to the nation – were also channeled toward maintaining the war effort. At the same time, the lines between combatant and civilian were blurred or erased to an extent not seen since the religious wars of the 11th century. Essential to this evolution of warfare were the transformative effects of the industrial revolution, which revolutionized not only armaments and their production but also transportation, medicine, and communication. In this view, the destructive potential of nationalism and new technologies was fully realized in the world wars of the 20th century. Other historians, however, have seen more continuity than change in the modes of warfare practiced in Europe from the early modern era to the 19th century. Certainly, there was more continuity than discontinuity when it came to the ways Europeans had been fighting and conquering beyond Europe since the 15th century. For those on the receiving end of European imperialism, warfare had always been "total."

Finally, there is evidence that attempts to regulate the conduct of war from the ancient to modern periods were occasionally effective where it mattered most – on the battlefield. But this was not the case when it came to certain types of armed conflicts and categories of belligerents. Modern codes and laws of war were formulated to apply in conflicts between perceived relative equals, that is, uniformed combatants representing their respective kingdoms or states. They expressly excluded domestic rebellions, wars deemed to be initiated for unjust causes, and wars of imperial conquest and colonization. This critically important distinction has proven to be the single strongest line of continuity linking the ancient world of warfare to the present. In simplest terms, the laws of war did not apply to outsiders, whether defined in ethnic, "civilizational," religious, or (in the modern world) racialized terms.

So what makes the modern laws of war distinctively "modern"? First, written codes of conduct became standard for the world's uniformed armed forces. Second is the creation of an international structure to define, investigate, and prosecute violations. This structure comprised treaties and conventions, institutions (e.g., the International Committee of the Red Cross [ICRC], the United Nations [UN]), *ad hoc* international tribunals, and a permanent **international criminal court** (the International Criminal Court [ICC]). Third is the role of sub-state and increasingly transnational actors – most notably **non-governmental organizations** (NGOs) and journalists – in exposing war crimes and other atrocities and amassing evidence for legal proceedings. Legal frameworks and diplomatic precedents for restitution and reparations have also been developed to a greater extent than ever before. Another distinctive development has been the expanded recognition in international law of the prevalence and significance of crimes against women. Finally, accelerating human-generated climate change has produced a movement to include crimes against the environment ("ecocide") as a crime against humanity.

Both old and new challenges confront those working to uphold and develop the legal frameworks for regulating the conduct of war and more generally protecting human rights. Hopes articulated in the aftermath of World War II that precedents like the Nuremberg and Tokyo international tribunals or the courts established for the former Yugoslavia have not deterred states from initiating unprovoked wars, as the United States did in Iraq in 2003 or the Russian Federation has done in Ukraine beginning in 2014 and culminating in the full-scale invasion of that country in 2022. Nor has the creation of the ICC deterred war crimes and crimes against humanity in Africa, the Middle East, and Asia. In short, there remains a fundamental tension between the sovereignty of states, which continue to act in their perceived best interests, and international law. A similar tension obtains among soldiers who are often forced to make split second decisions in the heat of battle. Nonetheless, defenders of institutions like the ICC and those who work to document and expose crimes against humanity argue that without laws and willingness and capacity to enforce them, atrocities would continue completely unchecked and their perpetrators would go unidentified and unpunished.

Conclusive military victories along with the willingness of states to cooperate have been the basic requirement of all successful international prosecutions: in post-World War II Europe and Asia, in the former Yugoslavia, and in Rwanda and several other African countries. In the absence of this condition, investigations and prosecutions, while not impossible, are extremely difficult. Further, the development of international law has lagged behind the development of new kinds of armed forces, notably transnational groups like Al-Qaeda and ISIL or Private Military Corporations (PMCs) and new technologies, notably unmanned vehicles (drones) and the weaponization of cyberspace. Finally, despite decolonization after World War II, the creation of the UN, and the development of international human rights law, the application of the laws of war continues to be highly selective. Those with a professional stake in IHL and war crimes, historians included, have yet to come to terms with the single greatest blind spot of the entire endeavor: the separation in law of colonial wars (and, in the postcolonial landscape, "counterinsurgency" wars) from the development and application of IHL and war crimes law.

Much of the scholarship on the international laws of war, especially that produced in the 1990s, offered a narrative of overall progress. This narrative presented the late 19th century as marking the first breakthrough, with the first international treaties signed to constrain the conduct of war. Progress faltered in the interwar years, but resumed – indeed, took a giant step forward – with the IMT and NMT in Nuremberg and the genocide and human rights conventions concluded in 1948. Progress faltered again during the Cold War, but thanks to the precedents set in the first postwar years, the development of international criminal law accelerated in the 1990s in the wake of the wars in the former Yugoslavia and the genocide in Rwanda, culminating in the creation of the first standing international criminal court, the ICC, in 1998. More recently, scholars have broadened their approach to studying war crimes and the law by reaching much farther back in time and by paying closer attention to atrocities other than the **Armenian genocide**, the Holocaust, or the Rwandan genocide. At the same time, more attention is being paid to heretofore lesser-known attempts at judicial reckoning, such as in post-World War II Eastern Europe and the Soviet Union or in much of Asia outside Japan. Particularly noteworthy has been the intensified interest in the history of colonial wars and the relationship between genocide as a concept in history, law, and diplomacy and its applicability to colonial contexts. The broader and more critical approach to assessing war crimes and international law reflected in recent scholarship will be essential for policymakers, diplomats, jurists, journalists, and activists as they navigate an increasingly uncertain and unstable world.

# Part I

# War crimes and the laws of war in the era of global war (1863–1945)

# 1 The 19th century in the United States and Europe

Constraints on the conduct of war had been imagined, written about, and in some cases observed in practice across the world's cultures for centuries. Yet developments in the 19th century – especially in the second half – marked a watershed in the history of the laws of war. One major achievement was the first codified body of the laws of war for armies in the field, drawn up in the United States in 1863. The second was the first international conventions, negotiated in 1899 and 1907, codifying the laws of land and maritime warfare. A related development was the creation of the modern **military commission** to try soldiers and civilians for violations of the laws of war. By the beginning of the 20th century, then, it had become possible for the first time in history to speak of the international laws of war as more than theory or aspiration. Yet the scope of the achievement was in reality limited to armed conflicts conducted between self-professed "civilized states." The newly codified rules of conduct were never intended to apply to what was at the time a global theater of warfare in colonized – or soon to be colonized – spaces, stretching from North America to New Zealand.

Why did these developments take place in the second half of the 19th century? All informed observers understood that the nature of warfare had changed. Professional national armies had emerged from the consolidation of nation states, and nationalism had proven itself to be a dangerous and powerful engine of aggression. There were striking (and ongoing) advances in weapons technologies and, by the end of the 19th century, a global arms race that was accelerating at a terrifying pace. And while there was no great power war in Europe from 1815 to 1914, there were multiple smaller-scale conflicts that nonetheless portended the possibility of wider wars, the fear of which the scramble for colonial possessions in Africa and Asia only intensified. Yet despite these worrisome conditions, there were strong currents that favored international cooperation of all kinds, including on questions of maintaining peace and regulating the conduct of war. A highly destructive war, most people had come to believe by the first decade of the 20th century, could not be allowed to bring an end to the general prosperity made possible by the second industrial revolution, expanded international trade, and decades of continent-wide peace. And for those who favored finally codifying

DOI: 10.4324/9781003118664-3

the laws of war, there was a rich tradition of writing from which to draw (Angell, 1910/2010; Bryant, 2021).

## The "Lieber Code" (1863)

It would be in the midst of the US Civil War (1861–5) that the first codification of the rules of war was drawn up for use by armies in the field. Formally titled "Instructions for the Government of Armies of the United States in the Field" and issued by the US War Department as General Orders [*sic*] No. 100, it was and remains known as the "Lieber Code" after its principal author, Francis J. Lieber (1798 or 1800–72), a German-born immigrant and scholar who had served in the Prussian army in its campaigns against Napoleon. Drawn to law and politics and an opponent of slavery, Lieber yearned to be part of the intellectual life of northeastern cities. But he could only find a position teaching history and political economy at South Carolina College (now the University of South Carolina) where he tried without success to keep his views a secret. In 1857 he accepted a position as a professor of history and political economy at Columbia College (now Columbia University) in New York. Here there were no constraints on his ability to express his views in public, including strong support for Abraham Lincoln (Witt, 2013).

When the war began, Lieber was writing and lecturing about the laws of war. Hearing of his lectures, Major General Henry W. Halleck (1815–72), then general-in-chief of the army, commissioned him to write a code of regulations for the Union Army. Lieber was not a pacifist and accepted Carl von Clausewitz's (1780–1831) dictum that, as Lieber put it, "the more earnestly and keenly wars are carried on, the better for humanity, peace, and civilization" (Finkelman, 2013: 2104). But he nonetheless wanted the violence and destructiveness of war constrained by a set of mutually observed rules. His code, comprising 157 articles, dealt with a wide range of issues related to the specific features of the Civil War but with clear implications for armed conflicts in general: notably the issue of military necessity, rules for occupying enemy territory, the treatment of prisoners of war (POWs), civilians, and property, enslaved people, irregulars (or guerillas), and armistices [*Doc. 1, p. 111*]. President Lincoln ordered the code to be included in the Union Army's General Orders, effective in 1863. Initially resistant, officials of the Confederacy eventually adopted it, though Confederate forces violated its provisions repeatedly.

How effective was Lieber Code in the field? Lincoln, for one, suspected that some "flexibility" in applying its articles would be necessary, particularly when it came to fighting irregulars (Crowe, 2014: 82). But two things are clear: that the code was distributed widely among Union officers and soldiers and that for the most part, the conduct of Union forces conformed to the code's articles. That does not mean, of course, that officers and soldiers read it carefully and then applied its provisions during and after combat. Some historians have pointed to the case of General William T. Sherman's advance across Georgia in late 1864 as evidence that written rules can regulate the conduct of soldiers in the field. Indeed, recent research has challenged a long-standing claim that Union forces devastated the state. The fact that Sherman issued a set of special field orders aimed at constraining the behavior of his troops seems to have had some effect, though it is also true that some soldiers committed wanton acts of destruction and pillage. Then and since, it was often difficult to determine what constituted permissible and impermissible acts in wartime and during occupations. And the question of whether Confederate forces would have behaved with less brutality had the Confederacy also distributed Lieber Code or something very similar more widely among its officer and soldiers cannot be answered (Dilbeck, 2016).

Much easier to establish is the relevance of Lieber Code to the development of the laws of war nationally – in the United States, the code remained in effect until 1914 and has influenced succeeding general orders – and internationally. It was the first codification of the laws of war for use by officers and soldiers in the field, and Lieber expected the code's influence to extend beyond a single conflict, considering it to be "a contribution by the United States to the stock of common civilization" (Crowe, 2014: 82). In short order, the militaries of Britain, France, Prussia, Spain, Russia, Serbia, the Netherlands, and Argentina adopted similar codes. The Swiss jurist Johann Caspar Bluntschli (1807–81), the co-founder of the influential **Institute of International Law** (established in 1873), was convinced that the code could inform the development of international law regarding the conduct of war.

## International declarations and conventions (1856–1929)

Around the same time as Lieber was developing his code, Great Britain and a handful of European states negotiated the first international agreements aimed at regulating the conduct of war. The Lieber Code provided something of a blueprint. Nearly a decade before Lieber wrote his code, however, Britain and France had agreed to a set of rules regulating naval operations during the Crimean War (1854–6). At the conference in Paris that ended the war, the plenipotentiaries signed the **Declaration Respecting Maritime Law.** The declaration abolished **privateering:** when states (through "letters of marque") authorize private ships to conduct military operations at sea, mainly the seizure of merchant shipping. It also included provisions to protect the property of neutral states and proclaimed that in order to be binding, blockades had to be implemented effectively. Representatives of 56 states, federations, and principalities ratified or at least agreed to abide by its provisions ("**accession**"), thus making the declaration the first multilateral treaty in history aimed at regulating the conduct of war. Despite not being among the signatories, the US government agreed to respect its provisions.

Six years later, a Swiss businessman named Henry J. Dunant (1828–1910), appalled by the lack of care provided to wounded soldiers on both sides of a short war fought between Austria and Piedmont in 1859, published a book about what he had witnessed. More than an account of the horrors of war, Dunant's book proposed the creation of a neutral, international organization of volunteer medical professionals dedicated to the care of wounded soldiers in wartime with the idea that belligerents would not interfere with the organization's work in the field. Fortunately, the book, *A Memory of Solferino*, was an international bestseller and inspired a small group of Geneva's elite to form the International Committee for Relief to the Wounded in 1863. The Swiss government then offered to host an international conference to promote the new organization's mission. Representatives of 16 states met in Geneva in August 1864 and signed the **Geneva Convention for the Amelioration of the Condition of the Wounded in Armies in the Field,** the first of what would be four Geneva Conventions. Its provisions sought to ensure the humane treatment of wounded and sick soldiers and protection for civilians providing treatment. It also established a red cross as the identifying symbol of civilians covered by the convention's terms. Within three years, all major European and many other states had ratified the convention. In 1875, the International Committee for Relief to the Wounded became the **International Committee of the Red Cross** (ICRC). In addition to its work in wars around the world, the ICRC became one of the most important sources of the development of the laws of war and its post-World War II embodiment, IHL. In 1901, Dunant was the co-recipient of the first Nobel Prize for peace (Dromi, 2020).

It would be a response to a particularly destructive new technology of war that prompted the next major advance in the international laws of war: a bullet that exploded upon contact with hard or soft objects. Though developed by the Russian military, its ability to cause grievous wounds prompted Tsar Alexander II (1818–81) to convene an international conference in 1868 in St. Petersburg. The resulting declaration – the **St. Petersburg Declaration Renouncing the Use in War of Certain Explosive Projectiles** – was signed by representatives of 14 European states and the Ottoman Empire, who pledged that their respective armies would not use explosive bullets of a certain size. The declaration was significant as it was the first international agreement to ban the use of a particular weapon for humanitarian reasons. While the focus was on a single type of projectile, the declaration's expression of a principal may have been its most important legacy: namely, that there were limits on what actions can be taken by the belligerents in a war and that it was "contrary to the laws of humanity" to deploy weapons that "uselessly aggravate the suffering of disabled men, or render their death inevitable" (Solis, 2022: 44).

In 1874, Alexander II and the German Emperor, Wilhelm I, agreed to organize another convention, this time to do no less than codify the laws of war. Though the attendees, representing 15 European states, failed to ratify a treaty, they did sign a non-binding statement, The *Brussels Declaration*. Modeled closely on the Lieber Code, the declaration was, as one historian characterized it, "the first collective European effort to agree on a common set of laws of war" and "a starting point for European discussions about a modern, codified body of the laws of war" (Crowe, 2014: 84). The newly created Institute of International Law, a Swiss-based organization of jurists co-founded by Johann Caspar Bluntschli and Gustave Moynier (the head of the ICRC), studied the declaration and drew up the **Manual of the Laws and Customs of War at Oxford** in 1880. Both documents would form the basis for the next landmark moment in international law: two **Hague Conventions** in 1899 and 1907.

The instigator of the 1899 convention was once again a Russian Tsar, Nicholas II (1868–1918), though his objective was not to codify the laws of war in an international treaty but to confront an accelerating arms race (in which the Russian Empire could not afford to compete) and defuse rising tensions among the European great powers. From May to July 1899, 100 delegates representing 28 nations convened in The Hague to consider disarmament, revisit the 1864 Geneva Convention, and otherwise explore ways to resolve international disputes peacefully, perhaps through the creation of a permanent international court to arbitrate disputes between states. While no progress was made on containing the arms race (except for banning the use of explosives delivered from balloons, poisonous gases, and certain types of bullets) or a permanent court, delegates from 23 states ratified what was the first codification in the form of an international treaty of the laws of war on land and sea. The convention defined belligerents, dealt extensively with the status of POWs and sick and wounded soldiers, and set limits on the "means of injuring the enemy," the status of spies, truces, capitulations, armistices, and occupations. Of particular significance was a clause (written by a Russian delegate, Fyodor Martens [1845–1909]) stating:

> [I]n cases not included in the Regulations adopted by them, populations and belligerents remain under the protection and empire of the principles of international law, as they result from the usages established between civilized nations, from the laws of humanity, and the requirements of the public conscience.
>
> (https://ihl-databases.icrc.org/ihl/INTRO/150)

In other words, the convention indicated that military commanders could not simply do as they wished should they encounter a situation not covered explicitly by the convention's terms (Meron, 2011).

A second international conference in 1907 – this one instigated by US President Theodore Roosevelt in the aftermath of the *Russo-Japanese War* (1904–5) and also held in The Hague – updated the first and added a few modifications [*Doc 2, p. 114*]. Taken together, the two conventions had greater long-term significance than immediate. Their articles had an uneven effect on the war in Europe between 1914 and 1918. German forces violated multiple provisions during the invasion of Belgium in 1914, and France, Germany, Britain, and Austria-Hungary all used poison gas. Another issue was the lack of detailed provisions for the protection of civilians, something future international conventions would address. And there was no mechanism to enforce the conventions' terms. A particularly glaring problem, though certainly not to most Europeans at the time, was that the signatories had no intention of applying the newly codified rules of war to armed conflicts in the colonies. It is easier to make a case for the long-term significance of the Lieber Code and the Hague Conventions. In addition to being the first such codes and conventions of their kind, they formed many of the legal bases for the major and minor post-World War II trials and the international tribunals for the former Yugoslavia and Rwanda. The conventions also played an important role in inspiring the creation of the **International Court of Justice** in 1945 as one of the principal institutions of the UN.

## Military commissions

It was also in the United States that the first modern **military commissions** were developed. The tradition of political and military authorities convening special courts to try soldiers for violating codes of conduct dates back to the Middle Ages. But it was not until the mid-19th century that the first formal military commission was convened by the US Army. While a **courts martial** is indeed a military court, they are convened by a given military for its own personnel accused of violating military law. A military commission (or tribunal – the terms are sometimes used interchangeably) is also a military court, but it conducts proceedings, usually during and shortly after hostilities, against enemy combatants and sometimes civilians accused of violating the laws and customs of war. Designed to be highly flexible instruments, they have traditionally been largely independent of civilian oversight and (until recently) have adopted less rigorous standards than civilian courts or **courts martial** (Witt, 2013; Prescott, 2003; Maguire, 2002).

It was during the US war with Mexico (1846–8) that the US military created the first military commissions. The commander of US forces, General Winfield Scott (1786–1866), who also happened to be a lawyer, established what he called "military commissions" and "councils of war" to try around 400 US soldiers and a small number of Mexican civilians for a variety of offenses that would have been tried by civilian courts had the alleged crimes been committed within the United States. It was during the Civil War, however, that military commissions were used on a significant scale. The legal gateway was provided by the Lieber Code, which allowed for the punishment of soldiers and civilians who violate the laws and customs of war "in a place or a district under martial law" (Witt, 2013: 386). Military commissions could be convened in such cases, as Lincoln had declared martial law in war zones, which in 1863 included portions of Confederate states occupied by Union forces. During and after the Civil War, nearly 3,500 military commissions were convened, including one that tried conspirators in the plot to assassinate Lincoln. The best-known commission tried

Captain Henry Wirz (1823–65), the warden of a Confederate POW camp in Andersonville, Georgia, where around 13,000 inmates died as a result of inhumane conditions. Less well-known were the hundreds of cases in which Native Americans were tried in the 1860s and 1870s during multiple wars on the western frontier.

Military commissions were again convened in significant numbers by the United States and other states after World War II. Jurists, legal scholars, and historians have debated all aspects of these courts. Some criticized them harshly, mainly for presiding over seemingly rushed proceedings, an absence of legal protections afforded to defendants in civilian courts, and lax standards regarding admissible evidence. Defenders have argued that in most cases of postwar US military commissions, defendants received reasonably fair trials. In any case, military commissions soon virtually disappeared until the aftermath of the 11 September 2001 terrorist attacks on the United States, when they were revived by the administration of US president George W. Bush as a tool in what he called the "war on terror." The targets were mainly members of Al-Qaeda, who, when captured in the aftermath of the US invasion of Afghanistan in 2002, were subjected to interrogation methods that constituted forms of torture, hence violating international law. These methods had been approved by the Bush administration on the grounds that protections normally afforded to enemy combatants did not extend to members of Al-Qaeda or the Taliban or undefined "associated forces." The US record was further besmirched by the dismal performance of military commissions convened at the US military base at **Guantanamo Bay** in Cuba, which have been beset by multiple legal challenges regarding jurisdiction, the legality of the courts, and the treatment of detainees. From 2002 to 2020, only eight commissions were conducted to completion, with no case completed since 2014. Civilian courts, by contrast, have concluded hundreds of trials of suspected terrorists (Maguire, 2002; Remy, 2017; Bravin, 2013).

# 2 Colonial wars

Historians in the western world have long characterized the 19th century as a period of sustained great power peace, a period that produced no general European war between Napoleon Bonaparte's final defeat in 1815 and the outbreak of World War I in the summer of 1914. But the characterization is as misleading as it is parochial. Wars to create, expand, defend, and resist empires and colonies increased in frequency, scale, and intensity in the mid- to late-19th century. By the beginning of the 20th century, a belt of imperial wars had encircled the world. These conflicts were generated by the expansion of European, American, and Japanese empires in North America, Africa, Asia, and the Pacific. This expansion provoked ongoing Indigenous resistance, which in turn provoked even greater levels of violence by imperial powers. The result was decades of armed conflicts in which war crimes and atrocities against civilians were committed on a vast scale. Western and Japanese imperial troops won most individual engagements, thanks mainly to superior technologies, effective anti-guerilla warfare doctrine, the deployment of large numbers of Indigenous auxiliaries, and the willingness to conduct warfare without regard to legal or humanitarian constraints.

## The imperial world at war

The astonishingly rapid expansion of empire from the mid-19th to early 20th centuries was driven by a number of factors. In some places – North America, Australia, and New Zealand – the objective was to conquer territory for settlement. But most imperial ventures in the era of the "new imperialism" were not aimed at settling large numbers of non-Indigenous peoples. Rather, the extraction of natural resources to meet demands generated by the second industrial revolution was the principal motivation. As more colonies were acquired, perceived strategic necessity became another incentive: to secure what had already been taken, it often became necessary to expand further. Also important were matters of prestige and status. Nationalists in the German Empire and Italy, for instance, increasingly felt compelled to acquire colonies as markers of great power status. Whatever the mixture of motivations, the new wave of empire building was justified

DOI: 10.4324/9781003118664-4

by all imperial powers with reference to their supposed civilizational and racial "superiority" over "savage," non-Christian, and "inferior" peoples.

In North America, US government forces and white settlers engaged in over 1,000 armed conflicts with native peoples from 1866 to 1891 and fought a brutal war with nationalist forces in the Philippines from 1899 to 1902. Great Britain consolidated its hold over India and, along with France and a few other European states, took control of nearly all of Africa. From 1869 to 1902, British colonial forces fought 40 colonial wars and "punitive expeditions," while the British Indian Army faced at least 77 major rebellions during the period of the Raj (1858–1947). Thirty military operations between 1893 and 1911 were undertaken to conquer Kenya, while 19 were conducted in Nigeria from 1900 to 1906. Imperial Russia conquered Central Asia from the 1850s to the 1880s. The Ottoman Empire was beset by revolts and attacks on the Arabian peninsula and in the Balkans, which was fracturing into mutually hostile independent states (Vandervort, 2005, 2009; Wesseling, 2004; Howard, 2017).

France, Britain, and the Netherlands extended their control or solidified it in South and Southeast Asia. Imperial Germany – a latecomer to the "scramble for Africa" – undertook 231 campaigns to secure control of German East Africa (today Burundi, Rwanda, and parts of Tanzania and Mozambique) from 1889 to 1910. In East Asia, the most important development was the expansion of Japanese imperial control, mainly at the expense of China and Korea. Alongside Japanese expansion came the imposition of informal empire by the European great powers in a greatly weakened China. Australia is something of an exception to the pattern of intensified warfare, with armed conflict between Europeans and Aboriginal peoples lasting from 1788 into the mid-1930s. New Zealand fits the global pattern more closely, as British and colonial forces conquered the north island from the Maoris from the 1840s to the early 1870s (Elkins, 2022; Quinn, 2001; Baranowski, 2010; Myers and Peattie, 1987; Silbey, 2013).

Imperial and anti-imperial forces developed modes of conducting war suited to the unique features of colonial conflicts. The result was a particular kind of warfare, one that had become less common in post-Napoleonic Europe and was highly destructive in terms of loss of human life, plunder, and environmental devastation. Colonial armies had to learn to fight in dangerous environments and over vast expanses of unfamiliar territory, and in most cases they had to make do with relatively small numbers of men and rely extensively on Indigenous personnel to do much of the carrying and fighting. So new doctrines and combat methods had to be developed [*Doc 3, p. 116*]. These doctrines and often the men who developed them (and their protégés) were transferred around the world and became sources of instruction and inspiration for officers in different imperial spaces. Colonial troops also resorted to a form of environmental warfare that greatly magnified the destructiveness of their campaigns. When imperial armies failed, as they nearly always did, to force opponents to engage in conventional, set piece battles, they turned to destroying the means of subsistence – mainly crops and livestock and the infrastructures that supported farming, fishing, and herding – with devastating short- and long-term consequences for Indigenous populations (Walter, 2017; Kreike, 2021).

Conversely, anti-imperial forces responded in strikingly similar ways across cultures and territories. The most consequential development was a turn to forms of guerilla warfare. Pre-colonial fighting traditions, the realities of the physical environment, and asymmetries of power *vis-à vis* the colonizers all made the resort to this form of fighting necessary and entirely rational. It is important to note that Indigenous peoples around the world had developed their own elaborate codes of conduct in wartime and in some cases attempted to observe them in conflicts with westerners. But Europeans and white North Americans had no interest in learning about or observing them and acted on the assumption that native peoples were by nature irrational and lawless, hence their resort to unrestrained forms of warfare. The perceived necessity of "fighting like the natives" in response became a major through-line in imperial and post-imperial wars from the 16th century to the present (Walter, 2017; Callwell, 1899/1996).

Guerilla warfare meant that the determination of imperial forces to meet their opponents head-on in the open field was consistently frustrated. Around the world, the results were similar: colonial wars were long, inconclusive, and often incredibly violent, with the distinction between combatants and civilians eroded or erased. A telling exception to this general pattern was Russia's late 19th-century campaigns in Central Asia. Whereas Imperial Russian forces in the Caucasus had been beset by opponents who had adopted guerilla warfare tactics, this was mostly not the case in the latter 19th century. Then, Central Asian forces either met the Russians head-on in the open or attempted to defend fortresses. In both cases they were unsuccessful, which explains the relatively short duration of Central Asian campaigns (Morrison, 2021).

Technological superiority in weapons, transportation, communication, food preservation, and medicine along with the claims of civilizational and racial superiority used to justify imperial expansion ran up against a hard reality: colonial forces were invariably outnumbered and operating in hostile, unfamiliar, and often physically dangerous environments. This combination of self-confidence and vulnerability acted as another accelerant to the dynamic of violence, mainly by inciting colonial forces to stage punitive expeditions and demonstrations of firepower. The objective was to "teach the natives" – who were presumed to be simple-minded, child-like, and highly impressionable – a "lesson." The superiority–vulnerability complex also incentivized colonial forces to seek decisive, total victories. The fact that such victories were so elusive made warfare in the colonies less identifiable as a formal "state of war" that would exist between two or more states and more so as an unending series of engagements in which final victory was never really achieved.

## War crimes and atrocities in colonial wars: exemplary cases

The following cases illustrate some of the most important features of colonial wars and the range of atrocities committed by colonial armies in the late 19th and early 20th centuries. A revolt against British rule in India in 1857 produced one of the most violent and consequential reprisals perpetrated by a western imperial power. Known variously as the Indian Mutiny, Sepoy Mutiny, and the First War of Independence, the rebellion was fueled by growing elite and popular discontent over various aspects of British rule. It was sparked in April when Indian troops (or Sepoys) serving in the Bengal army in Meerut were punished harshly for refusing to use new British rifle cartridges they believed – falsely – to have been lubricated with cow and pig fat, a grievous insult to both Hindu and Muslim religious and cultural sensibilities. Their fellow soldiers attacked British officers, marched to Delhi, and restored the former Mughal emperor. The revolt spread in northern India and involved the killing of British military personnel and civilians. British forces responded against rebels and civilians with extreme harshness. Historians now estimate that around 6,000 British subjects were killed in the 18-month-long rebellion and at least 800,000 Indians perished in the fighting and as a result of famines and disease. Following the mutiny's suppression, the British government abolished the East India Company, took direct control of India, began consulting with Indians on legislative matters, instituted other minor reforms, and continued to develop infrastructure such as railways and roads. British rule was assured for the time being, though the failure to decisively reject the imposition of western influences, combined with the reforms, laid the groundwork for a new Indian nationalism and independence movement (Peers, 2013).

In North America, settlers from the British Isles and Europe had been in conflict with native peoples beginning with the first sustained contact in the 17th century. It would be expansion westward in the second half of the 1800s that generated multiple wars that resulted in the removal, relocation to reservations, and, frequently, the mass murder of an uncountable number of native peoples. Exemplary in this period was the Great Sioux War (or Black Hills War) in 1876 and 1877, a stage in a longer running series of conflicts between the Lakota Sioux, Cheyenne, and Arapaho peoples, white settlers, and the US government. In 1868, the US government had concluded a treaty with the Sioux nation that created a 60-million-acre reservation and granted it access to the Black Hills region (present-day South Dakota and part of Wyoming). Though white Americans were barred from trespassing or settling on any Sioux lands, the discovery of gold deposits in the Black Hills drew prospectors, resulting in incursions that US officials did nothing to stop. At the same time, the government persisted in constructing a rail line to the Pacific coast (the Northern Pacific Railroad) (Gump, 2016).

An offer to buy the Black Hills from the Sioux was rebuffed, and in response, the US government required all Indians to report to a federal agency on the reservation. The US Army dispatched troops to round up those who refused and in June 1876 suffered two substantial defeats at the Battle of the Rosebud and Little Bighorn. As was nearly always the case in modern colonial wars, the colonizers had the advantage in weapons technology while Indigenous forces enjoyed superiority in mobility and intimate knowledge of the terrain. Sioux fighters also benefitted from being underestimated as "savages" by white forces. Yet US forces adapted and overcame Sioux resistance, in part by attacking and destroying villages in winter and restricting supplies of food. By 1877, US forces had broken Sioux resistance and captured its principal leaders. The Black Hills region was annexed from the Great Sioux Reservation. As in other colonial wars, white settlers and government forces also waged a form of environmental warfare by reducing the size of the vast reservation (to only 12.7 million acres by 1887) and slaughtering millions of buffalo – a critical resource for the Sioux people. One result was division among the Sioux between those who sought to cooperate with the US government (and the Bureau of Indian Affairs, the intrusive administrative arm on Sioux lands that pursued policies of forced cultural assimilation) and those who took up arms.

In southwest Africa, German colonial troops perpetrated what historians now refer to as the 20th century's first genocide. Imperial Germany took control of what it called German Southwest Africa (today Namibia) between 1884 and 1890. With few natural resources to extract, the German government aimed at creating a settler colony. Expanding settlements provoked conflict with the Indigenous and pastoral Herero people over scare resources in the largely desert environment – namely, water and arable land for grazing cattle. Fighting erupted in January 1904 and spread rapidly. The local German military commander, fully aware that his forces were outnumbered, advocated negotiating with the Herero (whose leader had attempted to prohibit the killing of German women and children by his troops) but was overruled by his superiors in Berlin. They demanded the violent suppression of the rebels and dispatched a new local military commander, Lieutenant General Lothar von Trotha (1848–1920), who had experience with suppressing revolts in other imperial settings. Von Trotha sought a single, decisive battle with Herero forces in which he expressly ordered their annihilation. Though vastly outnumbered, von Trotha's troops had the element of surprise and superiority in weapons. Herero fighters and non-combatants retreated into the Kalahari Desert, where thousands would perish (Hull, 2006).

Despite the victory, von Trotha would not relent and pursued the Herero, executing those who were captured or had surrendered, until his supply lines could no longer support the offensive. Instead, von Trotha prevented the Herero from exiting the desert and on 3 October issued an order stating

> [w]ithin the borders of German territory, any Herero, with or without a firearm, with or without livestock, will be shot; nor will I give refuge

*Figure 2.1* A memorial in the coastal Namibian town of Swakopmund for the victims of the Herero and Nama genocide perpetrated by German colonial forces (1904–7).

> to women or children any more. I will drive them back to their people or have them fired upon.
>
> (Zimmerer, 2021: 42)

News of the campaign provoked a rare instance of strong political opposition in Germany to the conduct of colonial forces, and Emperor Wilhelm II rescinded the order. German forces resorted to erecting **concentration camps** – a practice copied from the British experience in South Africa – in larger towns, in part to suppress the revolt and in part to create a pool of slave labor. As the Herero rebellion was suppressed in the fall of 1904, the Nama people in the southern part of the colony mobilized and struck at the Germans. They, too, were rounded up and imprisoned in concentration camps, mainly to the Shark Island camp. Mortality rates there reached 80 percent. Historians estimate that around 80,000 Herero and Nama perished between 1904 and 1908, amounting to 75 percent of the Herero population and perhaps half of the Nama.

The conquest of Indonesia by the Dutch began in the 17th century. One of the last parts of the vast archipelago to be targeted was the island of Sumatra. From the beginning, Dutch colonial forces targeted "environmental infrastructure" – that is, the human-created and managed natural resources such as farms and orchards – as a way to extract resources, control the

Indigenous population, and suppress organized resistance. When they encountered strong resistance in the Aceh sultanate on the northern part of the island in the 1870s, the Dutch resorted to a scorched earth strategy to destroy the ability of recalcitrant and rebellious local peoples to sustain themselves. This entailed the destruction of not only entire villages but also orchards, plantations, valuable fruit-bearing trees, rice fields, and stores of food. As a result, hunger and disease spread, and the Dutch were able to effectively suppress, though not eliminate, resistance and take control of the region by the end of the decade. One Dutch general estimated that between 1874 and 1880, 400 to 500 villages had been burned and 30,000 Acehnese had perished out of prewar population of 300,000 to 400,000 (Kreike, 2021).

When resistance continued in the 1880s, local collaborators advised Dutch officials to substitute the destruction of villages, crops, and food stores with the weaponizing of starvation by strictly controlling the sale of rice, fish, and other foods. In response, Acehnese rebels attempted, albeit without much success, to disrupt the flow of food to Dutch outposts. The inability of the Dutch to completely suppress Acehnese resistance combined with the mounting costs of supplying and defending Dutch positions resulted in retrenchment to Aceh's core region. The ensuing construction of new forts, roads, and railways in the 1880s entailed clearing land and razing farms and orchards with dire consequences for local Acehnese. The Dutch resumed a strategy of offensive military action in the 1890s and the first decade of the 20th century. Despite – or perhaps because of – the massive loss of life and the disruption to what had been an intricately constructed and maintained environmental infrastructure, Dutch control of the region was never entirely secure. As with the German war against the Herero and Nama, the Aceh campaigns provoked a political scandal in the Netherlands in the early 1900s after a disgruntled former Dutch officer accused the state of committing "volkerenmoord," or "nation murder," a forerunner of the term genocide (Kreike, 2012).

# 3 Between the Hague and Nuremberg

Despite intensifying nationalism, an international arms race, and crises over colonies in Africa, most Europeans in the first decade of the 20th century believed a general European war to be highly unlikely, if not practically impossible. The world was increasingly interconnected by trade, expanding communication and transportation networks, and international agreements over everything from intellectual property to standardizing weights and measurements, making the risk of a Great Power war in Europe seem unthinkable. Yet in the summer of 1914, a relatively minor diplomatic crisis in the Balkans sparked the first Europe-wide war in nearly a century. Predictions of a short, decisive conflict – made most confidently by the German emperor and his top military commanders – proved disastrously wide of the mark. The war cost the lives of around 20 million people, while its aftershocks led to the deaths of millions more. In the process, four empires collapsed, the first communist dictatorship took power in the former Russian Empire, and the United States emerged as a global superpower (if a rather reluctant one at first). It also created the conditions for a second and far deadlier world war.

In World War I, the killing and forced displacement of civilians were the most common form of war-related atrocity and were most prevalent – with one important exception – in eastern Europe and Anatolia, where conditions of imperial disintegration prevailed. The exception took place in Belgium in 1914. When the German army invaded and occupied that country and northern France from August to October, its soldiers massacred around 6,500 civilians, used them as human shields, burned thousands of buildings of no military significance, and in a few cases destroyed entire towns and villages. They did so in part because of a belief – held by the Emperor and the German army's Supreme Command and, most crucially, by officers and enlisted men in the field – that civilians had mobilized to wage a form of guerilla war against the invaders, which was in fact not the case (Horne and Kramer, 2001).

Civilian centers were subjected to sporadic and random artillery attacks by Germany throughout the war, though in ways that did not always violate international agreements or customary laws of war. The resort to poison

DOI: 10.4324/9781003118664-5

gas attacks by both sides, however, clearly contravened the second Hague Convention. Most novel was the use of aircraft by the British, French, and Germans to bomb industrial facilities and civilian populations. The stalemate in Europe combined with the belligerents' dependence on international trade produced opposing British and German naval blockades, now aided by the evolution of newer technologies, notably submarines. While naval blockades were not prohibited by international law, the British blockade of Germany's northern ports pushed the German government to resort to unrestricted submarine warfare. The main result of this policy was to move the United States from neutrality to a declaration of war on Germany in April 1917 (Hull, 2019; Strachan, 2005).

The Russian, Austro-Hungarian, and Ottoman Empires were multi-ethnic entities, and the pressures of the war produced a multiplicity of atrocities against ethnic and religious minorities. Sporadic attacks on civilians were conducted by Russian forces as they marched into East Prussia in 1914 and later in Austria and Bukovina, where Jewish communities were subjected to pogroms. The Russian army also deployed colonial war-style counterinsurgency operations against Kyrgyz and Kazakh Dungan populations in Semireche region (today southeastern Kazakhstan and northeastern Kyrgyzstan). Russian troops also massacred Muslims in the Caucasus and deported hundreds of thousands of ethnic Germans. Seeking revenge for the assassination of the Archduke and his wife and fearful of encountering irregulars, Austrian troops committed numerous crimes against civilians in Serbia in 1914 and 1915, while Bulgarian forces occupying Serbia's south engaged in a form of ethnic cleansing reminiscent of the Second Balkan War.

Entire states and large swaths of the Russian Empire were subjected to military occupation regimes, which resorted to the internment of civilians and forced labor practices as the war dragged on. The wording of the Hague Conventions prohibited forcing POWs or civilians to work for the enemy. And the deteriorating conditions in which laborers were held or civilians detained in what were concentration camps violated the conventions' requirements that captives be treated humanely. The deteriorating military situation for the German and Russian armies produced more depredations against civilians. The German army's Operation Alberich, which involved the withdrawal of German forces from a portion of the Western Front in March 1917, entailed the evacuation of some 160,000 civilians and scorched earth tactics. Similarly, the Russian army's retreat from Galicia and Bukovina in 1915 involved the deportation of around three million people, with ethnic minorities and Jews singled out.

As the Ottoman war effort faltered in the spring of 1915, Turkish nationalists (the Young Turks) seeking to establish an ethnically "pure" nation state in Anatolia lashed out at the Armenian population in eastern Anatolia in a series of premeditated attacks that continued until 1923. Recent research has produced estimates of the deaths of around 1.3 million Armenians out of a prewar population of about two million. The Ottoman Minister of the

Interior justified the measures as a response to alleged Ottoman Armenian assistance to Russia as part of larger campaign aimed at securing an independent Armenian nation state. The widely publicized atrocities resulted in the first time states – in this case Russia, France, and Britain – using the term "crimes against humanity" to describe the actions of another state. The term "genocide" was applied retrospectively. Turkish forces also targeted Syriac Christian populations for deportation or murder in Anatolia and northern Persia. Out of an estimated prewar population of 563,000 in the Ottoman Empire and Persia, one historian has estimated that 250,000 Syriac Christians were murdered or killed in fighting. Beginning in the spring of 1916, hundreds of thousands of Kurds were deported from eastern to western Anatolia with the objective of their assimilation as "Turkish" Muslims (Kevorkian, 2011; Morris, 2019).

## Trials and the prevention of war

During the war, Entente governments and jurists discussed holding war crimes trials and collected evidence for postwar prosecutions. When the war ended in November 1918, there was considerable popular support in Entente nations for holding German civilian and military leaders accountable for an array of well-publicized atrocities. But there proved to be limits to what could be done in practice. Some of the most notorious incidents of the war were not violations of the Hague Convention. While the German state could be held accountable for violating Belgium's neutrality in 1914 and resorting to unrestricted submarine warfare, as these acts violated agreements the German government had signed, there was no law or precedent for holding individual civilian or military leaders accountable for war crimes or acts that transgressed the customary laws of war. The taking and killing of hostages were not prohibited. The sinking of the passenger ship *Lusitania* in May 1915 was not legally a war crime, as it was carrying munitions and was thus a legitimate military target. Nor did German dirigible attacks on London violate the treaty, as London was a defended city. There were no provisions in the Hague Conventions regarding how states treated their own citizens, making prosecuting many of the war's atrocities against civilians seemingly impossible. The convention's terms could not be applied to the massacres of Armenians because a formal state of war between the Ottoman Empire and Armenians did not exist.

Moreover, the victors differed among themselves over prosecutions and how international law might – or might not – evolve after the defeat of the Central Powers. The idea of putting the former German emperor, Wilhelm II (then in exile in the Netherlands), on trial for starting the war and the creation of an international court caused the strongest disagreement, mainly due to the resistance of American officials to support either proposal. In the case of trying Wilhelm, they stuck to a narrow interpretation of the law, or, more precisely, the lack of any existing law – codified or customary – that prohibited the launching of a war. Further, there was no precedent for trying individual leaders of a state for war crimes. There was also a political dimension to the American objection: trying the former emperor might further destabilize Germany, making it vulnerable to a communist takeover. As for an international tribunal, the American Secretary of State worried that such a court could set precedents that might in the future be applied to the United States. Suspected war criminals, American officials insisted, should be tried by military courts convened by individual allied nations.

Lengthy negotiations produced a compromise in the form of five clauses in the **Versailles Treaty** that demanded Wilhelm be extradited from the Netherlands and tried by a special allied court for "a supreme offence against international morality and the sanctity of treaties." Other suspected war criminals would be handed over for trial by allied military tribunals. The fifth and best-known clause required the German government to accept full responsibility for starting the war in 1914. Yet the Dutch government refused to extradite Wilhelm. The refusal was only the beginning of what would be a sad denouement to the effort to hold war criminals to account and to set new precedents in international law (Schabas, 2018).

British, French, and Belgium officials had drawn up a list of 862 suspects to be handed over by the German government for trial by an envisioned international tribunal, a list that included Germany's most prominent military leaders and a former chancellor. Suspects were to be charged with responsibility for atrocities committed against civilians in Belgium and France, crimes against POWs, and the deportation of civilians for forced labor. When the list was made public in February 1920, the German Defense Ministry orchestrated what appeared to be mass public demonstrations. Given a desire not to further destabilize Germany and the fact that there was some significant popular and political support in Germany for domestic courts to hold trials of accused war criminals, the victors relented and dropped the extradition demand. Instead, trials would be held by Germany's Supreme Court, the Reichsgericht, in Leipzig (Kramer, 2006).

The **Leipzig trials** (May–July 1921) were a farce. Of the names on the original list of suspects, the court put only 12 on trial and convicted six. In these and other cases investigated but not tried, the Reichsgericht downplayed or simply ignored evidence. In the process, it bolstered the lie that German forces in Belgium and France faced hordes of irregulars and were forced to respond accordingly. It also defended the long-standing German military doctrine of achieving quick total victory at all costs, even if that meant violating agreements to which the German government was a party. Having decided to hand responsibility over to the Reichsgericht, British, French, and Belgian officials attending the proceedings could do little more than walk out in protest and (in the case of the latter two) hold trials of suspects *in absentia* in their respective countries.

In May 1915, officials of the Entente powers issued a warning to the Ottoman government that its leaders would be held accountable for atrocities committed against Armenians. For the British government, more than principle was at stake after the war ended, as it was in Britain's regional strategic interests to support the establishment of a Christian Armenian state situated between Bolshevik Russia and a Muslim Turkish nation. The first trials related to the Armenian genocide were held by Turkish military courts in Constantinople (which was then occupied by allied forces) in 1919 and 1920, and some even took place in Ankara, then the seat of a rival nationalist government. But Turkish public opinion – initially receptive to prosecuting the perpetrators – turned hostile to the trials. As part of a wider campaign against the foreign presence in the nascent Turkish state, officials in Ankara shut down the courts, released suspects awaiting trial, and even took British officials and civilians hostage until the British government agreed to release suspected perpetrators it had interned on Malta. The leader of the Ankara government, Mustafa Kamal, even made a point of appointing some of the worst perpetrators of the genocide to high-level government positions. In the end, the courts in Constantinople sentenced only 17 men to death (most of them in absentia) and carried out the execution of three low-ranking officers. When the final treaty with Turkey was concluded at Lausanne in 1922, the allies had neither the ability nor the political will to force the Turkish government try or extradite any perpetrators. Turkish delegates took the position that alleged Armenian subversion of the empire during the war justified whatever killings and deportations that took pace. The final injustice was a general amnesty passed in Lausanne that precluded the possibility of any future trials (Kramer, 2006).

There were, however, three significant legacies of the Leipzig and Turkish episodes. One was that the evidence amassed by the prosecutors proved to be of enormous value to historians of the war and the Armenian genocide. A second was that future advocates of international tribunals could point to the Leipzig debacle in particular as proof that leaving war crimes prosecutions to national courts was folly. Finally, the attempt to hold individuals accountable broke with a tradition in Europe that stretched back to the Treaty of Westphalia in 1648. This treaty, which ended the Thirty Years' War, included a clause that required "perpetual acts of oblivion," meaning that signatories pledged to consign what had happened to an irretrievable past. It followed from this that no one would be held accountable for his actions during the war. Forgetting, in other words, was considered essential to achieving and maintaining the peace. But demands for an extensive judicial reckoning that followed World War I began – however imperfectly – the process of breaking with this tradition, a process that would take a far more destructive war to be realized.

British and European jurists did not abandon the campaign to create an international criminal court. But in the 1920s, the idea of preventing war became a more attractive option than creating international mechanisms for punishing crimes committed during them. There was, of course, US President Woodrow Wilson's idea of a **League of Nations** to arbitrate disputes between member states before they exploded into war. The League's covenant did provide for the establishment of the **Permanent Court of International Justice** (PCIJ), which existed from 1922 to 1946 and arbitrated relatively minor disputes between states. In 1925, negotiations between Germany, Great Britain, France, Belgium, and Italy (the Pact of Locarno) produced arbitration agreements between multiple European states and, most important, affirmed the postwar borders between France, Belgium, and Germany. The highpoint of the movement to prevent war was the **Pact of Paris** of 1928, also known as the Kellogg-Briand Pact. It was signed by representatives of 44 nations (the Soviet Union was not a signatory) on 27 August 1928. The terms of the treaty did not "outlaw war," as is frequently stated. Wars of self-defense, for instance, were considered legitimate. Nor was there any provision for holding individuals accountable for starting a war or committing war crimes. Rather, the signatories pledged that their governments henceforth renounced war "as an instrument of national policy" (Cooper, 2010; Hathaway and Shapiro, 2017).

At the same time, there were relatively few new conventions and treaties in the 1920s and 1930s related to regulating the conduct of war or holding war criminals accountable. The **Protocol for the Prohibition of the Use in War of Asphyxiating, Poisonous or Other Gases and of Bacteriological Methods of Warfare** was signed by representatives of 38 nations in 1925. Two Red Cross conventions related to the treatment of wounded and sick POWs were also concluded, though the Soviet Union and Japan were not signatories.

There were also some notable failures. The United States, now a true world power, did not join the League of Nations and largely withdrew from an active role in trans-Atlantic security issues. In 1924, the Czechoslovak government proposed the Protocol for the Pacific Settlement of International Disputes, which proposed bolstering the PCIJ's ability to arbitrate disputes between signatories and recommended sanctions for those parties deemed aggressors in any armed conflict. The British government, however, refused to sign. In general, the League failed to prevent or respond effectively to such outright acts of aggression as Japan's invasion of Manchuria in 1931 and Italy's invasion of Ethiopia in 1935. A series of international conferences aimed at limiting the production of warships resulted in some initial progress in the 1920s but faltered in the 1930s. There was also a failed attempt to conclude international agreements on bombing by air and on submarine attacks on merchant ships.

It is also important to remember that while Germany sued for peace in November 1918, significant parts of Europe were consumed with war for years after making it very difficult to date the end of World War I with any exactitude. From 1918 to the mid-1920s, more Europeans died in armed conflicts than died in the years between 1914 and 1918 as wars raged in Russia, Finland, Central and Eastern Europe, Ireland, and Southeastern Europe. These conflicts were most often civil wars (Russia, Finland, Ireland) or conflicts to establish new boundaries in the wake of imperial collapse, or the result of attempts to new, ethnically homogenous nation states (parts of Eastern Europe, Turkey). A surge in anti-imperial mobilization in Africa and Asia produced revolts and a new round of colonial wars in Egypt, India, Morocco, Iraq, and Syria. But the League of Nations, treaties like Kellogg-Briand or Locarno, and the few agreements on weapons and the treatment of prisoners were all negotiated by and for the benefit of the great powers. War crimes and atrocities committed in colonial spaces remained, as they had been, untouched by the prospect of legal constraints and judicial reckoning (Gerwarth, 2016; Pedersen, 2017).

## World War II

It would be the actions of Nazi Germany and Imperial Japan that would have the greatest impact on the evolution of war crimes law. Since his entry into politics in the early 1920s, Adolf Hitler pledged to renounce the widely despised Versailles Treaty. As Germany's Chancellor in the 1930s, he proclaimed in public to be seeking peace, but his real objective was to rearm Germany and launch a war of territorial conquest aimed primarily at Eastern Europe and the Soviet Union. From 1933 to 1939, he led the country on a nearly uninterrupted string of diplomatic victories. The guarantors of Versailles, Great Britain, and France (the United States had removed itself from any meaningful role in supporting collective security in Europe) did nothing to stop him. War finally came in September 1939 with the invasion of western Poland by German forces, followed by an invasion of the eastern half of the country by the Soviet Union.

Germany's invasion of Poland and its ensuing attempt to conquer "living space" in the east entailed the commission of war crimes on a massive, and in some ways unprecedented, scale. The east was in many ways a classic campaign of imperial conquest. "Living space," as the Nazi Party's platform called it, was to be taken and settled by Germans. Resident populations of Slavic peoples and, above all, Jews were considered at best "sub-human" and at worst a mortal threat to the German "race." And to an even greater extent than in the colonial wars of the previous century, German forces erased the distinction between combatant and civilian. But the major difference with other modern imperial projects was that Hitler envisioned the complete removal of Slavs and Jews. Populations of the former were to be exploited as slave labor and allowed to die out, mainly through hunger and disease. The latter were to be physically removed, with Madagascar and somewhere beyond the Ural Mountain range being the two envisioned destinations. When mass deportations proved impossible, mainly due to the fact that the Soviet Union remained undefeated following the massive German invasion in June 1941, all Jews were to be murdered in place, mainly by shooting operations or by gassing in a small number of camps purpose-built to kill huge numbers of people as efficiently and quickly as possible. By the end of the war, around six million Jews – almost half of Europe's prewar Jewish population – had been killed (Baranowski, 2010; Bergen, 2009).

What became known after the war as the **Holocaust** was premeditated mass murder that in its ambition, scale, and speed was unprecedented in history. But it represented one of many crimes against humanity committed by the German army (Wehrmacht), Schutzstaffel (SS) units, and various auxiliaries along with non-German collaborators. In all 3.3 million Soviet POWs were executed or allowed to die. The regime dragooned over 12 million Europeans as slave laborers. The program of murdering mentally and physically handicapped Germans was extended to the east. Concentration and death camp inmates were subjected to gruesome medical experiments. The regime also pursued the total elimination of Europe's Roma and Sinti (or "Gypsy") populations. The physical infrastructure of exploitation and mass murder was vast: recent research has identified the existence of over 40,000 concentration camps, death camps, slave labor camps, and ghettos for Jews in Germany and German-controlled Europe. And as armed resistance against German occupation in eastern and western Europe intensified, so did the savagery of German reprisals against civilians.

The Holocaust was a German-led pan-European assault on a vulnerable minority. The Germans found collaborators everywhere, and they proved willing to replicate Nazi racial policies against Jews, Roma, and ethnic minority populations. Indeed, the Holocaust could not have been carried out as it was without the active (and passive) assistance of thousands, if not millions, of non-Germans. The Vichy government in France, the Slovak Republic, the Independent State of Croatia, the Government of National Salvation in Serbia, the Italian Social Republic, and the Iron Cross in Hungary were all collaborationist regimes that participated to varying degrees in the persecution, robbery, roundup, deportation, and murder of Jews. In German-controlled Europe, civil servants, policemen, and business owners formed a kind of local infrastructure of persecution. Farmers and homemakers betrayed and robbed their neighbors. Hundreds of thousands of non-Germans also served in the Wehrmacht and Waffen-SS or in various German-controlled auxiliary units. They guarded ghettos and camps and benefited from Jewish slave labor. Thousands of others perpetrated mass killings of Jews in the Baltic States, Poland, and the USSR. Most would never be held accountable for their roles in the genocide (Deak, 2013).

Fascist Italy's wars in Africa and the Balkans, though on a much smaller scale, also involved the commission of numerous war crimes, the vast majority of which went unpunished after the war. The murder of POWs and civilians was routine in Italy's invasion of Ethiopia, which included the use of poison gas against combatants and non-combatants. An uprising by Senussi tribesmen in what is today eastern Libya led to a ten-year-long war in which some 75,000 Senussi were killed. As with Japan's invasion of Manchuria and Shanghai, the League of Nations proved ineffective. Italy's occupation regimes in Greece, Slovenia, and along the Dalmatian coast were also brutal, particularly as partisan activity intensified in 1942 and 1943 (Strang, 2013; Gooch, 2005).

Japan's wars of imperial conquest began years before Germany's. Ultranationalist elements in the military spearheaded a resurgence of regional imperialism that aimed to contain the Soviet Union, prevent the unification of China by the Nationalists, and push Britain, the United States, and other western powers out of Asia altogether. The offensive began in September 1931 with the conquest of Manchuria. An attack on Shanghai four months later involved the first aerial bombardment of a large civilian center. The League of Nations did no more than form investigatory committees and pass toothless resolutions. When it attempted to broker talks between China and Japan, Japan withdrew from the organization. The conflict intensified in July 1937, when fighting broke out between Chinese and Japanese soldiers outside Beijing. The Nationalist capital of Nanjing was subjected to a ferocious attack in which 260,000–350,000 civilians were killed and around 30,000 POWs executed (the "Rape of Nanking"). The mass rape of some 80,000 Chinese women was a particularly notable feature of the occupation, provoking international condemnation at the time and close attention by prosecutors at the postwar international tribunal in Tokyo (Tanaka, 1996).

Contrary to Japanese expectations, the Nationalists refused to come to terms, and a long war of attrition followed, making China one of the most important theaters of World War II. But Tokyo's ambitions extended to Southeast Asia. Germany's invasion of the Soviet Union surprised the Japanese, but removed one looming threat. With Britain and its empire fighting the Germans alone and France and the Netherlands vanquished, only the United States remained to block Japan's expansion into Southeast Asia. The catalyst for war came with the US decision to embargo the sale of raw materials to Japan, a decision that provoked a Japanese attack on American naval installations in the Pacific. A wider offensive followed, with Japanese forces conquering Indonesia, the Philippines, Burma, Malaya, and Singapore by early 1942. In the process, the Japanese captured tens of thousands of Asian and western Allied soldiers, subjecting them to atrocious and often murderous treatment en route to and in POW camps. Prisoners and civilians alike were subjected to forced labor and horrific medical experiments. Mortality rates were greatly intensified by the unsparing tropical climate. After testing biological weapons on Chinese civilians, Japanese forces deployed them against Soviet troops. As with Nazi Germany – which continued to round up and deport Jews to Auschwitz as late as July 1944 – Japanese forces massacred civilians even as final defeat loomed, most notoriously from October 1944 to May 1945, when troops under General Tomoyuki Yamashita (1885–1946) murdered around 25,000 civilians in Batangas Province in the Philippines.

In postwar trials, many defendants, their lawyers, and critics of the trials repeatedly pointed out that Allied governments and militaries were responsible for crimes similar to those they now accused their defeated foes of committing. While the motives of such accusations were to undermine the trials or relativize, and thus minimize, the guilt of Axis soldiers and governments, they are not baseless. Allied soldiers maltreated and sometimes murdered POWs, raped women, and plundered the property of those they were presumably liberating. The strategic bombing campaigns of Germany and Japan, especially the use of two atomic bombs against the latter, elicit charges of rank hypocrisy to the present day. Yet there was no question that Imperial Japan and Nazi Germany had initiated and waged wars of unprecedented destructiveness. And unlike the period after November 1918, the victors would embark on an unprecedented effort to hold at least some of those responsible to account.

# 4 The Nuremberg and Tokyo tribunals

World War II in Europe and Asia was followed by thousands of trials of suspected war criminals and collaborators, a wave of judicial reckoning without parallel in history. There were three categories of trials. The first involved military courts. The second involved trials held by postwar civilian governments. The third, and the subject of this chapter, were international tribunals. The legal precedents set in the most prominent of these trials – the *International Military Tribunal in Nuremberg* (IMT), the *Nuremberg Military Tribunal* (NMT), and the **International Military Tribunal for the Far East** (IMTFE or Tokyo Tribunal) – continue to shape the course of international law relating to the conduct of war and the protection of human rights. And the two tribunals in Nuremberg were instrumental in documenting the base criminality of the Nazi regime and the reality of its responsibility for starting a general war in Europe and committing vast crimes against combatants and civilians alike.

## Planning the trials

As early as the fall of 1941, Allied governments issued statements that those responsible for committing crimes against combatants and civilians would face some kind of retribution. Plans for a formal judicial reckoning in lieu of uncontrolled acts of vengeance began to take shape the following year. In January 1942, the Soviet Union, Great Britain, the United States, and six governments in exile established the Inter-Allied Commission on the Punishment of War Crimes, which issued a demand for "the punishment, through the channel of organized justice, of those guilty of or responsible" for war crimes. The declaration included an explicit rejection of "acts of vengeance on the part of the general public" (UNWCC, 1948: 90). In August, the British government – its leaders were not enthusiastic supporters of an international court – proposed to the Americans that a United Nations* commission

* While the United Nations was not formally created until 1945, Allied governments used the term regularly following the signing of the Declaration of the United Nations on 1 January 1942 by the representatives of 26 nations.

DOI: 10.4324/9781003118664-6

be established to gather evidence of atrocities. In October, the British and American governments agreed that armistice terms with Germany and all Axis nations include a provision for the capture and surrender of accused war criminals. The point was to prevent a repeat of the situation after World War I when Kaiser Wilhelm II found sanctuary in the Netherlands, one of several important lessons Allied leaders believed they had learned from that embarrassing episode. Accordingly, neutral countries were warned not to shelter wanted war criminals (Kochavi, 1998; Plesch, 2017).

The **United Nations War Crimes Commission** was created in October 1943 and based in London, but it could do no more than gather evidence and was not well funded or staffed sufficiently. Josef Stalin's refusal to cooperate was another liability. He instead created a Soviet investigative body, the **Extraordinary State Commission for Ascertaining and Investigating Atrocities Perpetrated by the German Fascist Invaders and Their Accomplices.** This commission gathered evidence for what would be the first war crimes trials of the war. In 1943 and 1944, Soviet military courts tried thousands of suspects, the vast majority of them Soviet citizens accused of **collaboration.** A smaller number of trials were public and publicized widely. These were show trials in which guilty verdicts were a foregone conclusion. Yet the prosecutors foreshadowed some aspects of the IMT – notably the charges of common plan or conspiracy – when they pointed toward the Nazi regime's leaders as the men most responsible for the countless atrocities committed in the USSR. American and British officials, conversely, were more reluctant to hold trials while Germany and Japan remained undefeated, the main concern being the possibility of retaliation against Allied POWs (Hirsch, 2020).

During a conference held in Moscow in October 1943, the American, British, Soviet, and Chinese foreign ministers declared their determination to send accused German war criminals to the countries in which crimes had been committed but withheld for themselves the authority to pursue those whose "offenses have no particular location" (UNWCC, 1948: 108). Beyond this important distinction, however, their declaration lacked specifics, and at that point in the war, planning trials was not a high priority for the American and British governments. And despite agreement among most Allied leaders and governments-in-exile that trials were preferable to "acts of vengeance," the urge to resort to such acts remained very strong. The wording of the **Moscow declaration** contained the threat of summary executions by stating that many Germans would be "judged on the spot by the peoples whom they have outraged" (UNWCC, 1948: 107). Such language reflected British Prime Minister Winston Churchill's hostility to the idea of holding trials of Nazi Party leaders and German military officers. All British officials of Churchill's generation recalled the debacle of the Leipzig trials. And while they were amenable to the prospect of courts convened in different European nations for "lesser" criminals, they also advocated summary executions for leading Nazis on the grounds that their actions had placed them outside the boundaries of law.

Churchill's counterparts, however, favored trials for the major war criminals. An ailing and distracted Franklin Roosevelt, who had briefly given tacit support to a British summary execution scheme, changed his mind and backed the idea of an international tribunal. His successor, Harry Truman, was an even stronger supporter of high-level trials, as was Charles De Gaulle. An international trial would serve multiple purposes. Most important was to expose the crimes of Nazi Germany and Imperial Japan and hold accountable those most responsible for designing, ordering, and carrying them out. Also important was the opportunity to set new precedents in international law. And the promise of judicial reckoning would, ideally, deter future wars of aggression. From the American perspective in particular, the postwar order would be one dominated by the rule of law and international organizations created to promote international trade and resolve disputes peacefully. For French officials, participating in the trial would remind the world that France was a great power, further legitimize the post-liberation government led by De Gaulle, and focus attention on the crimes of the Germans and thus away from the ugly reality of France's four years of collaboration (Smith, 1982).

Stalin's determination to hold trials was of particular significance. Though he mused to Roosevelt and Churchill about summarily executing thousands of German military officers as soon as the war ended (he claimed to be joking), the idea of a public trial held considerable appeal. He thus took what Churchill referred to as an "ultrarespectable line" on dealing with major war criminals by backing plans for an international court, something his Foreign Minister, Vyacheslav Molotov, had called for in 1942. The hard-won prestige of the Soviet Union as a true global superpower could be showcased. And there was much to be said for calling the world's attention to the sacrifices endured by Soviet citizens, particularly as ignorance in the west about the extent of the suffering and destruction was shockingly vast, as dismayed members of the Soviet delegation would realize when the IMT convened. And then there was the belief that a high-visibility trial would bolster Moscow's case for extensive reparations from Germany (Hirsch, 2020).

Laying bare Nazi Germany's responsibility for planning and executing a war of territorial conquest would also distract the world's attention from some inconvenient facts, mainly that it was Stalin's non-aggression pact with Germany that allowed Hitler to first conquer Poland and then much of Western Europe. Stalin even made sure that the murder of nearly 22,000 Polish officers and intellectuals in and near Katyn Forest in 1940, carried out by Soviet secret police on his orders but blamed on the Germans, would be part of the Soviet indictment against the German defendants. Fully expecting a repeat of the infamous show trials held in Moscow in the 1930s and the wartime military tribunals – he would appoint the former chief prosecutor of the show trials, Andrei Vyshinsky, as the principal Soviet representative to the IMT – Stalin did not count on defendants being allowed to choose their own defense lawyers. They would not hesitate to accuse the

Soviets of the Katyn massacre and to remind the court of the non-aggression pact's existence, going so far as to reveal the once secret protocols that sealed Poland's fate and that of the three Baltic states.

It would be within the US War Department that the legal framework for the IMT was formulated. The existing foundation was the Hague Conventions. But they pertained only to states already at war, and there were no provisions to hold political leaders accountable for crimes committed by their states' militaries, let alone for starting a war in the first place. Here the Soviet jurist **Aron Trainin** (1883–1957) made a crucial contribution when he proposed including a charge of "**crimes against peace**" (or "aggressive war") in the indictment. Trainin recognized the charge as a way to indict the leaders of countries, men who might otherwise avoid prosecution for war crimes and other violations of international law. Trainin also hoped Germany's leading industrialists would be included in the charge. Crucially, his proposal was taken up with enthusiasm by his American counterparts, who very much wanted to put the highest-ranking Nazi party officials in the dock.

A US War Department lawyer, **Murray Bernays** (1894–1970), came up with another innovation. In September 1944, Bernays proposed charging Nazi Party organizations with "conspiracy to commit murder, terrorism, and the destruction of peaceful populations in violations of the laws of War" (Smith, 1982: 51). An individual could thus be found guilty on the basis of membership in a criminal organization, with the extent of his or her knowledge of or participation in its crimes determining the severity of punishment. Bernays had in mind principally the SS, the organization he and many other Allied government officials held most responsible for the Nazi regime's worst crimes.

The most important convert to Bernays' scheme was Secretary of War **Henry L. Stimson** (1867–1950). As a former federal prosecutor in President Theodore Roosevelt's administration, he had successfully prosecuted anti-trust cases on criminal conspiracy charges. Stimson understood that Bernays' proposal would facilitate the prosecution of crimes authorized by a state and committed by hundreds of thousands of individuals. Roosevelt seemed to favor the idea, but it faced strong resistance in the War and Justice Departments, with opponents favoring a much narrower interpretation of war crimes and skeptical about the need for an international tribunal. What tipped the debate in favor of including the criminal organization and conspiracy categories was a massacre of American POWs in Belgium in mid-December 1944 by a unit of the Waffen SS. News of the incident provided the critical leverage to supporters of the conspiracy charge, as it had been perpetrated by a branch of the SS, the principal Nazi Party "criminal organization" in the eyes of American officials. Also important was the widely held belief that the responsible SS battle group had been ordered to execute captured US soldiers. Two weeks after the bodies of the executed American soldiers were recovered in Belgium, the Red Army liberated Auschwitz, and

Allied armies soon overran the vast network of concentration camps in Germany, stoking yet more outrage at the soon-to-be-vanquished Nazi regime. Such events were charging the atmosphere in high-level Washington policy circles with a current of "utter hatred" for the SS (Taylor, 1992: 41–42; Remy, 2017).

It was in this atmosphere that Stimson and proponents of the criminal organization and conspiracy categories prevailed, allowing them to present the idea as American policy during negotiations with other Allied governments over an international tribunal's charter. In June 1945, the allies met in London to prepare for the trial. After two months of negotiations, they produced the court's charter: the **Agreement and Charter for the Prosecution and Punishment of Major War Criminals of the European Axis**, or the "**London Agreement.**" The accused could be charged with one or more of four counts. The first was conspiracy (or "common plan") to participate in the remaining three: crimes against peace (or crimes of aggression), war crimes (the killing of combatants and civilians for no military purpose), and crimes against humanity (another new category to account for atrocities committed against civilians). The four Allied governments would each appoint a judge and an alternate, with the four judges selecting a president (they would choose the British jurist Sir Geoffrey Lawrence). Decisions would be made by the majority vote of the judges, and there was no possibility of appeal. They also selected the location for the tribunal: the city of Nuremberg. It was chosen for its symbolic significance – it had been the site of annual Nazi Party rallies, and its name was associated with a series of race laws that formed much of the legal basis for the regime's persecution of Germany's Jews. Not least, the courtroom and its adjacent jail facility were undamaged (Taylor, 1992).

## The IMT in Nuremberg

At the end of August 1945, the chief prosecutors announced a list of 24 defendants, nearly all then in American custody. Adolf Hitler, Joseph Goebbels, and Heinrich Himmler were dead. Martin Bormann, the powerful chief of the Reich Chancellery, was unaccounted for (he was in fact dead) and charged *in absentia*. The most important defendants were Hermann Goering, head of the air force (Luftwaffe) and the Four Year Plan and without question the highest-visibility defendant, Rudolf Hess, the Deputy Party Leader and head of the Party Chancellery who had been in British custody since his ill-fated flight to Scotland in 1941, Alfred Jodl, Chief of the Wehrmacht Command Staff, Wilhelm Keitel, head of the armed forces High Command, Karl Doenitz, the Supreme Navy Commander who served very briefly as the President of Germany following Hitler's suicide, Hans Frank, the brutal Governor General of the General Government in occupied Poland, Wilhelm Frick, head of the Interior Ministry and Reich Protector of Bohemia and Moravia (most of the former Czechoslovakia), Alfred

Rosenberg, one of the Nazi Party's most prominent ideologues, Joachim von Ribbentrop, the regime's Foreign Minister, Albert Speer, the powerful wartime armaments minister, and Fritz Sauckel, the wartime organizer of slave labor. Only one SS officer was tried: Ernst Kaltenbrunner, head of all German police forces in the war's final years. The Nazi regime's most important organizations were also indicted: the SS, Gestapo, SA (Sturmabteilung, or SA, the Nazi Party's paramilitary wing), the Reich Cabinet, the Nazi Party's leadership, and the General Staff of the armed forces (Taylor, 1992).

The trial ran from 20 November 1945 to 31 August 1946 and held 216 sessions. The bulk of the prosecution's evidence was drawn from the huge quantity of German documents captured by the Allies. The accused all pleaded not guilty and based their defenses on a bundle of claims: that only states could be prosecuted for committing war crimes, that the tribunal was applying the law *ex post facto*, that they had been wrongly accused or ignorant, or that they had simply been obeying orders. Only one – Albert Speer – showed anything like remorse on the stand. In October 1946, the judges announced their verdicts on 22 of the original 24 defendants (one had committed suicide and the other had been deemed unfit to stand trial): 12 received death sentences, seven received prison sentences of four years to life, and three were acquitted.

*Figure 4.1* The document room at the International Military Tribunal in Nuremberg.

The accusation that the IMT imposed *ex post facto* law has been the most serious criticism leveled at the tribunal, one that its judges, prosecutors, and defenders never convincingly rebutted [*Doc. 4, p. 118*]. There was in fact no precedent for prosecuting someone on the charge of waging aggressive war, and crimes against humanity was a mostly novel legal concept. The charge that the defendants did not receive a fair trial has been far easier to rebut. Each was in fact entitled to legal representation of his choice or he could represent himself, and each had the right to copies of all documentation referred to in his indictment and could present evidence in support of his defense and cross-examine witnesses. Other critics of the IMT would later point to the lack of attention given to the Holocaust. Yet at the time of the trial, relatively little was known about the scope of the genocide. Indeed, one of the most important American prosecutors, Brigadier General **Telford Taylor** (1908–98), would confess that he only learned about it during the proceedings. The vast differences between the Anglo-American legal systems on the one side and the Soviet system on the other at times impeded the prosecution. Soviet prosecutors, after all, were accustomed to simply issuing pre-scripted denunciations of defendants without the expectation of serious challenge, and unsurprisingly they did not do well against the defendants' lawyers.

The IMT's critics failed to offer realistic alternatives to an international tribunal that established new legal standards for atrocities committed in wartime, particularly a war of unprecedented destructiveness. Mass executions were, in practical, legal, and moral terms, out of the question. Leaving prosecutions up to a new German government – even a democratic one – was unthinkable. Excluding the Soviet Union – the nation that had suffered and done the most to defeat the Nazis – from the tribunal was also impossible in 1945 and 1946. Even asking a neutral nation to host the trials would not have worked, as no nation in 1945 could be considered truly neutral and acceptable to all four Allied states. And scattered trials would not have had the international profile that the IMT would attract.

That the tribunal received the international media attention its designers hoped for was one of its greatest achievements. Extremely important in this respect was that it exposed the connection between the leadership of the Nazi Party and German military to the planning and execution of an unprovoked war of territorial aggression in which war crimes and atrocities committed against civilians were planned in advance. No future political or military leader anywhere – especially in Germany – could ever claim with any degree of credibility that the charges leveled by the court were fabricated. Finally, the IMT was a landmark moment in the evolution of international law and a model for future such tribunals. For the first time, individuals who violated international laws were held accountable. Neither the sovereignty of states nor claims of acting on superior orders were accepted as viable defenses. On 11 December 1946, the United Nations General Assembly affirmed provisions of the London Agreement as principles of international law.

Charges of hypocrisy, however, are more difficult to refute. This charge was not baseless. The issue of *tu quoque* was dealt with in the trial, though not in terms of public perception. Then and since, critics have pointed out that Allied armies were guilty of some of the crimes committed by those their governments were now prosecuting. The Allies' strategic bombing campaign in Germany, which killed around one and half a million Germans (mostly civilians) and did not produce the collapse of either German industrial production or civilian morale, was a particularly glaring example for the trials' critics. The host city was emblematic: an attack in January 1945 had destroyed its historic center.

World War II was in significant part a moral contest. The undeniable fact that it was Imperial Japan and Nazi Germany that had initiated the war and the savagery with which both regimes waged it and, not least, the reality of total Allied victory made it possible for certain deficiencies on the Allied side to be overlooked, at least for a time. The British and French policy of appeasing Hitler, culminating in the abandonment of Czechoslovakia in 1938 and 1939, meant London and Paris shared a significant degree of responsibility, albeit indirect, for the war's outbreak. During the war, Britain and the Free French were fighting not only for the survival and future of their nations but also for preserving control over hundreds of millions of colonial subjects in the Caribbean, Africa, and Asia. The United States was a nation segregated by race and one in which citizens of Japanese descent were incarcerated in concentration camps. The Soviet Union was ruled by a murderous tyrant who had authorized a pact with Nazi Germany that led directly to the start of the European war in 1939. In addition, the Soviet Union attacked Finland and Poland in 1939. During the war, Stalin ordered the deportations of seven ethnic groups in the USSR to the interior of the country. Bulgaria was attacked following a declaration of war on 5 September 1944 with the objective of occupying the country and installing a pro-Soviet regime. The Soviets also declared war on Japan two days after the bombing of Hiroshima, an act that fulfilled an agreement with the western Allies but was unnecessary from a wartime strategic standpoint.

Just as the war in Europe ended, British, French, and US forces initiated new wars in their respective colonies. On 8 May 1945 (Victory in Europe (VE) Day), French forces attacked Setif and Guelma in Algeria in response to anti-French protests. French and British forces fought pro-independence forces in Syria and Indochina (now comprising Vietnam, Laos, and Cambodia) while around one half million Dutch troops fought to hold on to Indonesia. In the Philippines, where **General Douglas MacArthur** boasted that the United States had "buried imperialism" upon the establishment of the Philippine Republic on 4 July 1946, the American military and covert intelligence operatives backed a corrupt and undemocratic regime in a bloody fight with a peasant-based insurgency. As with World War I, it is difficult to pinpoint when World War II really ended. What was clear was that Allied states had no intention of applying the standards to which they had held Germany and Japan to their own actions during or after the war (Burleigh, 2013).

The Axis, of course, included fascist Italy. Why was there no international tribunal for that country? Defenders of the IMT and its legacies omit reference to the lack of a similar court for Nazi Germany's most important ally. The Italian fascist regime was, after all, responsible for an array of war crimes and atrocities committed during its brutal invasion and occupation of Ethiopia in 1935 and later in the Balkans. But no trial – on either the IMT or NMT models – ever took place. For one thing, Benito Mussolini and the fascist regime had been deposed in 1943 following the Anglo-American invasion of Sicily. As American and British troops then advanced up the Italian peninsula, civil war conditions erupted in parts of the country as anti-fascist partisans fought both the Germans and Italian fascists. By 1945, Italy was occupied by the Allies (the Soviets were deliberately excluded from any role) and faced an unstable political situation in which the popular Italian Communist Party might conceivably come to power legally (Battini, 2007).

Communist successes in a series of local elections in the spring of 1946 only reinforced the fears of liberal and conservative Italians and American officials that a high-profile trial of Italians would further inflame popular anti-fascist sentiment to the benefit of the communists. Besides, tens of thousands of Italians had already been purged or tried in 1945, a fact that led government officials to conclude that the fascist period had truly come to an end and justice had been served. The post-fascist Italian government's reluctance to see Italians tried for war crimes was also evinced by its resistance to extradition requests by the governments of countries, notably Yugoslavia, where Italian forces had committed numerous atrocities. Complicating matters was the fact that the German army and SS had committed serious crimes in the course of anti-partisan warfare and the roundup of Jews for deportation to the ghettos and camps in the east. For a time, the British planned to hold two major trials of German army and SS personnel, but never did so. In the end, only a few trials were held by British military tribunals, with relatively lenient sentences handed down. There were clearly limits to the influence of the Nuremberg model.

## The Nuremberg military tribunal

Since the IMT tried only the highest-ranking surviving members of the Nazi regime, the legal fates of a large number of other important German officials remained undetermined. Notably absent from the IMT, for instance, was a single representative of German industry. And some of the regime's most serious crimes – notably the genocide of the Jews and the program to systematically murder the handicapped – went almost entirely unaddressed. Clearly, more trials and perhaps the convening of another international court were warranted, and the London Agreement included a provision for a subsequent international tribunal. But even before the IMT concluded its work, divisions among the wartime allies – mainly the US and Great Britain on one side and the Soviet Union on the other – precluded the possibility of another four-power tribunal.

So American officials took it upon themselves to create a new court to prosecute suspected war criminals in US custody. Also known informally as the "Subsequent Trials" or "Subsequent Proceedings," the Nuremberg Military Tribunal (NMT) comprised 12 tribunals that operated in Nuremberg between October 1946 and April 1949. The NMT's legal basis was a law promulgated on 20 December 1945 by the four power Allied Control Council (ACC, **Allied Control Council Law No. 10**) that authorized officials in each of the four occupation zones to arrest and try suspected war criminals in their respective zones. The proceedings were organized by a new entity – the Office, Chief of Counsel of War Crimes – and led by Brigadier General Telford Taylor, who had served as a prosecutor in the IMT. The OCC's most important responsibility was to select defendants. Given that around 10,000 designated war crimes suspects were at that time in American custody (a number soon reduced to 2,500) and that office faced budget cuts, ultimately only 185 defendants, nearly all of them men, were tried by the NMT (Priemel and Stiller, 2012).

Unlike the IMT, then, the NMT was not an international court, nor was it, strictly speaking, a military tribunal, as the judges were all civilians. In terms of its procedures and the rights accorded to the defendants, it modeled itself on the IMT. Yet while the IMT tried the surviving individual regime officials and military officers, the NMT mainly prosecuted individuals representing institutions: physicians in the "euthanasia" program, judges, officials in government ministries, directors of the IG Farben and Krupp industrial conglomerates, Wehrmacht officers, and various branches of the SS. And while the IMT focused on the crime of aggressive war, the NMT emphasized what one historian characterized as "crimes of atrocity" committed against civilian populations.

The NMT ultimately convicted 142 and sentenced 26 to death. Not only was its reach and operations hamstrung by budget cuts, its procedures, prosecutors, and legal bases received a great deal of criticism in and outside occupied Germany. As the trials netted prominent members of Germany's professional, legal, industrial, and military elite (and in some cases the long-established and widely esteemed institutions they represented (such as the Foreign Ministry)), the NMT became the target of a campaign spearheaded by ex-Nazi lawyers, veterans groups, and prominent clergymen to discredit its legitimacy and win amnesty for the convicted. This campaign and domestic criticism of the NMT and trials held by the US Army in Germany in the context of the emerging Cold War put American officials – particularly Military Governor General Lucius D. Clay (1898–1978) and his successor, High Commissioner for West Germany John J. McCloy (1895–1989) – under pressure to halt all executions and free the convicted men. McCloy oversaw the creation of a clemency and parole system as a substitute for a court of appeals. In the end, only 12 of the death sentences were carried out, and by 1958, every convicted defendant had been released from prison (Hutchinson, 2022).

In retrospect, it was the precedent set by the NMT and the documenting of Nazi crimes that comprised its most significant legacies. The court's records and proceedings and emphasis on "crimes of atrocity" informed the 1948 United Nations **Genocide Convention** and influenced crimes against humanity cases to a greater extent than the IMT. By producing a massive record of individual and institutional criminality, the proceedings made an incalculable contribution to the historical record. And while the Holocaust did not play a prominent role in the IMT's proceedings, it did so in the NMT's, above all in the Einsatzgruppen case, in which 24 former members of mobile execution squads were tried for murdering thousands of Jews and others in the USSR (Heller, 2011; Earl, 2010).

## The International Military Tribunal for the Far East

As with Nazi Germany, the Allied states fighting Japan issued repeated warnings of a harsh postwar reckoning. And as with defeated Germany, the victors believed prosecuting war criminals would be an essential component of Japan's transition to a peaceful member of the international community. The new Supreme Commander for the Allied Powers in Asia (SCAP), US General Douglas MacArthur (1880–1964), received the authority to put "major Japanese war criminals" on trial for committing crimes against peace, conspiracy, "orthodox" war crimes, and crimes against humanity. The IMT in Nuremberg was to be used as a model, but if no other Allied state wished to participate, the United States would act alone (Crowe, 2014).

In January 1946, MacArthur announced the creation of the International Military Tribunal for the Far East (IMTFE) and appointed nine (and later two more) judges from a list compiled by an Allied commission. While the tribunal's president was an Australian, Sir William Webb, the Americans would dominate the proceedings. The prosecutors targeted Japan's "principal leaders" – with one very significant exception – and created three categories: "Class A" war criminals to be charged with planning and committing crimes against peace and "Class B" and "C" for lower-ranking officials charged with committing war crimes and crimes against humanity. Another similarity to Nuremberg was the use of a version of the conspiracy and common plan scheme: individual defendants would be accused of committing war crimes and crimes against humanity as part of a wider conspiracy to wage wars of territorial conquest (Dower, 1999; Tanaka *et al.*, 2011).

The IMTFE ran from 3 May 1946 to 4 November 1948, holding 818 sessions in 417 days, a considerably longer trial than its counterpart in Germany. The 28 defendants included former high-ranking government officials and military officers, notably wartime Prime Minister Hideki Tojo and much of his war cabinet. All defendants were found guilty (one was determined to be mentally incompetent and two others died during the trial), with seven former leaders convicted and sentenced to death, 16 receiving life sentences, and the two other sentences of 20 and seven years. The death sentences were carried out, but otherwise no one served his full sentence and all convicted men were free by 1958.

The most notable absence in the dock was Emperor Hirohito. Why wasn't he indicted? There was no question that he bore responsibility for approving the imperial army's massively destructive wars against China and Southeast Asia and, by extension, the commission of countless crimes against millions of combatants and civilians. The main reason was that American officials, above all the powerful MacArthur, shielded Hirohito from any serious investigation into his culpability and any possibility of prosecution. MacArthur was convinced that Hirohito must be retained as emperor to lead Japan first to surrender and then to a peaceful – and anti-communist – future, a future that would be dominated by Japan's traditional conservative elites.

MacArthur's determination to protect Hirohito made a mockery of the principle of holding individuals – including national leaders – accountable for committing war crimes. And Hirohito's title and stature only magnified the hypocrisy of the Americans. For if, as American officials claimed, Hirohito was "the Symbol of the state and the unity of the people, deriving his position from the will of the people with whom resides sovereign power," then how could his role in the war go uninvestigated? (Dower, 1999: 326). Despite MacArthur's insistence that no convincing evidence linked Hirohito to any war crimes, American officials never conducted anything like a thorough investigation into the emperor's role in the prewar and wartime years. During the trial, American and Japanese officials, the defendants, and even the prosecution collaborated in protecting the emperor from any accusations that he bore ultimate responsibility for his country's wars and the countless crimes authorized by the government and military and committed by Japanese forces across Asia.

There were some dissenting voices. Two judges, Webb and the French Justice Henri Bernard, believed that Hirohito bore the ultimate responsibility for war, but their objections could not pierce the wall that the Americans and the defendants had constructed around the Emperor. Some prominent Japanese jurists and intellectuals stated publicly that Hirohito should have taken the responsibility for Japan's wars and abdicated, and some public opinion polls indicated significant public support for abdication. And there is evidence that Hirohito wrestled with the question, possibly considering abdication and even suicide. When such rumors reached American officials, the response was consistent and unequivocal: abdication would result in chaos and communism. In March and April 1946, Hirohito had in fact dictated a long account of his policies that avoided any hint of responsibility. Instead, he blamed his subordinates. Conversely, his subordinates went to great lengths to protect him. Blaming subordinates comported perfectly with the basic American position that the emperor's own military commanders had simply acted without his leave. Since they, as leaders of the truly guilty clique of war criminals, would now be held accountable by a tribunal, justice would be done and Japan's political and moral reconstruction could commence.

As with the Nuremberg trials, the prosecution presented an enormous quantity of documentary evidence and eyewitness testimony. Defendants were afforded the same rights, and defense lawyers were even permitted (albeit to no effect) to challenge the tribunal's legitimacy, something that was not permitted in Germany. Yet the IMTFE has been subjected, then and since, to even more withering criticisms than the Nuremberg tribunal [*Doc. 5, p. 120*]. Some of the justices were unqualified or had backgrounds that should have barred them from the bench or were absent for long stretches of the trial. Only three of the 11 justices were Asians, despite the fact that Asians comprised the vast majority of Japan's victims. Nor had the prosecution made a particularly convincing case for a conspiracy dating to the late 1920s and formulated at the highest levels of the Japanese government to wage aggressive war. As at Nuremberg, the prosecution was favored by greater resources, friendly judges, looser rules regarding admissible evidence, and other advantages. Defense lawyers and several justices also excoriated the tribunal for imposing *ex post facto* law (or "judicial legislation," as Webb labeled it) (Dower, 1999: 463). And the emperor was hardly the only notable absence in the dock. American officials also secretly extended protection from prosecution to members of a Japanese army unit that conducted horrific medical experiments on prisoners in exchange for their research, though the cover-up was not revealed for decades. Crimes committed in China, Taiwan, and Korea were ignored. The IMTFE never served the same educational purpose for the Japanese elite and wider public that the IMT and NMT did. One reason was the length of the trials: two and a half years. And unlike the Nuremberg IMT and the NMT, no version of the full proceedings was published until 1981. In short, to many observers in and outside Japan, justice appeared not impartial but arbitrary and capricious: the result of political and diplomatic calculations.

# 5 National trials in Europe and Asia

The Nuremberg IMT, the NMT, and the IMTFE represented the tip of the iceberg in terms of the post-World War II's judicial reckoning with war criminals and collaborators. Across much of Europe and Asia, occupiers and postwar governments put tens of thousands of people on trial. The targets of prosecution were either suspected war criminals or collaborators. Given the huge numbers of people involved in the war's countless crimes, it is easy to conclude that most perpetrators evaded punishment for the crimes they had committed or at least made possible, and the numbers do indeed support this depressing conclusion. Yet it is important not to lose sight of the unprecedented nature of this vast legal undertaking. Never before or since have so many people been prosecuted for committing war crimes and atrocities against civilians, or crimes against humanity. The convening of thousands of courts is all the more remarkable given the revenge-driven violence that surged in much of Europe for months, and in some cases years, after VE Day (Lowe, 2012).

The war's destructiveness is the main reason so many trials took place. Allied governments and their publics wanted to punish war criminals and perpetrators of atrocities against civilians. Trials also served political purposes, depending on where they were being held, in that they helped legitimize postwar governments, which had to respond to popular pressures to punish Germans and those who collaborated with them. And trials would help to distance the new governments from compromised wartime regimes. The sheer size of the undertaking in the difficult first postwar years, popular resistance to extending prosecutions more deeply into society and into institutions, and the Cold War's reversal of enemies and allies are the main reasons more trials did not take place.

## Trials in occupied Germany and Austria

In Germany and Austria, each occupier had the authority to hold trials in its respective occupation zone. Judicial reckoning outside of the IMT and NMT took two forms: **denazification** courts (run by the Allies and then by Germans under Allied supervision) and Allied war crimes courts. The policy

DOI: 10.4324/9781003118664-7

of denazification comprised automatic arrests, prosecutions, and employment bans implemented by all four allied states in the occupation years (1945–9) and carried over into the early years of the two German states. Denazification courts were authorized by the Allied Control Council to convict individual Germans in one of the five categories: "major offenders," "offenders," "lesser offenders," "followers," and "exonerated." Between 1945 and 1949, the courts handled over 3.6 million cases and convicted 1,667 as major offenders, 23,000 as offenders, 150,425 as lesser offenders, over one million as followers, and the rest either exonerated or not charged. British, the United States, and French authorities also convicted over 5,000 Germans of war crimes, with more than 800 sentenced to death and around 500 executed. The Soviets also took a two-pronged approach to prosecuting suspected war criminals, purging, convicting, and imprisoning in eastern Germany or deporting to the USSR hundreds of thousands of Germans (Taylor, 2011; Pendas, 2008).

In the US zone, most cases were handled by US Army courts. From 1945 to 1948, these courts tried 1,672 suspected German war criminals in 489 trials. Most of these were held in the former concentration camp at Dachau. There were six main concentration camp cases involving 200 defendants who had served in the Dachau, Buchenwald, Flossenburg, Mauthausen, Nordhausen, and Mülldorf camps. They were followed by some 250 trials of around 800 personnel from sub-camps. The "fliers" cases involved around 600 Germans, most of them civilians, accused of killing around 1,200 US military personnel, most of them US Army Air Force personnel shot down over Germany. In addition, there were a handful of special cases, including the widely publicized Malmedy massacre trial, in which former members of a Waffen SS unit were tried for executing hundreds of US POWs and civilians in Belgium in December 1944 and the trial of the staff of the Hadamar asylum who were charged with killing around 400 Polish and Soviet citizens. There was also a trial of members of German tank unit charged with donning American Army uniforms during the Battle of the Bulge (1944–5) for the purposes of sabotage and sowing confusion behind enemy lines. The United States also extradited nearly 4,000 suspected German war criminals to 16 European states (mainly to Poland and France) in 1946 and 1947 (Heberer, 2008; Remy, 2017; Jardim, 2012).

In the British zone, around 500 trials were conducted by British Military Commissions (BMCs). These were based on Field Court-Martial of the British Army but the rules of evidence followed those of civil courts, making convictions more difficult. The acquittal rate was almost double that of the US Army trials: 28.3 percent to 15.3 percent. The highest visibility trial was of personnel of Bergen-Belsen and Auschwitz camps (17 September to 17 November 1945). In these trials, almost half the defendants were women (and Polish citizens). The British also tried members of a company that manufactured Zyklon B (the poison gas used in death camps) and handful of high-ranking military officers. French authorities tried a small number of

Germans in France's occupation zone and Charles De Gaulle's interim government authorized military tribunals to try "enemy nationals" in France. The highest visibility trial of a German was that of Robert Wagner, the former Gauleiter (regional leader) of Alsace and six other officials. Not surprisingly, trials in France emphasized collaborators. In the period of liberation (summer and fall of 1944), around 9,000 accused collaborators were given hasty "trials" and executed. In 1945 and 1946, the new government held trials of the highest-level officials in the collaborationist (Vichy) regime, including Marshal Philippe Pétain, the former head of the Vichy government, Pierre Laval, prime minister in 1940 and 1942–4, Joseph Darnand, former chief of the paramilitary police force (the *Milice*), and René Bousquet, the former police chief who orchestrated the roundup and deportation of Jews from France in 1942 and 1943 (Crowe, 2014).

The Soviets took a particularly punitive approach in the immediate post-war years. Military tribunals operating in secret convicted around 18,000 Germans, and over 12,500 were convicted of war crimes by special Soviet courts. Hundreds of denazification commissions were authorized and dominated by the Soviet-backed Socialist Unity Party (formerly the Social Democrats and the German Communist Party and merged on Moscow's orders in 1946). Official figures show that over one half million Germans had been

*Figure 5.1* The Soviet Military Tribunal at the Sachsenhausen concentration camp war crimes trial in Berlin, October–November 1947.

purged by these commissions by 1948. Shortly after Germany's formal division in 1949, Soviet authorities transferred around 14,000 suspected war criminals to the East German government and deported another 20,000 to the USSR. The new state continued prosecutions long after they ceased in West Germany: around 13,000 were convicted between 1948 and 1964 (Naimark, 1995).

Austria's status as a separate state (it had been annexed by Nazi Germany in 1938) was restored and the country was occupied by the four Allied nations until 1955. An Allied declaration in 1943 identified the country as Hitler's "first victim," a falsehood that after the war very much worked to the benefit of the large number of Austrian war criminals. In the end, 130,000 Austrians were investigated for committing war crimes, with only 23,000 tried and just over half that number convicted. Forty-three people received death sentences, of which 30 were executed. As early as 1946, the occupiers turned control over war crimes trials and purges to the Austrian government. The leniency with which Austria was treated reflected not only by the widespread belief in its alleged victimization by Germany but also by the belief that the real source of German fascism lay in Prussia and "Prussianism." And Austria's strategic location in Central Europe as the Cold War divided the continent incentivized both sides to court public opinion, which was steadfastly opposed to trials and purges (Judt, 2005).

## Trials in post-occupation West and East Germany and reunified Germany

German courts in the western occupation zones issued over 4,600 convictions of Germans between 1945 and 1949. The new West German government, however, was steadfastly opposed to continuing war crimes trials. Denazification and war crimes trials were extremely unpopular. Accordingly, the moderate conservative party that dominated politics in the western zones and then West Germany (the Christian Democratic Union and its sister party in Bavaria, the Christian Social Union) adhered to a dictum: it was possible to have democracy or more memory of the Nazi years, but not both. So its leaders pushed very hard for an end to denazification, the rehabilitation of those who had been purged, an end to war crimes trials, and amnesties for imprisoned war criminals. And they got all of those things. There were, of course, oppositional voices, notably the moderate left of center Social Democrats, who took the position that "daring more democracy" required a more extensive reckoning with the past. But a majority of Germans in the west did not want this. In addition, convicted war criminals became the beneficiaries of determined and well-organized trans-Atlantic amnesty campaigns. And as thousands of former Nazis – including many guilty of serious crimes – reintegrated into German society and took up positions of influence, they proved adept at protecting themselves and each other. Finally, the Cold War incentivized American and British officials to look forward rather than backward in time, an inclination most Germans were more than happy to support. As a result, by the end of the 1950s, most war criminals convicted by the NMT or by zonal military courts or West German courts were released (Herf, 1997; Frei, 2002).

The East German government was initially aggressive in prosecuting suspected war criminals and continued holding trials into the early 1960s. As in West Germany, however, the government released thousands of convicted war criminals in the mid-1950s: from over 3,000 to just 34 in prison by the end of 1956. At the same time, the regime suppressed the memory of Nazi crimes against anyone other than the peoples of the Soviet Union and German communists. Scholars, novelists, and journalists, of course, could not research, write, or teach freely about the past. And while the East German state did make restitution payments to Holocaust survivors, it also supported Israel's Arab enemies – eventually including terrorist groups – with aid and training. The regime also directed a propaganda campaign at West Germany that called attention – accurately – to the enormous numbers of ex-Nazis then serving in the government, armed services, judiciary, and in the professions. The campaign had the effect of motivating the West German government to initiate the prosecution of ten former members of an SS mobile execution squad (Einsatzgruppe) in the Bavarian town of Ulm in 1958. The accused were charged as accessories in the murder of around 5,000 Jews in Lithuania (Herf, 2016; Pendas, 2010).

The trial caused a sensation in West Germany and generated increased public demand for more trials. This pressure, along with the East German propaganda campaign, led Chancellor Konrad Adenauer to authorize the creation that year of the **Central Office of State Judicial Administrations for the Investigation of National Socialist Crimes**. Based in the southwestern town of Ludwigsburg, the Central Office could only investigate crimes and provide names to regional prosecutors, as there was no special provision in West German criminal law for pursuing war crimes cases. Of the 120,000 investigations undertaken by the agency, 5,000 were eventually tried. West German courts would not prosecute former Nazis on charges of participating in genocide or committing crimes against humanity on the grounds that to do so would be to impose the law *ex post facto*. It became possible to charge accused war criminals with committing murder, the statute of limitations for all other crimes having expired. This greatly limited the ability of prosecutors' to bring charges against those who had played important roles in the vast machinery of the Nazi regime's programs of systematic, premeditated mass murder (Pendas, 2010; Weinke, 2018).

The Ulm trial was followed by the capture near Buenos Ares in 1960 of former SS Lieutenant Colonel Adolf Eichmann (1906–62) by the Israeli foreign secret service (Mossad). Like numerous other war criminals, Eichmann escaped from Europe to South America, where he lived quietly under an assumed name. Though he never killed anyone personally, Eichmann had combined bureaucratic efficiency with intense ideological commitment to deadly effect as a principal architect of the Holocaust. In a widely publicized trial held in Jerusalem, he was convicted of crimes against the Jewish people, sentenced to death, and executed. The publicity generated by the trial raised awareness of the Holocaust and reminded Germans that thousands of perpetrators had gone unpunished. From 1963 to 1965, Fritz Bauer (1903–68) – a state prosecutor and Jewish German who had survived incarceration in a concentration camp – led the prosecution of 22 former mid-ranking SS officers and capos who served in Auschwitz ("**Frankfurt Auschwitz Trials**"). Bauer had spent the last five years gathering evidence. The accused had been living openly in West Germany but had remained unprosecuted. They were charged not with committing war crimes or crimes against humanity, but with violating German law. Eighteen were convicted, with six sentenced to life terms and the others receiving sentences ranging from five to 14 years. Though the trial received extensive coverage by the West German and foreign press, much public opinion in the FRG was indifferent and even hostile to the proceedings. In 1969, the West German Supreme Court overturned the conviction of a former SS officer who served in Auschwitz on the grounds that serving as camp personnel was not itself a crime (Lipstadt, 2011; Pendas, 2010).

Once again, prosecutions in West Germany fell off precipitously over the next four decades. They were revived beginning in 2007 after a German court sentenced a Moroccan national for wiring money to one of the 9/11 hijackers. The accused had been convicted of being an accessory to murder. Investigators interested in pursuing Nazi era criminals saw an opening to challenge the supreme court's 1969 ruling. It was at this point that the case of John Demjanjuk (1920–2012) became particularly relevant. Demjanjuk was a Ukrainian-born Nazi collaborator who had served as a guard at the Sobibor death camp. After the war, he immigrated to the United States and lived freely for decades, though American investigators had known of his past since the 1970s. After years of legal wrangling, Demjanjuk was first extradited to Israel, where he was tried and convicted in 1987 as a camp guard at Treblinka, but the verdict was overturned on appeal as there was not sufficient evidence proving his service in that camp. He was deported to Germany in 2009, where he was convicted in 2011 of being an accessory to the murder of 28,000 Jews and sentenced to five years' imprisonment. He died in 2012. The trial was important because it set a new standard in German courts: despite the fact that it could not be proven that Demjanjuk killed anyone, he had served at a camp that was designed to murder its prisoners, meaning he – and other former personnel – could be charged as accessories to murder. The Central Office drew up a list of 30 former personnel of Auschwitz, a slew of new investigations followed, and former SS guards were convicted in 2015, 2016, and 2020. In June 2022, a court near Berlin convicted a 101-year-old man, Josef Schuetz, of more than 3,500 counts of accessory to murder in his role as a guard at the Sachsenhausen concentration camp between 1942 and 1945 and sentenced him to five years' imprisonment. Several similar cases are pending as of 2022 (Douglas, 2018).

## Trials in other European states

Accompanying waves of violence that continued outside Germany after VE Day – resulting in civil war conditions in Greece, Italy, and France and unprecedented instances of ethnic cleansing – were trials of suspected war criminals and collaborators. Most Germans who were tried by new postwar governments were tried in Eastern Europe and the Soviet Union. Tens of thousands of suspected collaborators, mostly men, were also targeted as members of now-criminalized organizations (the entire membership of Norway's fascist party, for example was indicted, including those who had belonged to the party before the war, when membership was legal) or as individuals. But purges and trials of collaborators quickly became controversial in Western Europe – too punitive or too lenient, depending on one's point of view. New communist regimes in Eastern Europe used them to solidify their hold on power by identifying "class enemies" as collaborators, regardless of the demonstrable guilt or innocence of an individual. With a few important exceptions, collaboration in the Holocaust was not addressed. Postwar governments had little desire for an extended legal reckoning with those who had aided and abetted the Nazis' "final solution." Everywhere, in short, trials were used by postwar governments in ways that promoted their particular interests. Extensive purges, trials, and the blacklisting of businessmen, technocrats, civil servants, policemen, army officers, and others would not have been conducive to rapid recovery, political stability, and social peace. In any case, most Europeans were consumed with rebuilding their disrupted lives. Few wished to be reminded that resistance was relatively rare. Fewer still wished to remember whatever roles they had played in the persecution, robbery, and murder of millions of people. Finally, there was the Cold War, which turned former enemies into allies, and vice versa (Deak *et al.*, 2000).

Yet in several places, close attention to the Holocaust did accompany trials of Nazis and collaborators. "People's Tribunals" in Hungary (1945–9) were exceptional for the attention given to perpetrators of crimes against Jews, as were Jewish Honor Courts convened across Europe and in Israel. In Eastern Europe, Poland was the site of the most extensive reckoning with German war criminals. The postwar Polish government put around 20,000 people on trial for war crimes, among them some 5,500 Germans, Austrians, and ethnic Germans. The underground Home Army also conducted trials of over 5,000 Poles for war crimes, passing death sentences on a majority of them. The government's trials were not show trials of the Stalinist type. Indeed, recent research has revealed the extent to which the courts adhered to norms and procedures followed by those in liberal democratic states. Strikingly, they also devoted considerable attention to the Holocaust, despite intensifying efforts by the communist regime to downplay the unique features of the persecution and mass murder of Polish Jews. It was in four cases held by the Supreme National Tribunal between 1946 and 1948 – out of a total of seven public trials of 17 Germans – that the charge of genocide appeared prominently: those of Jürgen Stroop (1895–1952), Amon Göth (1908–46), Hans Biebow (1902–47), and Rudolf Höss (1901–47). Stroop was a high-ranking SS officer who suppressed the Warsaw ghetto uprising in 1943, Göth was the commandant of the Plaszow concentration camp, Biebow was the officer in charge of running the Lodz ghetto, and Höss was a commandant of Auschwitz. It would not be until the Eichmann trial that an individual of these levels of responsibility for the Holocaust was put on trial (Peto and Barna, 2015; Finder and Jokusch, 2015; Finder and Prusin, 2018).

Extensive trials also took place in the Soviet Union. Between 1943 and 1952, Soviet courts – military and civilian – prosecuted around 82,000 people as Nazi war criminals and as collaborators. Most of the accused were Soviet citizens. Unlike the western allies, the Soviets held highly publicized war crimes trials – of Germans and of Soviet citizens accused of collaboration – during the war. And while Soviet officials were very well informed about the Holocaust, the mass murder of Jews did not figure prominently in the cases or in the publicity they were given. Many of these trials were little more than drumhead courts martial in which the accused were sentenced to death or terms of hard labor with little by way of due process. Beginning in December 1945, at the same time the IMT was convening in Nuremberg, the Soviets opened public trials in multiple cities with great fanfare and with the full intention of showcasing the very real suffering endured by the population and Red Army in defeating the vast bulk of the German army. The courts were based on Soviet law but prosecutors also made reference to international law. This time, however, the Holocaust received considerable attention and in a way that called attention to the roles of multiple arms of the Nazi regime, namely, the SS and special police units, the Wehrmacht, and the civilian administration. Prosecutors relied on documentation, eyewitness testimony, and – more problematically – confessions, which had often been obtained under various forms of duress. Defense attorneys could not defend the accused as they would be able to in western democracies, and the press or other outside observers could provide no independent reporting or critical commentary on the proceedings. Yet the fact that the crimes of the accused were corroborated by a large quantity of various sources has led recent historians to reject dismissing them as nothing more than show trials (Prusin, 2003).

The legacy of the postwar national trials in Europe is ambiguous. On the one hand, the extent of judicial reckoning was unprecedented and more extensive than previously thought. Zonal and national trials capped off the decisive turn away from the tradition, established in 17th-century Europe, of tying the conclusion of a war to forgetting in order to maintain peace. They showed that it was possible to prosecute more than leaders, but everyone from low-ranking soldiers to high-ranking officers to bureaucrats and other administrators of atrocity for war crimes and crimes against humanity. Over the longer term, the records of these proceedings have proven to be an invaluable source for research on the Nazi regime, collaboration, the war, and the Holocaust. Yet the inaccessibility until very recent years of many of the most important records – in Eastern Europe and the USSR, or those of the UNWCC, which were not opened until 2019 – obscured the historical record for decades after the war and, not least, impeded investigations.

While it is true that most perpetrators and collaborators were never prosecuted, it is difficult to see how holding even more people accountable would have been possible. One obstacle was purely practical: namely, the problem in conducting far more thorough and fair proceedings in the materially deprived conditions of the first postwar years. Another involved the legal problems of prosecuting collaborators, given how extensive and complicated collaboration was in reality. Yet another was political. Trials became unpopular at a time when new postwar governments were most interested in securing social peace, establishing their legitimacy, and seeing through reconstruction. Then there was the reality of the Cold War, which disrupted the brief postwar consensus among the allies that the perpetrators of the single most destructive war in history be held accountable. Finally, the vast majority of perpetrators and those who facilitated their crimes who were prosecuted only served a fraction of their sentences and then reintegrated into their societies. In many cases, they protected each other and impeded investigations and prosecutions.

## Trials in Asia

Large parts of Asia also witnessed thousands of local trials of war criminals and collaborators, with similarly ambiguous short- and long-term results. About 50 military tribunals were convened by the Americans, British, Dutch, Chinese, Australians, French, and Filipinos between 1945 and 1951. In total, historians estimate that around 5,700 Japanese nationals and collaborators of varying ranks were tried for war crimes, particularly against POWs and civilians in areas under Japanese occupation. Most – around 4,000 – were convicted. In 1953, all prisoners then held outside Japan were transferred to Japanese prisons, where the terms of their incarceration were still controlled by the states that convicted them. Yet by 1958, all remaining prisoners – including those convicted by the IMTFE – were released (Wilson *et al.*, 2017).

The Soviets also conducted trials, as did the Communist government in China. The Soviet trials were held in secret and were of a summary nature. The accused were Japanese military personnel captured in Manchuria, Korea, and on Sakhalin Island. Perhaps 3,000 were executed. Trials in China began during the Civil War, with Nationalist and Communist governments each undertaking prosecutions of suspected Japanese war criminals. The Nationalists were particularly aggressive in targeting Chinese who collaborated with the Japanese, trying over 25,000 and convicting around 15,000. Yet both Nationalists and Communists treated Japanese suspects with relative leniency, the main reason being a desire to establish good future relations

*Figure 5.2* Former Japanese soldiers on trial in Darwin, Australia, in March 1946 for committing war crimes in Timor during World War II.

with the former enemy. As with trials held by other states, nearly all Japanese war criminals convicted by Soviet and Chinese courts were released by the end of the 1950s (Crowe, 2014).

One case held by the United States was of particular significance for the development of war crimes law: that of General Tomoyuki Yamashita. In late 1944, Yamashita was charged with defending the Philippines. Though he had ordered nearly all troops to relocate from Manila to the north of Luzon Island, thousands of Japanese troops remained in the city, where they went on a murderous rampage against American POWs and Filipino civilians. Around 100,000 civilians and 1,000 US soldiers were killed, as were nearly all of the Japanese soldiers, while Manila was devastated. Fighting continued on Luzon for months, with appalling levels of casualties suffered by all sides, combatant and civilian. An outraged General Douglas MacArthur convinced President Harry Truman that Yamashita should be tried by a military commission. The single charge leveled against him was that he had failed to control the actions of the men under his command. What made the case distinctive was that it was the first time an officer had been charged with being accountable, indirectly, for war crimes committed by his troops. Moreover, the proceedings were rushed and the court ignored evidence that Yamashita had little to no effective control over the actions of his troops in

Manila. Predictably, he was convicted in December 1945 and sentenced to death. His lawyers appealed the verdict to the US Supreme Court, but the justices upheld Yamashita's conviction with reference to provisions of the Geneva and Hague Conventions. The unfairness of Yamashita's trial notwithstanding, a precedent had been established. Command responsibility has since become an important part of IHL, though since 1945 it has been applied selectively (Ryan, 2012).

In some significant ways, the prosecution of war crimes in Europe and Asia took similar trajectories. The desire for retribution against the Japanese military across Asia and among the governments and publics of the west was extremely high, and the thousands of trials reflect the intense anger. And as in Europe, judicial reckoning soon took a back seat to other considerations. But postwar Asia's fate took a very different course from Europe's. While Europe achieved stability relatively quickly, armed conflicts in Asia continued or broke out on a wide scale. Civil war in China resumed until 1949. A civil war on the Korean peninsula led to the Korean War of 1950–3. British, French, and Dutch forces attempted – ultimately without success – to regain colonies in Indochina and Indonesia. The British departure from India in 1947 and the country's ensuing partition led to massive violence between Hindus and Muslims. In many of these conflicts, former Japanese soldiers and officers became combatants, if only temporarily, a situation unthinkable in the European context (Spector, 2022; Chamberlin, 2018).

# Part II

# The world of war crimes and international law after World War II

# 6 War crimes and international law in the Cold War and the era of decolonization

In the decades following World War II, a broad new international framework aimed at constraining war – particularly its impact on civilian non-combatants – came into existence. The foundations of this framework were two international agreements: the **Genocide Convention** of 1948 and the two *Geneva Conventions of 1949* and their additional protocols adopted in 1977 and 2005. The former made the deliberate attempt to eliminate entire groups of people a violation of international law while the latter emphasized regulating the conduct of war among combatants, including important new provisions for protecting non-combatants. These agreements, which greatly expanded upon the Geneva and Hague Conventions of the late 19th and early 20th centuries, and the body of international law that emerged from them comprise what has become known as IHL. A complementary development was the emergence in the 1970s of international human rights activism and law, which aims to institute protections of a universal set of rights for all people in all circumstances. Despite these advances, however, the period of the Cold War was wracked with often incredibly violent wars, particularly in what was known as the "Third World," with very little by way of formal investigations and prosecutions of war-related atrocities. In short, war continued to outpace attempts to constrain it and punish those whose actions transgressed customary and codified law.

## The Genocide Convention (1948), the Geneva Conventions (1949), and contemporary human rights

The term "genocide" – a portmanteau combining the Greek prefix "genos" (race or tribe) and the Latin suffix "cide" (killing) – was first proposed by the Polish-born lawyer Raphael Lemkin (1900–59) in his 1944 book *Axis Rule in Occupied Europe*. Lemkin, who would lose most of his family in the Holocaust, emigrated to the United States in 1941 to teach at Duke University but was soon working for the US War Department. By the end of the war, he was advising the US Army's Judge Advocate and the chief prosecutor for the IMT at Nuremberg. Lemkin defined genocide as "a coordinated plan of different actions aiming at the destruction of essential foundations of the

DOI: 10.4324/9781003118664-9

life of national groups, with the aim of annihilating the groups themselves." The definition was based on two related conclusions about the nature of the war in Europe: that it was directed at civilian populations and that Nazi Germany had targeted an entire group of people, defined as members of a biologically determined "race," for complete elimination. In Lemkin's view, genocide involved two main phases (the "destruction of the national pattern" of the targeted group and the "imposition of the national pattern" of the perpetrator) and the deployment of political, social, cultural, economic, biological, physical, religious, and moral "techniques." Of central significance to Lemkin's conception was that genocide was a premeditated act and not simply a description of the outcome of a particularly destructive armed conflict (Lemkin, 1944/2005).

For Lemkin, there was nothing in existing international law that could account for such an atrocity. So he became determined to establish genocide as a crime in international law. He was unable to get it included by name as a charge in the indictments of the Nuremberg or Tokyo IMTs, but its essence was incorporated into count 3 (war crimes) of the Nuremberg IMT:

> They conducted deliberate and systematic genocide, viz., the extermination of racial and national groups, against the civilian populations of certain occupied territories in order to destroy particular races and classes of people and national, racial, or religious groups, particularly Jews, Poles, and Gypsies and others.
>
> (https://avalon.law.yale.edu/imt/count3.asp)

Undaunted, Lemkin worked relentlessly to get the new United Nations to adopt a resolution on genocide. The General Assembly approved a draft resolution in December 1946, and Lemkin was asked to serve on a commission to draw up a convention. Following lengthy deliberations among representatives of multiple states, the Genocide Convention was approved by the General Assembly in December 1948.

The convention defines genocide as

> any of the following acts committed with intent to destroy, in whole or in part, a national, ethnical, racial or religious group, as such: (a) Killing members of the group; (b) Causing serious bodily or mental harm to members of the group; (c) Deliberately inflicting on the group conditions of life calculated to bring about its physical destruction in whole or in part; (d) Imposing measures intended to prevent births within a group; (e) Forcibly transferring children of the group to another group.
>
> (Convention on the Prevention and Punishment of the Crime of Genocide, 1948)

In addition to the act of genocide, a conspiracy to commit it, incitement, an attempt to carry it out, and complicity were all considered punishable acts. This definition tracks closely with Lemkin's, with one major exception: Lemkin hoped that a genocide convention would accommodate the targeting of the "cultural foundations" of a group's collective existence. This category, however, was excluded from the language of the UN convention [*Doc. 6, p. 122*]. And there were other significant weaknesses. A formal charge of genocide must prove intent to be considered a violation of the convention, and establishing this has been extremely difficult. A related problem is that in practice, intent has been linked to states and plans by states, despite the fact that the convention's language does not require this connection to exist. But the most significant problem was the lack of any provision for an international institution charged with investigating and prosecuting alleged instances of genocide. The convention left this up to individual states.

Representatives of 14 states signed the convention in 1948 and 1949, though in some cases did not ratify the treaty for years. Most notably, the United States only joined in 1988, a delay that greatly weakened the convention in terms of its international authority and, not least, the ability of the UN to enforce its terms. As of 2019, a total of 153 states (including Palestine, a non-state member of the UN) have acceded to the convention, with most of the holdouts in Africa and Southeast Asia.

At the same time the Genocide Convention came into existence, the UN turned to expanding upon the Hague Conventions of 1899 and 1907. The driving force was the International Committee of the Red Cross (ICRC). In 1944 the ICRC resumed its efforts, interrupted in the 1930s, to expand protections for combatants and civilians in wartime. At a conference in Geneva in 1947, representatives of 15 nations charged three committees with drafting the language for a set of new conventions aimed at revising the 1929 treaties on treatment of wounded and sick combatants and of POWs. One of the committees was to create an entirely new convention dealing with the protection of civilians in wartime. The committees attempted to break with the long-standing separation of international wars and civil and colonial wars by proposing that "in any part of the home or colonial territory of a Contracting party, the principles of the convention shall be equally applied by the said party, subject to the adverse Party also conforming thereto," adding that the convention would be "equally applicable to cases of occupation of territories in the absence of any state of war" (Crowe, 2014: 312). Not surprisingly, the British and other governments rejected these provisions out of hand.

From April to August 1949, representatives of 59 states met in Geneva to consider four conventions related to (1) care of the wounded and sick in armed forces in the field; (2) care of the wounded, sick, and shipwrecked members of armed forces at sea; (3) the treatment of POWs; and (4) the protection of civilian persons in time of war. These would become the four Geneva Conventions of 1949. One of the most problematic issues involved defining the kinds of conflicts to which the convention's terms would apply. Predictably, the recommendation that the convention's provisions apply in "cases of civil war, colonial conflicts, or wars of religion" generated considerable controversy and resistance, though not from delegates from the USSR and its allied states in Eastern Europe (Crowe, 2014: 313). After months of reworking, the committees working on the convention's language proposed that "in the case of armed conflict not of an international character occurring in the territory of one of the High Contracting Parties" each party would be obliged to treat "those not actively engaged in the hostilities" (including those who have surrendered or were injured or too ill to fight) humanely (Crowe, 2014: 315). As with the Genocide Convention, there was no provision for an international tribunal to investigate and prosecute violations, though the door to the creation of such courts was left open. Over the course of the 1950s, 74 states ratified the conventions, with over 100 more added over the following four decades. As of 2022, 194 states and non-state entities have become states parties to the conventions, though not all have ratified the additional protocols.

The proliferation of wars in Asia and Africa over the next two decades – discussed later – made it clear to a growing number of human rights law advocates that the 1949 conventions needed revising. Once again, the ICRC was the instigator, with its attention focused on expanding the protection of civilians in time of war (particularly medics and aid personnel) and constraining the use of certain categories of highly destructive weapons (e.g., chemical, bacteriological, and radioactive). By the late 1960s, momentum in the UN and ICRC had built for adding protections for a category of armed combatant long excluded from military codes and international conventions: that is, those engaged in independence struggles. This movement represented a major break with the centuries-long tradition of limiting the laws of war to a narrowly defined category of armed conflicts and combatants. Not surprisingly, it immediately generated resistance, even within the ICRC, which had to shelve a proposal to create a set of "standard minimum rules" applicable in "guerilla warfare" (Crowe, 2014: 330).

The setback, however, proved to be temporary. From 1974 to 1977, the Diplomatic Conference on the Reaffirmation and Development of International Humanitarian Law Applicable in Armed Conflicts convened four times to draft the language of what would become two additional protocols to the Geneva Conventions. The biggest division among the delegates reflected the realities of the new post-colonial landscape, with representatives of recently liberated states arguing for the applicability of IHL to "armed conflicts in which peoples are fighting against colonial domination and alien occupation and against racist regimes in the exercise of their right of self-determination, as enshrined in the Charter of the United Nations" (Crowe, 2014: 324). Opponents of including such language, notably the United States, France, the United Kingdom, and Israel, held that the law already accommodated this category of combatant.

For the first time in such a setting, the anti-colonial contingent won the argument. Additional Protocol I, which applies to international conflicts, extends protections to women, medical professionals, children (it prohibits the recruitment of child soldiers), and journalists. It bans the use of certain types of weapons that "cause superfluous injury or unnecessary suffering" and for the first time specified environmental infrastructure like food supplies and sources of water for protection. Sites of cultural significance like places of worship and artifacts were included in the protocol's provisions. Another victory for this side was the inclusion of irregular combatants (specifically, those who did not display a "fixed distinctive emblem recognizable at a distance") as entitled to POW status. It was this provision that led the US government to refuse to ratify the additional protocol that contained this language (Additional Protocol I) for fear that it would, in the words of the US State Department, "grant recognition and protection to terrorist groups, and would result in a 'politicization' of humanitarian law by such organizations" (Crowe, 2014: 325).

While the first additional protocol dealt with international wars, the second focused on extending protections to combatants and environmental infrastructure in *non-international* conflicts. It also included a provision to ban the displacement of civilians from their own land. In the case of this protocol, however, it was representatives of recently independent nations that offered the most resistance, as many of their governments were facing internal rebellions. Despite the reservations, the vast majority of states would eventually become signatories to both additional protocols. A third was adopted in 2005 that added a neutral symbol – a red crystal – to the symbols (red cross, a red star and crescent, and a red lion and sun) used by UN and ICRC personnel.

Parallel to these developments was the emergence of a widespread movement of human rights advocacy and law. The idea that all individuals possess certain inalienable rights long predates the modern period, and historians have debated whether the origins of the modern concept of "human rights" emerged from the Enlightenment and the French Revolution or two centuries later. What is not in doubt is that in the post-World War II era, the world witnessed the proliferation of international declarations, laws, scholarship, activism (often by dissidents and subjugated peoples), and work by non-governmental organizations aimed at protecting a basic set of rights that should, according to advocates of the cause, belong to all peoples, regardless of nationality, race, ethnicity, religion, or any other form of identity. The influence of this new paradigm is difficult to delineate precisely, but there is no doubt that the rhetoric, activism, reporting, and lawmaking related to the protection of human rights informed and accelerated the expansion of IHL (Hunt, 2008; Moyn, 2012; Hopgood, 2006; Dromi, 2020; Davies, 2014).

## The Third World War

Warfare – international and civil – was omnipresent in significant parts of the world during the Cold War (1945–90). While Nazi Germany and

Imperial Japan were completely defeated by the summer of 1945, it is otherwise difficult to locate the "end" of World War II. Armed conflicts continued in Europe in the forms of localized civil wars. Fighting between Nationalist and Communist forces in China resumed and continued for another four years, resulting in victory for the communists and the establishment of the People's Republic of China. Beyond Europe and China, it would be the Cold War and the wars of decolonization that determined the course of what might be considered a third world war. The relative positions and military capabilities of the United States, the USSR, and – after 1949 – China prevented the eruption of a war between those states. With few exceptions, the armed forces of the United States, the USSR (and its client states in Eastern Europe), and China did not fight each other in these regions, nor did they deploy large number of their own troops. The exceptions were the Korean War, which involved a brief period of intense fighting between mostly US and Chinese forces, fighting between Soviet and Chinese forces along the Sino-Soviet border in the 1960s, the American war in Vietnam in the 1960s and early 1970s, and the Soviet invasion of Afghanistan in 1979 (Chamberlin, 2018; Spector, 2022).

The geographic center of global armed conflict thus shifted to Africa, Asia, and eventually to parts of Latin America. In the case of the latter two regions, the US, Soviet, and Chinese governments supported local actors with arms, advisers, and other kinds of aid with the objective of either extending or preventing the spread of communism, thus fueling decades of regional wars. Armed struggles for independence launched by the subjugated peoples of Africa and Asia formed the other dimension to this new global conflict. Greatly weakened by World War II, the British, French, and Dutch governments proved willing to engage in extraordinarily violent campaigns to retain their colonies. While Great Britain walked away from India and Palestine in 1947, it resorted to fighting in Malaya, Africa, and other parts of the Middle East. Around a half million Dutch soldiers attempted, unsuccessfully, to retain control of Indonesia, and France fought, also unsuccessfully, to hold on to Indochina and Algeria. Postcolonial states in much of Africa became the sites of often extremely violent internal or regional conflicts, though the support of proxies by the United States or USSR was far more limited than it was in Asia and the Middle East.

All conflicts of the third world war shared two characteristics related to the history of war crimes and crimes against humanity: (1) civilians comprised the majority of casualties and (2) war was waged without regard for the new frameworks of international law and human rights. One recent survey of the Cold War era's wars estimates that 20 million people lost their lives, with perhaps 70 percent of that figure perishing in a crescent-shaped region stretching from Lebanon in the west through the greater Indian Ocean region and Southeast Asia to the Korean peninsula. Whether the wars were international or civil or some combination, atrocities against civilians were pervasive. American troops committed an uncounted (and almost entirely unprosecuted) series of massacres of civilians in the Korean and Vietnam Wars, as did French and Soviet forces in Algeria and Afghanistan, respectively. Thousands of Indonesian civilians were abused and murdered by Dutch forces during the Indonesian National Revolution (1945–9). And while the United Kingdom was far less willing (and able) to wage war to hold its colonies, British forces were responsible for massacres of civilians in the long fight against communist insurgents in Malaya (the "Malayan Emergency," 1948–60) and especially in Kenya in the 1950s (the "Mau Mau uprising") and in counterinsurgency operations in Cyprus, Aden, and British Guyana. Moreover, the British government had close ties with a private military company (KMS, Keenie Meenie Services) that perpetrated numerous atrocities in multiple civil conflicts, notably during Sri Lanka's long civil war (1983–2009). Atrocities against civilians were widespread in the many international and civil wars and rebellions in Africa, the Middle East, Asia, and Latin America that did not involve the great powers directly or indirectly (Chamberlin, 2018; Luttikhuis and Moses, 2014; Elkins, 2005; Miller, 2020).

## The Cold War and the laws of war

There was something eerily familiar about the post-World War II period in terms of the conduct of war and attempts to regulate it through international law. In the late 19th and early 20th centuries, a watershed was reached with the first international conventions aimed at protecting combatants. Yet even before the eruption of a general European war in 1914, significant parts of the world were wracked with war, with civilians increasingly bearing the brunt of the violence. Since the terms of the new conventions did not apply to colonial wars (and in any case there were no enforcement mechanisms), there were hardly any prosecutions. And only very rarely did atrocities perpetrated by colonial troops generate significant protest or political controversy in the metropoles. After 1945, another watershed in international law was achieved while warfare continued on a global scale, again with few prosecutions. While the direct participation of French or American or Soviet troops on the ground in Algeria, Vietnam, or Afghanistan did cause significant political controversy in the aggressor states, proxy wars generated little significant public interest, despite the high levels of death and physical destruction. In some cases, as with British actions in Kenya in the 1950s or with the decision of the US government to sanction torture in the "war on terror" in the 2000s, the publics in those countries seemed either largely indifferent or supportive of what were clearly violations of international law.

There were only a few instances in which the provisions of the Genocide and Geneva Conventions were applied, albeit either with little success or without much wider impact. In 1960, a report by the International Commission of Jurists on years-long acts of violent suppression in Tibet – particularly against its Buddhist establishment and culture – constituted "acts of genocide," though at the level of cultural destruction and hence not a violation of the Genocide Convention. Succeeding decades of high-visibility human rights activism around the world has not deterred China from continuing to repress the Tibetan people and their culture. It was also in 1960 that agents of Israel's Mossad captured Adolf Eichmann, who was living under a false identity in Argentina. Eichmann was transferred to Israel, where he was charged with 15 counts of crimes against the Jewish people, crimes against humanity, war crimes, and membership in a hostile organization. The court and the prosecution based the case against him on Israeli law and multiple precedents in international law, the latter including the Genocide Convention (Crowe, 2014; Lipstadt, 2011).

A third example involved the 36-year-long civil war in Guatemala (1960–96), during which the country's Mayan population was subjected to a reign of terror by a US-backed military dictatorship for its alleged support of Marxist insurgents. The UN-brokered treaty that ended the war mandated the creation of a truth commission to investigate and document the many atrocities committed principally by government forces. The commission's final report included accusations of genocide against one or more ethnic groups of Mayan peoples. In this case, however, the commission's main purpose to "encourage peace and national harmony in Guatemala" by recommending "measures to preserve the memory of the victims, to foster a culture of mutual respect and observance of human rights and to strengthen the democratic process." The commission added a demand for reparations for surviving victims. Though the government established a National Day for Victims' Dignity and some reparations payments have been made, there has been no judicial reckoning with the perpetrators, many of whom continued to occupy positions of influence in the government and military. A significant, if singular, achievement was the conviction in 2013 of General Efraín Ríos Montt, the military dictator in the 1980s, by a Guatemalan court for attempting to exterminate a Mayan community (the Ixil). The conviction was overturned and Montt died in 2018 as a new case was being brought against him (Crowe, 2014).

Several factors explain the disconnect between the new frameworks and the massive surge in unchecked wartime and war-related violence after 1945. First, states – especially powerful states – would not allow international law to override military and national security interests. Second, the Genocide and Geneva Conventions had no mechanism in place to enforce their provisions. A third problem involved the matter of defining the nature of a given armed conflict: was it an international war, an "internal" matter, or a civil war? Though Additional Protocol II of the Geneva Convention did focus on non-international wars, affected states were reluctant or simply unable to prosecute war-related crimes. The prosecution of General Montt in Guatemala was the exception that proved the rule. Nonetheless, the Additional Protocols represented a significant step toward ending the fatal distinction in international law between wars between states on the one side and rebellions and wars of imperial conquest on the other. Moreover, the language of the post-World War II, international laws of war, and the new human rights paradigm was deployed, with mixed results, by subjugated peoples to justify their struggles for independence. But all of this was not enough to prevent a continuation of colonial era-style modes of warfare into the Cold War, a mode of warfare in which civilians and environmental infrastructure remained the principal targets. The tradition, established in the ancient world, of one set of rules for warfare between "civilized" states and another for wars against the "uncivilized" was shaken but not unbroken.

# 7 From International Criminal Tribunals to the International Criminal Court

It was not until the early 1990s that new international courts inspired by the Nuremberg and Tokyo models came into existence. While the catalysts were the wars that accompanied the break-up of Yugoslavia and an instance of genocide in Rwanda, it was the end of the Cold War, the spread of liberal democracy worldwide, and the willingness of a significant number of states – particularly the United States – to support the creation of international tribunals and a permanent International Criminal Court (ICC) that provided the essential context for the creation of a new legal architecture with global reach. By the second decade of the 21st century, the precedents established in Nuremberg and Tokyo had been upheld and what constitutes violations of international criminal law was expanded. But ongoing and new armed conflicts and other crises taking place in the context of changing global power balances – namely, the relative decline of American power *vis-à-vis* China and the determination of Russia to reassert itself as a great power – have presented serious challenges to the achievements of the first post-Cold War decades.

## The former Yugoslavia

By the late 1980s, the multi-ethnic and multi-religious Federal People's Republic of Yugoslavia (a federation comprised six republics: Bosnia and Herzegovina, Croatia, Macedonia, Montenegro, Serbia, and Slovenia) was coming apart. In 1991, Slovenia and Croatia seceded, producing short wars with Serbia. The following year the government of Bosnia and Herzegovina declared independence. Two factors made the situation explosive. One was that Yugoslav leader and president of Serbia Slobodan Milošovic (1941–2006) had already been stoking the fires of nationalism and extreme prejudice within Serbia as it became clear that the Yugoslav federation was heading toward breakup. The other was Bosnia's ethnic map. Most of the population was Muslim (Bosniaks), but Serbs were a substantial minority (around 1.3 million). Milošovic used Bosnia's move toward independence as an excuse to achieve the old Serb nationalist dream of a "greater Serbia" by trying to take control of a substantial part of Bosnia and a small part

DOI: 10.4324/9781003118664-10

of Croatia. In the process, the Bosnian Serb Army (BSA), backed by Serbia's military, conducted a campaign of ethnic cleansing on a scale not seen in Europe since World War II. By 1994, they had taken control of about 70 percent of Bosnia (Judah, 1997; Glenny, 2017).

While atrocities were committed by all sides, the vast majority were perpetrated by Serbs. The BSA forcibly removed thousands of peoples from their homes, executed thousands of civilians, constructed concentration camps, and engaged in the mass rape of Bosnian women. Most notoriously, in July 1995, the BSA massacred at least 7,000 Bosniak men and teenagers in the town of **Srebrenica**, which was part of a supposed UN "safe haven." In response, NATO conducted a series of airstrikes on BSA positions to force Serbia to negotiate an end to the war. A year later, when a treaty (the Dayton Accords) was signed by the presidents of Serbia, Croatia, and Bosnia, around 250,000 people had been killed and two million displaced (Holbrooke, 1999).

The widely publicized massacres, reports of mass rape, and population displacement spurred the United Nations Security Council to authorize the creation of an international tribunal (Security Council Resolution 827) for all of the former Yugoslavia to prosecute violations of international law and to "restore and maintain peace" (Crowe, 2014: 346). Based in The Hague, the *International Criminal Tribunal for the Former Yugoslavia* (ICTY) in the period of its mandate (1993–2017) charged 161 individuals (all but one

*Figure 7.1* Ratko Mladic (with binoculars), then a lieutenant colonel general in the Army of Republika Srpska, Bosnia-Herzegovina, April 1994.

of them men) with committing one or more of four crimes: genocide, crimes against humanity, violations of the customs of war, and grave breaches of the Geneva Conventions. Ninety were convicted and sentenced, most of them Bosnian Serbs, including several high-ranking political and military officials, among them Slobodan Milošovic [*Doc. 7, p. 123*]. The ICTY was the first of its kind since the Nuremberg and Tokyo trials and the first war crimes court created by the UN. It confirmed the main achievement of the Nuremberg IMT: that heads of state and government officials can be held accountable for their actions under international law. The tribunal also set important new precedents, namely, by affirming that violations of international law could be prosecuted in cases of civil war, that rape constitutes a form of torture in IHL, and that command responsibility applies to military and civilian commanders. Finally, the ICTY also served as the model for future international tribunals (Hazan, 2004).

## Genocide in Rwanda

In the spring and summer of 1994, thousands of members of the Hutu ethnic group in Rwanda murdered hundreds of thousands of Tutsis and other Hutus. Tensions and sometimes violence between the majority Hutu population and the minority Tutsis (perceived by the former as holding a disproportionate share of political and economic power) extended to the pre-colonial period, were exacerbated by German and Belgian rule, and continued into the post-colonial decades. By the first years of the 1990s, a Hutu nationalist government had become determined to eliminate the Tutsi on the baseless grounds that the Tutsi were planning to murder the Hutu population. Making matters worse was the intensification of violence between the two groups in neighboring Burundi. Following an invasion of Rwanda in 1990 by a Tutsi rebel force, a peace agreement and power-sharing arrangement between Hutu and Tutsi political parties failed to gain the support of the most extreme Hutu elements (Mamdani, 2020).

The catalyst for the genocide was the killing of Rwandan president Juvénal Habyarimana (1937–94) (a Hutu) on 6 April 1994, most likely by Hutu extremists' intent on eliminating the Tutsi minority. In the course of 100 days between April and July, around 200,000 Hutu civilians, members of militias, policemen, and army personnel (known collectively as *genocidaires*) killed an estimated 500,000 to 800,000 Tutsis and 50,000 moderate Hutus. Victims were often killed with machetes or blunt objects, and the rape of women was pervasive. Some two million people were made refugees. As in Bosnia, a small UN peacekeeping force proved totally ineffective at protecting civilians. The genocide ended in July when a Tutsi army invaded from Burundi and seized Kigali, the Rwandan capital city.

On 8 November 1994, the UN created the **International Criminal Tribunal for Rwanda** (ICTR) to "prosecute persons responsible for genocide and other serious violations of international humanitarian law committed in the territory of Rwanda and neighbouring States, between 1 January 1994 and 31 December 1994" (https://ihl-databases.icrc.org/ihl/INTRO/565). The court is based in Arusha, Tanzania, with offices in Kigali and an appeals court in The Hague. Since 1995, it has indicted 93 individuals charged with violations of IHL and convicted 62. Those indicted included high-ranking military and political officials and numerous civilians. At the same time, national and local courts (the latter known as *Gacaca*) in Rwanda tried thousands of cases. The ICTR achieved four notable firsts. One was that the tribunal was the first international court to prosecute and convict individuals responsible for committing genocide. A related achievement was the prosecution of former prime minister Jean Kambanda (b. 1955) as the first head of state to be convicted on the charge of perpetrating genocide. Third, the ICTR was the first court of its kind to recognize rape as a tool of genocide. The fourth involved holding the media responsible for inciting the public to commit mass murder (Scheffer, 2011).

## Other cases: Liberia and Sierra Leone, Chad, East Timor, and Cambodia

A number of other special courts were created in the early 2000s. Civil wars in the west African nations of Liberia and Sierra Leone that began in the late 1980s resulted in the creation in 2002 by the UN of the **Special Court for Sierra Leone**. The court, based in Freetown, operated between 2002 and 2013 and convicted eight members of three armed factions involved in that country's civil war for war crimes and violations of IHL. The highest-visibility defendant was Charles Taylor (b. 1948), the former president of Liberia, who supported a rebel faction in Sierra Leone. Taylor was charged with 11 counts related to war crimes and crimes against humanity, convicted on all counts in 2012, and sentenced to 50 years in prison. He became the first head of state to be convicted by an international tribunal (Malu, 2022).

Another landmark trial took place in 2015–6 in Senegal. The case involved the former dictator of Chad, Hissène Habré (1942–2021). In power from 1982 to 1990, Habré was ousted in a *coup d'etat* and took refuge in Senegal. A truth commission convened in 1991 and 1992 reported that around 40,000 people had been killed and thousands more tortured by the regime, and revelations by the NGO **Human Rights Watch** revealed a more extensive record of abuses. Yet Habré was not arrested and charged until 2015. The timing is significant. Victims and NGOs had been pressuring the Senegalese government for years to deport Habré to Chad or The Hague. But the ICC had no jurisdiction in the case, as its mandate limited it to crimes committed after its formal creation in 2002. In any case, the ICC had come under fire from a number of African states for targeting only nationals of African nations. Yet to allow Habré to live freely in Senegal reinforced a perception that African states had no interest in holding Africans accountable for crimes against humanity and human rights violations. Hence a new

Senegalese government, backed by the **African Union**, chose to take the unprecedented step of prosecuting in one of its own courts the former head of another state. The involvement of the African Union was significant, as it allowed the government of Senegal to claim that it was prosecuting Habré on behalf of all of Africa (Malu, 2022).

The precedent for Habré's arrest was the detention of former Chilean dictator Augusto Pinochet (1915–2006) in London in 1998 at the request of the Spanish government, which wanted him extradited to Spain to be tried for the disappearances of Spanish citizens during his rule from 1974 to 1990. While a British court ruled Pinochet unfit to stand trial and allowed him to return to Chile, where several more years of legal wrangling prevented him from standing trial before his death in 2006. Habré enjoyed no such protections and in May 2016, the Dakar-based court convicted him of crimes against humanity, torture, and sex crimes and sentenced to life in prison. Around the same time, a court in Chad tried and convicted former member of Habré's security services. Human rights activists and advocates of expanding international criminal law hailed the trial in Senegal as a landmark moment for war-related atrocities cases. Both courts awarded millions of dollars in compensation to the victims, though payments have not been made (Roht-Arriaza, 2005; Malu, 2022).

The end of the 1990s witnessed yet another instance of mass violence, this time in **East Timor**, a province of Indonesia. After decades of violence and deprivations resulting from the Indonesian occupation, the UN sponsored an independence referendum in September 1999 in which a majority voted for independence. Though the Indonesian government agreed to rescind the province's annexation, anti-independence elements in the Indonesian army and Timorese militias killed an estimated 1,000 to 2,000 Timorese around the time of the referendum. UN personnel were also targeted. One half million people were forced to flee their homes. A UN commission recommended the establishment of an international tribunal while Indonesia's National Commission on Human Rights conducted its own investigation and identified Indonesian and East Timorese individuals as alleged perpetrators of crimes against humanity. The Indonesian government rejected the idea of an international tribunal and pledged to hold trials by Indonesian courts, assuring UN Secretary General Kofi Annan that the process would be credible and fair (Kiernan, 2007).

The results were reminiscent of the national trials held by Turkey and Germany after World War I. The Indonesian *ad hoc* court handed down 12 verdicts, of which only two were convictions, both resulting in lenient sentences. International pressure pushed the Indonesian government to create a special Human Rights Court (albeit to operate within the country's judicial structure). This court indicted seven more officials (nearly all East Timorese) but convicted only one, leading to renewed calls for an international tribunal. In line with a long-standing tradition in Indonesian politics, high-ranking military officers who may have committed atrocities have gone unprosecuted. To date, no international tribunal has been convened. Prosecutors in East Timor, with UN assistance, have created a local hybrid Timorese-international court and have had some success in prosecuting over 100 individuals, despite a lack of resources and cooperation from the Indonesian government.

The case of Cambodia was unusual in that an international court was convened several decades after the alleged violations of IHL took place. Between 1975 and 1979, Cambodia was ruled by the Khmer Rouge, a communist group that was responsible for the deaths of nearly two million Cambodians (around 21 percent of the population) in one of the most radical attempts in history to create a peasant-based utopia (**Cambodian genocide**). Though Vietnam invaded in 1979 and toppled the regime, the Khmer Rouge was not completely destroyed and a lengthy civil war followed. A peace treaty in 1991 and two elections in 1993 and 1998, along with the death of its leader, Pol Pot, finally eliminated the Khmer Rouge as a threat to Cambodia's stability. At the same time, US president Bill Clinton signed legislation (The Cambodian Genocide Justice Act) in 1994 that pledged American support for investigating and prosecuting crimes committed by the Khmer Rouge between 1975 and 1979. In 2003 and 2004, talks between the Cambodian government and the UN produced the Law on the Establishment of Extraordinary Chambers in the **Courts of Cambodia for the Prosecution of Crimes Committed during the Period of Democratic Kampuchea** (ECCC). This international court would try "senior leaders" and other culpable individuals for "crimes and serious violations of Cambodian penal law, IHL and custom, and international conventions recognized by Cambodia" committed in the 1975–9 period (Crowe, 2014: 360; Kiernan, 2007).

The results of the court's proceedings were meager compared to those of the ICTY and the ICTR. For one thing, the court did not hold its first trial until 2007 and indicted only five aging suspects. One was declared mentally unfit to stand trial and another died during the proceedings, while the other three were all convicted. A disagreement over further prosecutions between the French judge and his Cambodian counterparts, who believed that more trials would have a destabilizing effect on the country, combined with the fact that many perpetrators have died effectively ensured that no more cases will be brought before the ECCC (Maguire, 2005).

## The International Criminal Court

The idea of a permanent international criminal court was not a new one, having originated with a proposal by Gustave Moynier, a founder of the International Committee of the Red Cross, in 1872 and taken up by jurists in the 1920s and 1930s and again shortly after World War II. The catalyst for the creation of the ICC was a proposal in 1989 to the UN by the government of Trinidad and Tobago to create a permanent court to deal with drug trafficking and terrorism. The proposal generated nearly a decade of work by the UN and NGO's resulting in the **Rome Statute** in July 1998. The treaty established the first permanent international criminal court and was signed by representatives of 120 states. It formally came into existence in 2002 after 60 nations ratified the treaty. By 2022, 137 states had signed the treaty and 123 are states parties. Thirty-five states, including the United States, the Russian Federation, and China, never became parties to the treaty.

Based in The Hague, the ICC began operating in 2003. It is an independent entity (and not a UN organization, as is often assumed) charged with investigating and prosecuting individuals accused of one or more of four international crimes: genocide, crimes against humanity, war crimes, and the crime of aggression committed in a state party's borders or by nationals of a state party. It claims jurisdiction only when a state party has not investigated its own nationals for the most serious violations (the principle of complementarity), though the UN Security Council can authorize an expansion of the ICC's jurisdiction. The court is funded by member states and private sources. It does not maintain any kind of police force and relies entirely on cooperation by state parties. For a case to be considered, it may be referred to the court by the UN Security Council, be initiated by the ICC Prosecutor, or be taken up by the court based on a request by one or more state parties to the treaty. Defendants are presumed to be innocent until proven guilty and have the rights to counsel, to remain silent, to introduce evidence and question witnesses, and to appeal guilty verdicts, and are protected from double-jeopardy. The court does not try any cases *in absentia*.

As of July 2022, the ICC has opened investigations in 16 states: Venezuela, Mali, Cote d'Ivoire, Libya, Sudan, Kenya, Uganda, the Central African Republic, the Democratic Republic of Congo, Georgia, Ukraine, Bangladesh, Myanmar, Afghanistan, Palestine, and the Philippines. Though it has conducted a relatively small number of investigations and prosecutions – ten convictions and four acquittals – in the first 20 years of its existence, it is widely regarded as a milestone in the evolution of IHL. The court is permanent and in terms of its purpose and structure, it promotes due process, accountability, the rule of law, fair trials, global governance, and the protection of human rights. It has upheld the Nuremberg principles and expanded the range of prosecutable war crimes and crimes against humanity (such as sexual and gender-based crimes). It has established what most informed observers consider to be an important track record of cases. And the ICC's influence has extended beyond its offices and courtrooms, as the principal of complementarity has encouraged state-level investigations and in some cases trials. And as with war crimes trials going back to the post-World War I period, the investigations have amassed collections of evidence that will be of potentially great significance to the future development of international criminal law and, not least, the historical record (Schabas, 2020).

Yet significant roadblocks to the court's operations and success have mounted since 2002. Three of the world's most powerful nations have refused to become parties to the treaty. Though China welcomed the creation of the court and has been engaged in its development as an observer, it did not become a party to the treaty. The main concern is the possibility that membership could interfere with the government's ability to act in areas it considers to be of purely "internal" concern, namely, the status of Tibet and Taiwan and the situation with regard to the Uighur ethnic minority in Xinxiang. The Russian Federation signed the Rome Treaty in 2000 and was moving toward joining the court until 2016, when the ICC opened an investigation into the Russian war in Georgia in 2008 and ruled that the 2014 annexation of Crimea in Ukraine amounted to an "ongoing occupation." Any possibility of the Russian Federation becoming a state party while Vladimir Putin serves as President was ruled out by his authorization of a full-scale invasion of Ukraine in February 2022.

Since 2002, the United States, one of only seven countries to vote against the Rome Treaty (along with China, Israel, Yemen, Iraq, Libya, and Qatar), has worked consistently to undermine the court. The attacks of 11 September 2001 were the catalyst. The main concern among American officials from the start was that the court could attempt to prosecute members of the US armed forces or otherwise interfere with the ability of the US military and the Central Intelligence Agency to gather intelligence and operate against Al-Qaeda and other international terrorist groups. In 2002, President George W. Bush notified the UN that the United States had no intention of ratifying the treaty. This was followed two years later by a legislation (the American Service Members Protection Act) that placed strict limits on cooperation with the ICC. The United States has also pressured other governments to pledge not to surrender any US nationals to the court. Hostility to the court and its officials was even greater during the administration of Donald Trump, particularly when the ICC was considering investigations in Afghanistan and Palestine. As the United States has long played a crucial role in the development of international institutions and law, its hostility to the court has invited charges of hypocrisy, particularly in the wake of Russia's invasion of Ukraine and the claim made by President Joseph Biden that Vladimir Putin is a war criminal.

The ICC has also been unable to do anything in response to war crimes and atrocities committed in the course of the Syrian civil war, which began in March 2011. Though critics have accused it of not taking a more assertive position regarding investigations and prosecutions, the main problem has not been the court but the fact that the conflict is ongoing and that China and Russia have used their positions on the UN Security Council to block it from creating a special tribunal. As in the case of other recent conflicts, NGOs, journalists, and private groups have attempted to collect evidence for future prosecutions (see Chapter 13). Also important has been two trials held in a German court in 2021 and 2022 of two former Syrian government officials. In February 2021, the Higher Regional Court in Koblenz found Eyad al-Gharib, a former low-ranking intelligence service officer, guilty of aiding and abetting a crime against humanity. A year later, the same court convicted Anwar Raslan, the former head of the Syrian General Intelligence Directorate's investigation department, for committing crimes against humanity when he oversaw detention centers where torture was routine. The Raslan trial was particularly significant as he was the first high-level official in regime of Bashar al-Assad to be convicted of crimes against humanity. Equally important was that in both cases, the court claimed **universal jurisdiction**, a principle in **customary international law** that provides a state with jurisdiction over violations of international law even when those violations did not take place on that state's territory or when the perpetrator or victim is a national of that state (Rabinovich and Valensi, 2021).

A major controversy erupted in 2017 when the African Union (AU) passed a resolution advocating the withdrawal of its members from the court. The issue was the fact that at that point the ICC had issued arrest warrants or summons to appear and criminal charges solely against nationals of African countries: ten individuals from the Democratic Republic of Congo, eight from Kenya, six from Sudan (including the sitting president), four from Uganda, three each from Libya and Cote d'Ivoire, and one each from Rwanda and Mali. Since the AU's resolution, four Central African Republic nationals and one Malian have been taken into ICC custody with their cases pending. In 2016, the governments of South Africa, The Gambia, and Burundi had decided to withdraw (only Burundi did so). While in November 2017 a large number of African and international NGOs issued a joint statement to all African states parties to the ICC supporting continued membership, it was hard to avoid the perception that the court was a neo-colonial enterprise [*Doc. 8, p. 127*]. The AU's resolution also suggested that a long-standing tradition had been turned on its head: modern war crimes law was created to apply to armies of "civilized states" and not to actions by colonial forces in the colonized world. Now it appeared that the rules were to apply solely to Africans committing crimes against other Africans (Malu, 2019; Clarke, 2019).

The Russian invasion of Ukraine in late February 2022 has presented the ICC with its most serious challenge to date. When the Russian military did not achieve an expected quick and decisive victory, it turned to tactics it had developed in Chechnya and Syria. Civilians became targets of indiscriminate air and artillery attacks and summary executions. Thousands of Ukrainians have been forcibly deported to Russia. Immediately after the invasion began, over 40 states belonging to the ICC submitted state party referrals requesting the court to investigate "any acts of war crimes, crimes against humanity and genocide alleged to have occurred on the territory of Ukraine from 21 November 2013 onwards" (therefore including the occupation of Crimea) (O'Toole, 2022). While addressing the UN Security Council in September 2022, Prosecutor of the International Criminal Court Karim Khan indicated that his office was making the investigation of forced deportations of Ukrainian children a priority. In March 2023, the ICC's Pre-Trial Chamber issued arrest warrants for Vladimir Putin and Maria Lvova-Belova,

Commissioner for Children's Rights in the Office of the President of the Russian Federation, on the grounds that both bore criminal responsibility "for the unlawful deportation and transfer of Ukrainian children from occupied areas of Ukraine to the Russian Federation, contrary to . . . the Rome Statute" (https://www.icc-cpi.int/). While Ukraine is not a party to the ICC, its government accepted the court's jurisdiction, and Ukrainian government officials and civilians along with individuals and groups from other countries have been collecting evidence of war crimes and atrocities.

In May 2022, the first trial of a Russian soldier took place when a district court in Kiev convicted a 21-year-old contract soldier for killing an unarmed civilian. A week later, two Russian artillerymen were convicted by another court for indiscriminately shelling civilian targets. The Ukrainian Prosecutor General reported in June 2022 that in roughly the first four months of the invasion, 18,000 conflict-related crimes had been registered with its office and that over 80 cases were being investigated. The limitations on the ICC's ability to act during and after the conflict may mean that the bulk of investigations and trials will take place in Ukraine or other countries with courts willing to prosecute on the grounds of universal jurisdiction.

The prospects for the kind of international cooperation that made the ICTY and ICTR, the *ad hoc* courts, and the ICC possible – flawed as they all were and are – have been diminished by familiar and newer challenges. The old problem of state sovereignty and national interests taking precedence over international law and global governance continues to impede the development of international criminal law. This impediment has been exacerbated by the fact that the ICC and states are attempting to investigate and prosecute violations as they are taking place, whether in the context of armed conflict (as with Syria or Ukraine) or in the absence of formal states of war (Myanmar, China). A more recent – though not unprecedented – development is the climate of intensifying xenophobic and isolationist nationalism. Such an environment impedes the kind of broad-based cooperation across borders and cultures necessary for the further development of IHL. And while the often extremely dangerous work of NGOs, journalists, and private citizens in collecting evidence of war crimes and atrocities has been essential to publicizing atrocities and laying the groundwork for prosecutions (see Chapter 13), these efforts have often been uncoordinated, sometimes amateurish, and may ultimately not be helpful to prosecutors in bodies like the ICC or national courts. Finally, there is the issue of the ICC's priorities – which to date have been on the most extreme crimes and high-level officials – and the capabilities of its offices to handle an expanding caseload.

# 8 Women and war crimes

War has always been planned and conducted primarily by men while women have always been the principal non-combatant victims, mainly as targets of abduction, enslavement, and especially rape. Whether the incidence of sexual violence increased in the wars and genocides of the modern era *vis-à-vis* the ancient, medieval, and early modern periods is difficult to determine. However, there is no question that the rape of women has been pervasive in the world's armed conflicts from the 19th century to the present. Girls and women have been made particularly vulnerable for several interlocking reasons, most of them not unique to the modern world. At the most basic level there the seemingly timeless willingness of male combatants of all cultural backgrounds to commit various forms of sexual assault, primarily against women. A second is the great degree to which civilians have been ensnared in warfare as deliberate targets and as victims of collateral damage. Another has been the significance of religious and secular ideological justifications for attacks on women. A related reason is the use of sexual assault as a weapon of war in the service of belligerent's ideological, strategic, and tactical objectives. A fifth has been an unwillingness among perpetrators, most victims, eyewitnesses, and the victors and vanquished alike to confront the pervasive reality of sexual crimes in war. To be sure, this situation has changed significantly since the 1990s. Yet expanded awareness and the inclusion of sexual crimes in military codes of conduct and international law have not had any appreciable deterrent effect on the behavior of soldiers in regular and irregular armed forces.

## Women as victims

Sexual violence against women in the colonial wars of the 19th and 20th centuries remains an under-researched subject, but there is no question that it was widespread. World War II and its aftermath represented something of a turning point, if not in terms of the laws of war but in wider public awareness of the prevalence of rape, particularly during military occupations. Ignoring ideological and legal restrictions on contact between "aryans"

DOI: 10.4324/9781003118664-11

and "subhuman" populations, personnel of the two principal land-based armed forces of Nazi Germany – the Wehrmacht and the SS – and various auxiliary units perpetrated countless sexual crimes during and after the invasion of Poland and the Soviet Union. Similarly, the armies of Imperial Japan perpetrated mass rape and sexual enslavement in China, Korea, and the Philippines. Rumors and well-substantiated reports of the mass rape of women – especially German women – by soldiers of the Red Army as it advanced westward circulated widely during and after the war. Recent scholarship has revealed that rape by American soldiers was far more common than has been acknowledged. Conversely, false accusations of rape directed at black African and African-American soldiers serving in the Free French and US armies, respectively, were used as a tool of intimidation and control by deeply racist institutions shaken by years of war and increasing challenges to white supremacy worldwide (Muehlhaeuser and Spengler, 2022; Naimark, 1995; Roberts, 2013).

As with wars of colonization, the instances of sexual crimes in the wars of *decolonization* or during the many internecine conflicts of the Cold War have been largely underreported and unprosecuted at the time they were committed and since (Zaalberg and Luttikhuis, 2022). The commission of sexual crimes has remained a pervasive reality in the many civil and international wars of the post-Cold War period. Most recently, the government of Ukraine, journalists, and NGOs have reported widespread instances of rape of Ukrainian women by Russian forces following the February 2022 invasion.

Sexual crimes also became a central feature of modern genocides. Instances of rape, sexual slavery, and forced marriages were widespread before and during the Armenian genocide. Perpetrators represented multiple levels of Ottoman military and civilian hierarchies, and the atrocities served to weaken Armenian resistance to the Ottoman objective of creating an ethnically "pure" pan-Turkish state. Rape was also used as a tool of ethnic cleansing in the former Yugoslavia and in Rwanda in the 1990s. In the 2000s, non-state armed forces operating in sub-Saharan Africa, notably those connected to the Islamic State of Iraq and the Levant (ISIL) such as Al Shabab and Boko Haram, have abducted hundreds of girls and women in Mozambique and Nigeria, forcing them to endure "sale," assault, and forced marriages. In 2014, ISIL forces attacked the Yazidi ethnic minority in northern Iraq, perpetrating what a UN investigative team (**Investigative Team to Promote Accountability for Crimes Committed by Da'esh/ISIL** [UNITAD]) determined to be genocide. The attack involved the abduction of around 7,000 women, with several thousand missing as of 2022 (Derderian, 2005).

## Sexual crimes and the laws of war

Prohibitions against rape by armed forces go back a long time. In Medieval and early modern Europe, some states issued decrees explicitly prohibiting rape by soldiers and singling out women, along with children, clergy, and peasants, as members of a protected category. There were exceptions, however, notably following the capture of a besieged town or fortress, a situation in which individual commanders had the discretion to be merciful or not. One early modern theorist, the Italian theorist Alberico Gentili (1552–1608), went so far as to propose that rape be prohibited in any circumstance and those guilty of the crime be held accountable by "those sovereigns who wish to observe honorable causes for war and to maintain the common law of nations and of nature" (Bryant, 2021: 133). As always, however, any codes, informal admonitions, or laws related to rape did not apply in cases of rebellion, wars against non-believers, and wars of imperial conquest.

Despite its long-standing prevalence in war, it took a long time for rape to be incorporated in international law. It was identified as distinct crime in the Lieber Code, but does not appear in the provisions of the two Hague Conventions, nor is it named in the charter of the international military tribunals at Nuremberg or Tokyo. But the wording of the conventions and charters left open the possibility of including sexual crimes as prosecutable offenses. The Martens Clause of the 1899 Hague Convention stipulated that

> [t]he inhabitants and the belligerents remain under the protection and the rule of the principles of the law of nations, as they result from the usages established among civilized peoples, from the laws of humanity, and the dictates of the public conscience.
>
> (www.icrc.org/en/doc/resources/documents/article/other/57jnhy.htm)

Similarly, the charter of the IMT listed "crimes against humanity: namely, murder, extermination, enslavement, deportation, and other inhumane acts committed against any civilian population, before or during the war" as crimes that would fall under the tribunal's jurisdiction (https://ihl-databases.icrc.org). Incidents of rape were described at the Nuremberg and Tokyo tribunals, and while no individual was convicted specifically for committing sexual crimes, official and public awareness of their prevalence in war had been broadened.

It was Allied Control Council Law Number 10, which authorized each of the four Allied states to prosecute war criminals in their respective zones of occupation in Germany, that added "rape" to the language of the IMT's charter. The 1949 Geneva Convention represented the next significant turning point. The possibility of prosecuting individuals for committing sexual crimes was implied in article three: "[p]ersons taking no active part in the hostilities . . . shall in all circumstances be treated humanely, without any adverse distinction founded on race, color, religion or faith, sex, birth or wealth" with "violence to life and person, in particular murder of all kinds, mutilation, cruel treatment and torture" and "outrages against personal dignity, in particular humiliating and degrading treatment" being named as prohibited acts. Another article (27) went further, stating that "[w]omen shall be especially protected against any attack on their honor, in particular against rape, enforced prostitution, or any form of indecent assault" (https://ihl-databases.icrc.org). Others in the 1949 convention and the 1977 additional protocols make references to mostly unspecified forms of "inhumane treatment," though rape (along with "forced prostitution" and "any other form of indecent assault") is listed in article 76 of the additional protocols (https://ihl-databases.icrc.org).

It was not until the 1990s that sexual crimes became a prominent part of war crimes and crimes against humanity prosecutions by international tribunals. In the former Yugoslavia, the instance of rape by all sides was widespread, particularly by Bosnia Serb forces against Bosnian Muslim women. Extensive reporting during the wars combined with a greater openness to confronting sexual crimes in general and, not least, the fact that the wars were taking place in a European country played a decisive role in prompting the UN to create the ICTY. The tribunal then made a landmark ruling in 1998, namely, that rape and sexual enslavement constituted torture and could be prosecuted as a war crime. Consequently, in 2001, the tribunal sentenced three Bosnian Serb men for war crimes and crimes against humanity because of their roles in the rape, torture, and sexual enslavement of Bosnian Muslim women. The judgment represented the first time an international court had based convictions exclusively on the commission of sexual crimes.

The ICTR also confronted the extraordinarily high levels of sexual crimes committed during the Rwandan genocide. The proceedings were notable in this context for the powerful testimonies of victims and by the prosecution in 1998 of Jean-Paul Akayesu (b. 1953), a former mayor of the Taba commune. Akayesu was accused of doing nothing to protect women being raped by members of Hutu militias (known as "interahamwe") around his office and of ordering fatal attacks on women. Not only was Akayesu, who received a life sentence, the first person to be convicted and sentenced under the terms of the Genocide Convention; his case established sexual violence as a crime against humanity and instrument of genocide. The precedents set by the ICTY and ICTR were codified in the International Criminal Court's charter (article 7), which identifies rape and other forms of sexual violence as crimes against humanity (Bryant, 2021).

These legal advances were made possible and then augmented since by other important developments. Extensive reporting during and after the conflicts in the former Yugoslavia and in Rwanda by journalists and NGO personnel was essential to raising international awareness of sexual crimes and influencing the actions of the tribunals. The willingness of victims to speak out and testify was of fundamental importance. Another critical factor was the presence of women judges on the ICTY and ICTR. Throughout the 2000s, a significant number of books, scholarly articles, and documentary films have continued to call attention to sexual crimes in the former Yugoslavia, Rwanda, and in the civil wars that wracked the Democratic

Republic of Congo in the late 1990s and early 2000s. NGOs dealing with all manifestations of sexual crimes have proliferated around the world. In 2000, a coalition of women's NGOs, the Violence against Women in War Network, sponsored a **Women's International War Crimes Tribunal.** Held in Tokyo, the tribunal was not a formal court of law but a venue for giving voice to the victims of wartime sexual crimes (64 survivors from nine countries participated in the proceedings) and further calling attention to their experiences and to the lack of prosecution of the perpetrators (Chinkin, 2001; Knop and Riles, 2017; Sakamoto, 2001). The heightened international visibility of the persistent problem of sexual crimes in war was reflected by the awarding of the 2018 Nobel Peace Prize to **Nadia Murad** (b. 1993), a Yazidi woman, activist, and wartime rape victim, and to Dr. **Denis Mukwege** (b. 1955), a Congolese surgeon who has pioneered medical and social-psychological treatments for rape victims.

## Women as perpetrators

Women have also been perpetrators of war crimes. The most extensive research to date on this little-known dimension of war has been on Nazi Germany. Around one half million German women served in various agencies in Germany's occupation of Europe, mainly in the east. For the most part, they worked in lower-level administrative capacities and as nurses, positions that often involved them in the identification of Jews for deportation or execution or as perpetrators in the program to murder the mentally and physically handicapped ("Operation T-4"). In addition, around 3,500 served as concentration camp guards and some 10,000 more as SS auxiliaries (Helferinnen). Yet relatively few German women were prosecuted after the war. No women were charged by the IMT at Nuremberg and only two in the 12 subsequent trials. Very few were tried by allied courts in the four occupation zones with a total of 21 executed between 1945 and 1949 (Lower, 2013).

Several factors explain the paucity of prosecutions. For one thing, women did not serve as soldiers or SS officers or in auxiliary police forces, in the higher echelons of concentration camp administration, or as high-level bureaucrats whose work organized and facilitated the regime's crimes. That is, they were not among those most responsible for war crimes, crimes against humanity, and genocide. And in any case the IMT determined that lower-level support staff (such as secretaries) in the regime and camp administration posed no threat to the stability of postwar Germany. Yet there is no question that a significant number of women sought and took advantage of opportunities – limited as they were by long-standing gender norms and the regime's inclination to limit women to child-rearing and homemaking – to participate in and benefit materially from the Nazi imperial project. Had there been more such opportunities and fewer restraints, there would have likely been many more female perpetrators. Another reason was that the nearly all male investigators and prosecutors believed that women by virtue of being women could not commit war crimes as understood at the time. In court, female defendants played to this form of gender bias in their demeanor and appearance, a practice repeated over 50 years later in prosecutions against women suspected of perpetrating crimes against humanity.

Since the immediate aftermath of World War II, only two women have been prosecuted for war crimes by international courts. The first was **Biljana Plavšić** (b. 1930), a former member of the Supreme Command of the Armed Forces of Republika Srpska. She was not a top-level decision maker, but "embraced and supported the objective" of ethnic cleansing and "contributed to achieving it," as prosecutors in her trial by the ICTY put it in 2003 (Smeulers, 2015: 225). The ICTY indicted her on nine counts, including genocide, but most of the charges were dropped. This was in part because of her subordinate position vis-à-vis the all-male political and military leadership and in part because Plavšić was a cooperative defendant who was able to manipulate assumptions about the supposed impossibility of middle-aged white European women perpetrating war crimes. In the end, she pleaded guilty to one count (persecution on political, racial, and religious grounds), was sentenced to 11 years, and released in October 2009. While serving her sentence, however, she published a memoir in which she presents herself as an unapologetic and unrepentant Serb nationalist, even claiming that Bosnian Muslim women were not raped but willingly engaged in a form of prostitution (Steflja and Darden, 2020).

The second was **Pauline Nyiramasuhuko** (b. 1946), a former minister in the Hutu Power government in Rwanda (serving as minister for the family and women's development). She was accused of encouraging her son and the group of *genocidaires* he commanded to rape Tutsi women in the town of Butare. Like others before her, she played to stereotypes of women (especially mothers) as essentially pacifistic and incapable of committing crimes against humanity. But in 2011, she was convicted on seven charges and sentenced to life in prison, which was later reduced to 47 years. Her conviction was significant in that she was the first woman to be convicted by an international court for sexual violence committed in connection with genocide (Steflja and Darden, 2020).

Nyiramasuhuko's case was also unique because she, similar to Plavšić in the Republic of Serbia, occupied a high-level position in the Hutu Power regime. But there is evidence that female participation in the genocide was relatively extensive. Other higher-level female regime officials, notably Agathe Kanziga (the widow of President Juvenal Habyarimana, an ethnic Hutu whose assassination in 1994 provided the catalyst for the genocide) and Agnes Ntamabyaliro (a former Minister of Justice), encouraged and abetted the genocide. Ntamabyaliro was tried by a Rwandan court, convicted, and given a life sentence. Further, as early as 1995, the NGO African Rights reported that many Hutu women – exact figures could not be given – were complicit in the genocide, if not as killers then by supporting

*Figure 8.1* Rose Karushara incites Hutu *genocidaires* in Rwanda, 1994.

and encouraging male perpetrators in a variety of ways, such as cheering on men or betraying those seeking shelter. The proceedings of local tribunals in post-conflict Rwanda (the **Gacaca courts**, see Chapter 11) support this assessment: of the two million suspects tried, around ten percent were women. Two of the first four Rwandans to be tried for crimes against humanity in courts outside Rwanda were women: two nuns accused of betraying Tutsis who had sought refuge in their convent to extremists intent on killing them were tried and convicted in a Belgian court in 2001 [*Doc. 9, p. 129*].

Only one woman has been among those investigated and prosecuted by the ICC: Simone Gbagbo. The UN had already been investigating her for human rights abuses committed during the civil war and questioned by French authorities in 2008 regarding the disappearance of a French-Canadian journalist. In 2012 she was charged with four counts of crimes against humanity (murder, rape and other sexual violence, persecution, and other inhuman acts) in connection with post-election violence in Cote d'Ivoire in 2010–11. Simone Gbagbo was the wife of former president Laurent Gbagbo, who refused to accept his election loss in November 2010, a situation that threatened to reignite the country's civil war. ICC investigators accused Simone Gbagbo of bearing individual criminal responsibility as an indirect co-perpetrator for participating in what it considered premeditated attacks on supporters of her husband's opponents in the election. But the charges were dropped in July 2021. In the interim, she was tried by an Ivorian court, convicted, and sentenced to 20 years imprisonment for crimes against humanity but then acquitted and pardoned in an amnesty issued by the Ivorian president in 2018. She returned to an active role in Ivorian politics.

# 9 Future war

## Private military companies, drones, cyberwar, and ecocide

The organization of armed forces and the technologies of war have evolved constantly, if unevenly, since prehistoric times. Attempts, from the ancient world to the contemporary, to regulate the conduct of war have lagged behind organizational and technological changes. In the 21st century, four developments have presented in some ways unprecedented challenges to advocates of developing the laws of war and protecting human rights. While they have deep historical roots, they have undergone rapid evolution and growth only in very recent years. One is the proliferation of **private military companies** (PMCs, also known as private security companies) since the 1990s, a development that has supplanted the millennia-old tradition of the mercenary with a new organizational basis for conducting war. A second is the increasing use of unmanned flying and submersible vehicles for surveillance and use as weapons of war. A third, and certainly the most recent and unforeseen phenomenon, is that of cyberweapons and **cyberwar**. Finally, there is the movement to make **ecocide** – the destruction of the physical environment in both war and peacetime conditions – an international crime. Less a result of new ways of organizing and fighting wars, the growing prominence of the concept of ecocide represents a change in perceptions of humanity's relationship to the environment, if not yet changes in international law.

### Private military companies

Mercenaries are soldiers hired to fight for entities such as individual rulers, states, or private entities to which they do not belong as subjects or citizens. The use of hired soldiers dates to classical antiquity and became a prominent feature of warfare in Medieval, Renaissance, and Early Modern Europe. As states began to monopolize the use of force in the 19th century, mercenaries virtually disappeared from armed conflicts, of which there were relatively few in the period between the final defeat of Napoleon in 1815 and the outbreak of World War I in 1914. Nor were they a prominent feature of 19th- and early 20th-century colonial wars or post-World War II decolonization wars. Their use surged in the 1960s and 1980s, above all in Africa, as newly independent states fought each other or faced internal

DOI: 10.4324/9781003118664-12

rebellions. A few individual mercenaries even earned a kind of minor celebrity status for their exploits. Michael Hoare (1919–2020, known popularly as "Mad Mike" Hoare), an Irish World War II veteran, became one of the best-known Cold War-era mercenaries for his role in fighting communist rebels in the Congo in the mid-1960s and then for a failed attempt to topple the government of the Seychelles in 1981. Another was the Frenchman Gilbert Bourgeaud (1929–2007), who went by the *nom de guerre* Bob Denard and fought in multiple conflicts in Africa. In the 1970s and in 1995, Denard led three *coups d'etat* in the Comoros Islands, the third resulting in his arrest by French troops deployed to restore order in the former French colony (Thomson, 1996; Urban, 2015; Percy, 2007; Geraghty, 2009).

Years before Denard's arrest, individual mercenaries or loosely connected bands of them were being replaced with what would become known as private military companies. The first were formed during World War II, but regional conflicts in Africa and the Middle East combined with the end of the Cold War and the global movement toward the privatization of a growing number of state functions all fueled the rapid growth of the industry. Contemporary PMCs are multinational corporations that contract with governments, international organizations, and private enterprises to provide a range of security services. These services most often involve training, logistical support, the protection of personnel and properties, and varying levels of engagement in armed conflicts, with personnel recruited from state military services, especially counterinsurgency and special force units. By 2021, hundreds of PMCs were operating in nearly every part of the world, with the industry's market size estimated at nearly 250 billion US dollars and growing (McFate, 2017).

In general, PMCs have been used as proxies by states when those states wish to influence the course of an armed conflict or occupation but do not want to involve their own national forces. This situation is a continuation of a pattern set during the Cold War, namely, the connections between the intelligence services of major powers like the United Sates and the United Kingdom and mercenaries. In the post-Cold War world, the relationship between national governments and PMCs is much clearer. Moreover, eyewitnesses, UN investigators, NGOs, reporters, and foreign government sources have implicated the personnel of PMCs in multiple war crimes and crimes against humanity. The first important PMC to operate in the 1990s was the South African company Executive Outcomes (EO). In the Angolan Civil War (1975–2002), EO was hired by the ruling Popular Movement for the Liberation of Angola party (Movimento Popular de Libertaçâo de Angola [MPLA]) to train soldiers and pilots for combat against rebel forces (Uniâo Nacional pela Independência Total de Angola [UNITA]). During the period of EO's involvement in the war in the early and mid-1990s, the number of civilian deaths increased significantly, and the NGO Human Rights Watch and the UN accused EO personnel of participating in attacks on civilians and possibly committing war crimes (Singer, 2007).

Most other important PMCs have originated in the United States and the Russian Federation. The US firm Military Professional Resources Incorporated (MPRI), established in 1987 by former US military officers, has contracted extensively with the US government. With Washington's encouragement, the government of Croatia hired MPRI to provide training and logistical support to Croatian forces in the war with Serbia (1991–5). As with EO in Angola, MPRI support seems to have been a crucial factor in the final Croatian victory over Serbian forces in 1995. And, similar to EO, there is evidence that MPRI personnel were involved directly in the main Croatian military operation ("Operation Storm") and may also have been complicit – if indirectly – in the largest single instance of ethnic cleansing in the entire conflict: the forced removal of ethnic Serbs from Krajina, a self-proclaimed Serb proto-state. In 2010, a group of Serbs who had lived in Krajina filed a class action lawsuit in a US court against MPRI, though a judge ruled the court did have jurisdiction to hear the plaintiffs' claims.

In 1996, the former US Navy officer Eric Prince created the Blackwater Lodge and Training Center. Following the invasion of Iraq in 2003, the US government contracted with Blackwater to guard installations, individuals, and convoys of military vehicles. The latter responsibility led to an incident in September 2007 in which Blackwater personnel guarding a convoy killed 14 Iraqi civilians and wounded dozens more in what its officials claimed was an act of self-defense. Subsequent investigations by American and Iraqi government agencies concluded that the shootings were unjustified. An investigation by the US Congress accused Blackwater personnel of using "frequent and extensive force" in Iraq "resulting in significant casualties and property damage" and they frequently fired their weapons "preemptively." In 2014, four Blackwater operatives involved in the shootings were convicted of first-degree murder and multiple counts of voluntary manslaughter in a US federal court, though all four were pardoned by President Donald Trump in 2020 (Ageli, 2016; Scahill, 2007).

In the 2000s, PMCs have increasingly operated as an unofficial arm of the Russian Federation's security and resource acquisition policies. The Russian Federation has made extensive use of PMCs in Africa, the Middle East, and Ukraine, the best known of which is The Wagner Group. In Ukraine, PMC operatives have provided combat support to separatists in the eastern Donbas region. Following the February 2022 invasion, Ukrainian, German, and British sources have identified Wagner Group operatives as complicit – along with the regular Russian Federation forces – in the killing of civilians in several Ukrainian towns. Wagner Group and personnel of other PMCs have also been accused of committing war crimes in the Central African Republic and Mali in 2021 and 2022, respectively (McFate, 2019).

International conventions have addressed the issue of mercenaries in stages. The 1907 Hague Convention stipulated that "[c]orps of combatants cannot be formed nor recruiting agencies opened on the territory of a neutral Power to assist the belligerents" in an armed conflict (https://ihl-databases.icrc.org/applic/ihl/ihl.nsf/ART/200-220005?OpenDocument). A state employing mercenaries to fight another state violates the provision of the UN Charter, which obligates members to "refrain . . . from the threat or use of force against the territorial integrity or political independence of any state, or in any other manner inconsistent with the Purposes of the United Nations" (https://legal.un.org/repertory/art2/english/rep_supp7_vol1_art2_4.pdf). The 1949 Geneva Convention requires that anyone in international or non-international conflicts who has ceased to be a combatant be treated humanely, though states are not obligated to accord POW status to captured or surrendered mercenaries. The 1977 additional protocol to the Geneva Conventions defined "mercenary" but did not specifically outlaw their use. This was attempted by two international conventions. The first was a regional agreement sponsored by the African Union (the Convention for the Elimination of Mercenarism in Africa, adopted in 1977 and entering into force in 1985) and the second (the International Convention against the Recruitment, Use, Financing, and Training of Mercenaries) adopted by the UN in 1989 and coming into force in 2001, with 35 states having ratified the latter convention (Solis, 2022).

The proliferation of PMCs since the 1990s has presented the ICC and other parties interested in developing international criminal law with a set of new challenges. The conventions defining and outlawing mercenaries did not account for PMCs as they have evolved in the 2000s. But the main problem is not that IHL has not accounted for PMCs. Nor is there a lack of evidence that PMC personnel have committed war crimes and other violations of IHL. Indeed, the ICTR set an important precedent when it ruled that non-military personnel could be charged with committing war crimes or crimes against humanity. The main problem is that prosecutions are extremely difficult, if not usually practically impossible. PMCs often incorporate immunity clauses into their contracts. States can run interference on behalf of PMCs, and much secrecy surrounds their operations. Journalists investigating the activities of Wagner Group operatives in Africa have been killed. PMCs cannot be charged as entities, and it can be difficult to trace the ownership of some companies (the purported head of the Wagner Group has denied the organization's existence). PMCs also often disband and then reform as new corporations, further complicating investigations and prosecutions. Some states have taken action to regulate the activities of PMCs, and in 2008, representatives of 17 states (since joined by 41 more and NATO, the EU, and the Organization for Security and Co-operation in Europe) signed the **Montreux Document**, a non-binding re-affirmation of international laws as they relate to the operations of PMCs. Yet as of 2022, no employee of a PMC anywhere in the world has been charged by the ICC for violations of IHL, and convictions in domestic courts are rare (International Committee of the Red Cross, 2009).

## The "Kill Cloud:" drone warfare and international law

Unmanned flying devices designed to deliver explosives were first deployed in the mid-19th century. During Austria's siege of Venice in 1849, the Austrians launched around 200 balloons designed to automatically drop 11 to 24 kilograms of explosives over their targets (only one is known to have hit its target). It would not be until 1916 that the first pilotless aircraft was developed by the British engineer Archibald Low, who also devised the first wireless guidance system. The US Army also designed a flying missile (the "Kettering Bug"), though it could not be deployed in the European theater before the war ended in November 1918. British and US military engineers continued to develop pilotless aircraft in the 1930s and during World War II, but the Germans would make the most significant technological leap forward with the construction of jet propelled autopiloted missiles launched against London and other British cities late in the war. The US military, with the assistance of ex-Nazi engineers, further developed the technology after the war. During the Vietnam War, the American Air Force deployed the first unmanned reconnaissance aircraft. The United States and Israel advanced the combat and reconnaissance capabilities of unmanned aircraft considerably in the 1980s and 1990s.

By the 2000s, the use of increasingly powerful drones for surveillance and combat purposes was transforming armed conflict around the world. The US military and the CIA have developed substantial capabilities, particularly with the Predator model (introduced in 2000) and used these extensively in Afghanistan, Somalia, and Yemen. Since 2001, the United States has conducted over 14,000 drone strikes on suspected terrorists alone. By the second decade of the 21st century, the US Air Force was training more human drone operators than aircraft pilots. The technology is proliferating widely and has not only been weaponized by the most powerful states. Turkey has also developed a sophisticated drone (the Bayraktar) it has used against Kurdish separatists and sold to combatants in Libya, Syria, Azerbaijan, and Ukraine. Iran and its regional allies have made use of drones in operations against Israel, US forces, and Sunni Arab states. In addition, the United States, the United Kingdom, China, and Russia are developing unmanned underwater vehicles (UUVs) for underwater mapping, mine laying, anti-mine and anti-submarine operations, surface warfare, and electronic warfare. UUVs may also be constructed to carry deliverable nuclear weapons (Solis, 2022).

IHL has few specific provisions to account for the use of drones. The additional protocol (I) to the Geneva Conventions does require new weapons systems to comply with the laws of armed conflict and urges all states to implement a rigorous review process in developing any new weapons. Moreover, the basic requirements of legal military operations would apply to the use of drones and **lethal autonomous weapons** (LAWs, weapons that can operate without direct human control): distinguishing between combatants and non-combatants, proportionality, military necessity, and avoiding unnecessary suffering. Complicating the application of the laws of war to drone and LAWs operations is the accelerating development of artificial intelligence (AI) systems capable of operating weapons systems autonomously or semi-autonomously. To date, nearly all weapons systems with AI-based autonomous capabilities rely on human operators to monitor their operations and, most crucially, make decisions on the use of lethal force. Yet a few fully autonomous systems have been deployed in conflict zones, and there seems to be no question that multiple nations are pursuing more advanced LAWs capabilities. In the spring of 2020, for instance, a Turkish-made drone capable of fully autonomous operations was deployed against Libyan National Army forces. As only individuals are held accountable for ordering, abetting, or committing war crimes and crimes against humanity, the central legal question when it comes to drones and LAWs is who would be prosecuted should such a weapon violate the laws of war? In addition, the CIA has employed civilian contractors to operate drones in military operations, a violation of the laws of war, which require military aircraft to be operated by a state's armed forces (Wittes and Blum, 2015).

Defenders of drone use argue they are now essential tools for conducting surveillance and targeting non-state actors, like individual terrorists or terrorist groups. And there is evidence that drone operations are an effective way to fight terrorists. Supporters also claim that LAWs operate in a way that restricts collateral damage to a far greater extent than ever possible in modern warfare. In July 2022, for instance, a US drone strike killed Ayman al-Zawahiri, a senior Al-Qaeda leader and key planner of the 11 September 2001 attack. Despite the fact that the drone struck a private home in a residential area of Kabul, Afghanistan, Zawahiri was the only certified casualty. Critics, however, have pointed out that civilians are often killed by drone strikes. Of the over 14,040 confirmed drone strikes carried out by the United States between 2001 and 2022, an estimated 8,858 to 16,901 people have been killed, with 910 to 2,200 of them civilians (and 283–454 of that total being children) (www.thebureauinvestigates.com/projects/drone-war). In addition to the moral, ethical, and legal problems civilian casualties present, critics point to evidence that drone strikes in particular generate a great deal of anger among affected civilian populations and thus become counterproductive to anti-terrorist operations. And there is a problem of perception. As in the period of global colonial wars, conflict zones in the global south remain testing grounds for developing new weapons systems, and it is in poorer parts of the world that drones have been deployed and caused the most casualties, most often in non-international armed conflicts. And video footage of the attacks has increasingly been distributed on the Internet, increasing the awareness of the deadly capacities of what is otherwise a highly stealthy weapon of war.

## Cyberwar

As with drones, the capacity of states and individuals to use communications and information technology to not only spread disinformation or disrupt political processes like elections but conduct attacks on military and civilian targets also expanded enormously in the 2000s. Lagging far behind have been the capacity of states, private enterprises, and individuals to defend themselves and the expansion of IHL to respond to this rapidly evolving form of high-tech warfare. Distinct from "cybercrime," "cyberwar" involves the use of computers and computer networks as offensive or defensive weapons. A "cyberattack" is any form of cyberwar that can be expected to produce injuries to persons or result in their deaths and/or damage or destroy physical objects. An attack on vital cyber infrastructures might also be considered part of an attack on physical objects, while theft of data falls into the category of cyber operations. The distinction is an important one, as the former legitimizes acts of armed self-defense. Again like drones, cyberattacks are not by themselves violations of the laws of war. How the rules of war may or may not apply depends on how the particular weapon is used.

The UN General Assembly, the G20, the EU, the OAS, and ASEAN have all confirmed that international law applies to the use of information technologies and NGOs, and businesses have investigated how it might be applied in practice. Beginning in 2009, the NATO-sponsored Cooperative Cyber Defense Centre of Excellence (CCDCOE) has produced multiple guides for policymakers and lawyers regarding cyberspace and international law (the "**Tallinn manuals**"). Private tech companies have an unusually high stake in the development of international law in relation to cyberwar. In 2017, the president of Microsoft, Brad Smith, issued a call for a "**digital Geneva Convention**" to protect civilians and civilian infrastructure from attack [*Doc. 11, p. 133*].

In March 2022, a group of lawyers and activists based at the University of California's School of Law requested that the ICC investigate cyberattacks conducted by hackers working for Russian military intelligence (GRU) against targets in Ukraine as possible war crimes. Russian hackers have launched hundreds of cyberattacks since 2014, targeting power grids, satellite systems, government agencies, media outlets, and businesses. They have also deployed a highly destructive malware program (NotPetya) and used others (Industroyer, Crash Override) in attacks on power grids. During the 2022 invasion, hackers coordinated attacks with the Russian military's ground and air operations. Specifically, the petitioners have pointed to two blackout attacks in eastern Ukraine in 2015 and 2016 conducted by the Russian hacker group Sandworm in which critical civilian infrastructure was the principal target. Should the ICC decide to investigate, it would be the first such action of its kind taken by an international body. Yet prosecuting the perpetrators of cyberattacks that violate the laws of war will undoubtedly prove to be extremely difficult. For one thing, single-actor cyberattacks or those conducted by small groups that are not state-sponsored might be held accountable for their actions by domestic courts but do not constitute a party to a conflict in terms of the laws of war. And while it is widely known that individual hackers and groups of hackers may be utilized by a state's military or intelligence services, these connections tend to be very well hidden (Al-Rawi, 2021; Arquilla, 2021).

## Ecocide

For centuries, belligerents in armed conflicts have attempted to damage or destroy the enemy's environmental infrastructure – that is, the human-engineered or human-cultivated production of food, potable water, fuel, and other essential natural resources like timber or pastureland. It has only been since the 1970s that activists, jurists, and a small number of states have advocated defining the destruction of the natural world, whether as part of a war or not, as a violation of international law. The idea was first articulated in 1970 by antiwar activists in response to the US military's extensive use of an herbicide and defoliant chemical ("Agent Orange") as a weapon in the Vietnam War (known in Vietnam as the American War). In that conflict,

*Figure 9.1* Environmental warfare: US Air Force planes spray defoliants and herbicides in South Vietnam ("Operation Ranch Hand") to deprive North Vietnamese and Viet Cong forces of cover and food.

the objective was to clear the dense foliage concealing the Ho Chi Minh trail, the main conduit used by North Vietnam to supply troops fighting in the south of the country. Though the United States failed to seriously disrupt supply operations, the damage to the surrounding environment was extensive and long lasting, extending to the bodies of several generations of Vietnamese and Laotians (Figure 9.1). With reference to Vietnam, the Swedish Prime Minister Olof Palme (1927–86) became the first head of state to propose the idea of ecocide as an international crime at the 1972 UN Conference on the Human Environment.

Over the following decades, scholars paid closer attention to the environmental impact of war while activists pursued criminalizing acts of environmental destruction. In 2010, one of the most influential activists, the Scottish lawyer Polly Higgins (1968–2019), offered what has become a widely accepted definition of ecocide: "extensive damage to, destruction of or loss of ecosystem(s) of a given territory, whether by human agency or by other causes, to such an extent that peaceful enjoyment by the inhabitants of that territory has been severely diminished" (Higgins, 2010: 63). By that point, the UN had debated making ecocide a violation of international law and ten states had criminalized ecocide (Vietnam, not surprisingly, was one of them). The term was, of course, inspired by the term genocide, albeit in a way that called attention to Raphael Lemkin's original definition, which was not incorporated into the 1948 UN Genocide Convention, namely, that genocide was

> a coordinated plan of different actions aiming at the destruction of essential foundations of the life of national groups, with the aim of annihilating the groups themselves. The objects of such a plan would be the disintegration of the political and social institutions, of culture, language, national feelings, religion, and the economic existence of national groups, and the destruction of the personal security, liberty, health, dignity, and even the lives of the individuals belonging to such groups.
>
> (Lemkin, 1944/2005: 79)

While Lemkin did not mention the physical environment, its destruction could easily be considered a mortal threat to the "essential foundations of the life of national groups." Two related core assumptions underpinned this interpretation of Lemkin's definition: (1) that the term genocide cannot simply apply to human beings and (2) there is no meaningful distinction between the worlds of humans and non-humans, with the survival of the former dependent upon the continued healthy existence of the latter (Eichler, 2020).

Since 2010, the strongest support for adding ecocide to the four core crimes prosecuted by the ICC has come from NGOs and a handful of small island nations faced with destruction as a result of rising sea levels. The most recent attempt to propose an amendment to the Rome Statute that would add ecocide to the ICC's four core international crimes took place in June 2021 [*Doc. 10, p. 131*]. To a greater extent than any other area of conflict-related international law, establishing ecocide as an international crime faces enormous obstacles. For one thing, most forms of environmental destruction do not take place during times of war. Another relates to the issue of intentionality at the core of the definitions (Lemkin's and the UN's) of genocide and how it could be determined legally. The biggest obstacle, of course, is the deeply entrenched – and in some respects growing – human dependence on the burning of fossil fuels and unsustainable forms of food production as the earth's population climbs steadily toward the ten billion mark.

# 10 Memory, transitional justice, and the investigative turn

The purpose of the first codes and conventions related to the conduct of war was to constrain its excesses against combatants and civilians. After World War II, the unprecedented wave of trials in Europe and Asia was driven first and foremost by a desire for a judicial reckoning with the crimes of the Axis states and those who collaborated with them. The international conventions that followed returned to the problem of regulating the conduct of war, this time emphasizing the protection of civilians, while the creation of new international tribunals to investigate and prosecute crimes against humanity took place only in the 1990s. That decade also witnessed the development of what has become known as **transitional justice**. The objective was to combine the administration of justice (or at least the investigation of alleged crimes) with public memory, memorialization, and forms of restitution in order to establish a peaceful post-conflict political and social order.

Outside the contexts of courtrooms and international conventions, the memory of war crimes and crimes against humanity has been preserved, denied, and debated around the world. What might be called "memory work" has, particularly since the 1990s, taken place in diplomacy, in politics at all levels, in various forms of memorialization, in public and private institutions, in communities, and within families. The work has been undertaken by remarkably wide range of institutions, such as governments, NGOs, museums and archives, and individuals such as scholars, lawyers, journalists, artists, and ordinary people. They have been motivated by a desire to seek justice and recompense for the victims and by the belief that an honest reckoning with the past is essential to creating a peaceful present and future. There has been, however, a darker side to the impulse to remember: that is, the deliberate distortion of the past in the service of political ends. While there is nothing new about denying or suppressing free discussions of war-related atrocities, the propagation of lies and false narratives about what did and did not happen in past (or ongoing) wars has accelerated worldwide since the "memory boom" of the 1990s.

DOI: 10.4324/9781003118664-13

## The memory of war crimes after World War II

The three postwar German states have been the sites of an extended and extensively studied experiment in transitional justice. The liberation of concentration camps in 1945 and the Nuremberg trials laid bare to the world – and, not least, to a German public largely unwilling to confront the truth – the base criminality of the Nazi regime. Two postwar German governments – the Federal Republic of Germany (West Germany), a liberal democracy, and the German Democratic Republic (East Germany), a communist dictatorship – took dramatically different approaches to the past. While the East German regime was initially aggressive in prosecuting suspected war criminals, it soon suppressed the memory of Nazi crimes against anyone other than Soviet Union and German communists. Scholars and journalists, of course, could not research, write, or teach freely about the past. And while the East German state did make restitution payments to Holocaust survivors, it also supported Israel's Arab enemies – eventually including terrorist groups – with aid and training. In West Germany through the 1950s, governments dominated by moderate conservatives sought to draw a clear line between the new state and the Nazi past by ending denazification purges and pressuring Allied governments to end war crimes trials and release convicted war criminals. This was the best way, it was argued by German, American, and British officials, to ensure that West Germany would remain a stable member of a trans-Atlantic alliance of states mobilized against the Soviet Union and its allies in Eastern Europe and a productive partner in a new economic unification project. The government also negotiated restitution payments to Holocaust survivors and the state of Israel and, contrary to East Germany, became Israel's most important European supporter (Herf, 1997; Moeller, 2001).

At the same time and to a greater extent than in East Germany, former Nazis flooded back into the West German government and into the professions. Most had no interest in discussing whatever roles they had played in the years of Nazi rule. Yet neither did most Germans join nor vote for far right parties, which remained on the fringes of West German politics for the next 60 years. Overall, former members of the Nazi Party or ex-Wehrmacht or SS officers were content to live in what one historian called the "security of silence." Throughout the 1950s, there was little by way of broader public discussions about the past in the form of memorialization, public school curricula, research by historians, and cultural productions like films, novels, or museum exhibits. The silences began to be broken in the late 1950s, with the first domestic trials of former SS personnel and then by the Eichmann trial. More trials in West German courts followed and by the mid- and late-1960s, a younger generation of Germans representing a "new left" showed themselves willing to ask questions about the past and point to the considerable influence former Nazis exerted across West German society (Frei, 2002; Fulbrook, 2018; Neiman, 2019).

Despite the high visibility of the Eichmann trial, the central crime of the Nazi regime – the Holocaust – only began to take up a prominent place in West German political and cultural life in the 1980s, though not without generating considerable controversy, as when prominent conservative intellectuals attempted to relativize the genocide of the Jews and provoked a fierce public debate about its significance to German and world history. This situation changed dramatically in the 1990s. After the end of the Cold War, historians were able to learn a great deal more about the Holocaust in the places where the vast majority of the genocide took place: eastern Europe and the former Soviet Union. The newly unified Germany committed itself to building an enormous memorial to the murdered Jews of Europe in the center of the restored capital city of Berlin and soon sponsored the construction of memorials to other persecuted groups, notably Roma and Sinti people and homosexuals. Public memorials – state-sponsored and otherwise – appeared across much of Germany in the 2000s.

It was also in the 1990s that German and non-German scholars revealed – often in the face of considerable resistance and hostility – the extensive involvement of every significant German institution with the Nazi regime and its genocidal war of conquest: the medical establishment, industrial concerns, banks and insurance companies, the Christian churches, and universities and scientific institutions. Particularly notable in this context was a traveling exhibit titled "War of Annihilation: Crimes of the German Wehrmacht 1941 to 1944" (known informally as "Crimes of the Wehrmacht"). The exhibit, organized by a highly respected German research institution, focused on the responsibility of the Wehrmacht for war crimes in World War II, above all on the eastern front. It premiered in 1995, was briefly suspended following revelations of misidentified photographs (quickly corrected by the sponsors), and then resumed until 1999, eventually visiting 33 German and Austrian cities and receiving some 800,000 visitors. The exhibit shocked many viewers and generated a great deal of controversy, with neo-Nazi groups regularly staging protests and even firebombing one of the exhibition sites. Much of the controversy can be attributed to the fact that the exhibit challenged a deeply entrenched myth in German society: that it was the SS that was responsible for the worst crimes of the regime and not the regular German army, which most Germans believed had acted as a "normal" fighting force throughout the war (Bartov, 2013).

The exhibit's success, however, along with the outpouring of scholarship and memorialization on every aspect of the Nazi regime and the Holocaust, is evidence that by the 2000s, a consensus had been achieved in Germany, namely, that the Nazi past must be discussed honestly, taught about in schools, and never forgotten. Most recently, much attention in Germany has been devoted to the history and legacies of the genocide of the Herero and Nama peoples in Imperial Germany's colony of German Southwest Africa (present-day Namibia, see Chapter 2). Beginning in 2004, the German government began issuing apologies and has since pledged restitution payments while German museums have begun returning looted cultural artifacts. Yet there are grounds to challenge this admirable record of memory work. There is evidence of a kind of popular exhaustion with the various manifestations of Holocaust memorialization, even among those who are not Holocaust deniers and do not support the far right. And while Holocaust denial has always been a central feature of the post-World War II German far right, it – along with the refusal to acknowledge the German army's complicity in war crimes – has been augmented by recent attempts by the country's most successful postwar far right political party, Alternative for Germany (Alternativ fuer Deutschland, AfD), to downplay the significance of the Nazi period and reject what its leaders consider a culture of constant self-flagellation about the past. The intensification of violence – arson, assault, and murder – perpetrated by the far right across Germany since the 1990s and at best consistently downplayed and at worst overlooked by politicians and law enforcement agencies has also called into question the extent to which the country has really "come to terms" with the Nazi past (Hughes, 2022).

Three other battles over the memory of war crimes and other war-related atrocities merit attention in this context. The Armenian genocide remains a highly contested landscape of memory politics in and outside of the Republic of Turkey and Armenia. It is important to remember that the attack on Armenian populations in Anatolia in 1915 was well publicized around the world as it was taking place. In 1920, the Turkish government recognized that "massacres" had been perpetrated and pledged itself (as per the terms of the Treaty of Sevres, which concluded the war between the victorious allied states and the Ottoman Empire) to prosecute the perpetrators, but it reversed course three years later in the Treaty of Lausanne. Few perpetrators were ever prosecuted, either in or outside the Republic of Turkey. Indeed, many occupied high-level positions in the new republic. Successive governments continued to oppress surviving Armenian communities. Suppression extended to evidence of the massacres and discussions of it in public. Outright denial (up to the present day) that massacres constituting genocide has been the most consistent feature of official memory (Ackam, 2007).

Conversely, successive generations of Armenians have kept the memory of the genocide alive within Armenian communities (including the Armenian diaspora). In the 1970s and 1980s, the US Congress, the UN, the European Parliament, and multiple individual European governments all adopted resolutions that commemorated the atrocity and even recognized it as an instance of genocide. The US government, wary of damaging relations with an important Cold War and post-Cold War ally, did not officially apply the term genocide until April 2021, when US President Joe Biden recognized the massacres as genocide. In hindsight, the long battle over the memory of a major crime against humanity reveals not only the power of a state to suppress and shape public memory (in and outside its borders) but also the potential of the victims to challenge decades of denial and maintain their cause at a high level of international visibility.

Another ongoing battle over the memory of a notorious war crime involves the sexual enslavement of women by the forces of Imperial Japan in World War II. During the Asia-Pacific war, perhaps 200,000 women from several Asian states were kidnapped or tricked into a form of sexual slavery by the Japanese military. The military and private contractors ran "comfort stations," hence the term "comfort women," with the main objective being the maintenance of discipline among Japanese soldiers. Despite the high visibility accorded to rape at the Tokyo IMT and an abundance of evidence about the existence of the comfort stations, crimes committed against comfort women were never prosecuted. Similar to the situation in Turkey, postwar Japanese governments backed by conservative nationalist historians and publicists have to the present day denied that the Japanese military was responsible, and hence liable in any legal sense, for such highly organized sexual crimes. Unlike the memory of the Armenian genocide, however, there was silence about the issue in Japan until the "memory boom" of the 1990s. This absence of public memory and memorialization was part of a wider silence about the Japanese military's record of committing atrocities on a massive scale between 1937 and 1945 (Soh, 2009; Hicks, 1995).

Silence on the memory of comfort women was broken in the early 1990s when a Korean woman, Kim Hak-Sun, spoke publicly about her abduction at age 17 and enslavement in a comfort station run by the military. Several lawsuits – none of them successful – against the Japanese government followed, as did a profusion of media coverage and academic studies. In 1992, the Japanese Prime Minister issued several public apologies and a year later, the Japanese government's Chief Cabinet Secretary issued a formal apology to the Korean victims following the publication of an official report on the ordeal of comfort women. Another formal statement directed at a wider audience in Asia was issued in 1995, and the Japanese government created a compensation fund for surviving victims, though it was to be funded by private donations. The following year, the Ministry of Education approved including references to comfort women in middle school-level textbooks. Broader official recognition was accompanied by an outpouring of scholarship, films, television shows, and other media. There is evidence of broadening public support at that point for the acts of official acknowledgment and compensation, particularly since official silence on the issue had remained a significant impediment to improved relations with China, South Korea, the Philippines, and other Asian states. Beyond Japan, there is no doubt that the visibility of the issue contributed to the establishment of rape as a crime against humanity in the statute of the ICC (1998). The Women's International War Crimes Tribunal, held in Tokyo in 2000 (see Chapter 9), capped off this first wave of public and private memory work (Henry, 2013).

Beginning in the mid-1990s, however, a remarkable turnaround was already underway. Conservative nationalist politicians and publicists struck back against what they considered to be a culture of self-imposed national humiliation and began to downplay, deny, and lie about the wartime sexual crimes of the Japanese military. At the forefront of this reaction was the two-time Prime Minister Shinzo Abe (1954–2022). Before his first term (2006–7), Abe had denied the existence of comfort women. In 2007, he adopted the position that women "working" in military brothels had not been coerced. In the meantime, demands for greater recognition from the South Korean government intensified and anti-Japanese sentiment grew in China. This only hardened the resistance of deniers like Shinzo Abe.

A similar dynamic has become evident in Bosnia since the conclusion of the civil wars of the 1990s. In November 1995, the United States brokered a peace agreement between Bosnia, Serbia, and Croatia that ended the war in Bosnia. Bosnia remained a sovereign and unified state but its administration was to be shared by its three ethnic groups – Bosnian Muslims (also known as "Bosniaks"), Serbs, and Croats – and divided into two largely self-governing entities: Republika Srpska and a Bosnian federation comprising ten cantons run by Bosnian Muslims and Croats. In recent years, Serb nationalism has surged, spearheaded by the Serb Member of the Presidency of Bosnia and Herzegovina since 2018, Milorad Dodik. Like other Serb nationalists before, during, and after the wars of the 1990s, Dodik portrays Serbs as the victims of Bosnian Muslims and more generally of the UN, the United States, and most European states. He also denies that Bosnian Serb forces committed war crimes in the 1990s. While the United States was the main driver of the peace negotiations (and the NATO airstrikes against Bosnian Serb forces that made them possible), it has long since turned its attention away from the region. Authoritarian governments – namely, Russia, Hungary, China, and some Arab states – have stepped into the breach and contributed to the centrifugal forces threatening to undo Bosnia's intricate post-conflict political architecture.

Developments in Japan and Bosnia related to the past are symptoms of a worldwide surge in the popularity of nationalist authoritarianism and authoritarian leaders. In general, these leaders and their parties have challenged and in some cases done away with rights fundamental to liberal democracies, attempted to manipulate fair elections, denigrated international institutions like the UN and EU, taken effective control of once-independent judiciary systems, and demonized "outsiders," notably migrants, refugees, and asylum seekers. In the case of the Russian Federation and its leader, Vladimir Putin, the most significant manifestation of authoritarian nationalism has been the multi-stage dismemberment and invasion of Ukraine. An integral part of the authoritarian turn has been an attack on memory work that excavates and memorializes past crimes and atrocities, whether war-related or otherwise (e.g., slavery in the United States). The Russian government, for example, has persecuted journalists, shut down NGOs that work on memorialization, and outlawed public speech that challenges a state-approved narrative of the Soviet war effort in World War II. Another example is contemporary Poland, the site of a powerful nationalist backlash following revelations by historians that the Christian population was more widely complicit in the persecution and murder of the country's Jewish population during and after World War II than most Poles had known or were willing to admit. The backlash has taken the form of attempts by the conservative nationalist Law and Justice Party to criminalize public statements deemed (by a conservative nationalist judiciary) to denigrate the Polish nation.

## Truth commissions, restitution, and the return of looted cultural artifacts

Enmeshed in the broader fabric of memory work has been the development of new approaches to post-conflict recovery and reconciliation. The first is the proliferation of truth commissions: *ad hoc* state-sponsored institutions charged with investigating political violence, usually during the negotiated transition from some form of autocracy to a liberal democratic system or in the aftermath of war. Indeed, proponents claim that the work of **truth commissions** is essential to the principal objectives of transitional justice. Truth commissions are not courts, nor are they alternatives to courts. Their main purpose is to gather evidence – documentary and eyewitness – and make recommendations for legal action, institutional change, compensation for victims, and memorialization. Finally, while truth commissions are government-sponsored entities, their creation and work have been influenced strongly by non-governmental actors, namely, victims and victims' groups and NGOs (Hayner, 2009; Bakiner, 2016; Bisset, 2012).

The first self-proclaimed truth commission was created in Uganda in 1974 to investigate killings and disappearances in the wake of the 1971 *coup d'etat* that brought Idi Amin Dada (c. 1925–2003) to power. Lasting only six months, it was dominated by members of the police and military and issued no public final report. The first effective commissions were established in South America in the 1980s, beginning with Argentina's National Commission on the Disappearance of Persons (1983–4), which investigated human rights violations committed by the military dictatorship that ruled the country from 1976 to 1983. Dozens of others in Latin America and Africa followed, the best known among them being the Commission of Truth and Reconciliation in South Africa (1995–2002), which was the only such commission to be empowered to grant amnesty to perpetrators of crimes who confessed openly. Truth commissions have not been limited to the global south. In 1980, the US Congress established the Commission on Wartime Relocation and Internment of Civilians to investigate the history of the incarceration of US citizens of Japanese descent in special camps during World War II. The post-unification German government created two truth commissions in the 1990s to investigate the East German communist dictatorship. The Truth and Reconciliation Commission of Canada (2008–15) documented the history and ongoing impact of the country's Indian residential school system, which attempted to force Indigenous children to assimilate into the dominant culture.

Though truth commissions are a relatively recent mechanism of transitional justice, scholars and activists have debated their effectiveness. Some have argued that given the tenuous political circumstances in which most commissions operate, simply completing the work and releasing a final report to the public (which occasionally does not happen) is a significant accomplishment. Others have taken the position that trials alone are punitive in nature and thus do not promote reconciliation. Moreover, they emphasize the individual perpetrator at the expense of exposing systems of injustice and criminality and, not least, giving a voice to victims. Supporters also insist that truth commissions, while not courts of law, nonetheless play an important role in supporting the rule of law, transparency, accountability, and respect for human rights. But even the most ardent champions cannot agree on what tangible contributions commissions have made to political and social reconciliation. Indeed, there is little evidence that recommendations made by commissions have been widely implemented. Some critics have warned that truth commissions undermine the potential of the ICC to investigate and prosecute crimes against humanity or have suggested that some governments may resort to commissions – which in nearly all cases have no enforcement mechanisms – to avoid legal prosecution. Finally, a few skeptics have asked whether truth commissions contribute to the perpetuation of grievances rather than to their amelioration, suggesting that a degree of forgetting can be an important component of reconciliation and the maintenance of peace (Brahm, 2007; Rieff, 2016).

A unique experiment that attempted to bridge the gap between courts of law and truth commissions has been the Gacaca courts in Rwanda (2001–12). Some of the highest-ranking individuals most responsible for organizing the genocide in 1994 were tried by the ICTR. That left the vast majority of perpetrators untouched and living openly in Rwanda or neighboring states. The established system of courts in Rwanda was simply unable to handle the huge number of cases, with only 1,292 suspects tried by 1998. The Gacaca initiative thus aimed at bringing as many foot soldiers of the genocide to justice as possible, albeit in a unique way. A total of around 12,000 local courts were created, each comprising a panel of judges – who were not required to be trained in the law – drawn from the local community. The courts ultimately presided over nearly two million cases, tried around one million people, and achieved a conviction range of 86 percent. The convicted were sentenced to prison terms or to terms of manual labor.

Defenders of the system argued that it administered justice to far more perpetrators than would otherwise have been possible while allowing many victims and their relatives to participate directly in the process of judicial reckoning. Moreover, the quantity and highly localized nature of the courts meant that a great deal was revealed about how the genocide took place. Anecdotal evidence suggests that a degree of reconciliation was achieved when victims were able to confront their tormentors, who in many cases admitted their guilt and asked for forgiveness. Yet since the system was shut down in 2012, many Rwandans, international scholars, and human rights activists have leveled a number of damning critiques at the entire endeavor, most notably regarding the absence of basic protections for the accused (who were not, for example, entitled to counsel) and the lack of legal qualifications for judges. Critics have also pointed out that the system evolved into a means of securing the Tutsi-controlled Rwandan Patriotic Front's (RPF's) control of the country. The RPF and its networks of patronage influenced the selection of judges, and in the end only members of the Hutu ethnic group were prosecuted, despite the fact that crimes against Hutus were also committed by Tutsi forces in the war that ended the genocide and overthrew the Hutu Power government (Chakravarty, 2015)

A second development has involved **restitution and reparations.** There is nothing new about former belligerents seeking compensation for material damages in wartime. What was new in the post-World War II context were two related forms of compensation provided to civilian victims of crimes against humanity and genocide. One has been referred to as *restitution*, defined as the return by states or private institutions (i.e., banks, museums) of something – usually property, assets of some kind, or artifacts of cultural significance – that had been taken by force or illegally from its rightful owner(s). *Reparation* entails attempting to restore or in some way repair what has been damaged. Reparation may also include forms of compensation for damages incurred by individuals or groups of people (and their descendants) victimized in wartime or various forms of non-war-related oppression (i.e., forced labor or hereditary chattel slavery). The postwar German states, which ultimately paid out billions of their respective currencies to victims of the Nazis, the state of Israel, and to the international Jewish Claims Conference, were pioneers in restitution and reparations and in some ways exemplary. Since then, the right to both forms of compensation has become widely accepted by various states and international bodies, namely, the UN, the ICC, and human rights NGOs, as important components of transitional justice. The ICC was the first international criminal body to authorize **reparations and restitution** to the victims of individual perpetrators of war crimes and crimes against humanity (Ferstman and Goetz, 2020; Neiman, 2019).

In practice, however, securing compensation for victims has proven difficult at best. Two court decisions in Chad in 2015 and Senegal in 2016, for instance, awarded around 250 million US dollars in compensation to thousands of victims of the former Chadian president Hissène Habré and members of his regime's security service. Yet only a small percentage of the total funds, which were supposed to be raised and held by an African Union trust fund, have been collected from the confiscation of Habré's assets and contributions and as of 2022, no payments have been made. The Chadian government, moreover, has not yet fulfilled an obligation – mandated by a Chadian court – to construct a monument and museum to honor the memory of the Habré regime's crimes. In addition, there remains the problem of defining the parameters of reparations. Should, for instance, nations and ethnic groups victimized by colonial rule be eligible for reparations paid by the former colonizers? In recent years, the United States has been the site of renewed calls for reparations for the descendants of enslaved peoples. Compensation in the form of property was promised to freed slaves in 1865 but neither states nor the federal government ever provided any kind of material compensation. Instead, political and economic inequality for Black Americans was institutionalized by laws, informal codes and customs, and extreme violence. It was only in 2021 that the US House of Representatives authorized the creation of a commission to do no more than study the effects of slavery and racial discrimination on Black Americans and recommend "appropriate remedies," including reparations.

In recent years, more attention has been paid to the return of cultural artifacts looted in the period of the new imperialism (the late 19th and early 20th centuries) and held in the collections of mainly British, European, and North American museums. The case of the Benin bronzes in the United Kingdom and Germany is of particular importance. In 1897, a British expeditionary force occupied and sacked the city of Benin (part of present-day Nigeria) and stole over 4,000 pieces of sculpture. The loot was dispersed to over 160 museum collections and private homes in Britain, Europe (notably Germany), the United States, Japan, Senegal, and the United Arab Emirates. British and German institutions with significant holdings of the stolen artifacts have until very recently steadfastly refused requests from colonial and post-colonial Nigeria for their return. But international pressure in the wake of Black Lives Matter protests and the broader movement to expose the ongoing legacies of colonialism and racism in cultural institutions has prompted multiple British, Scottish, and German museums and universities to return hundreds of stolen objects of cultural significance to Nigeria (Hicks, 2020).

## The "investigative turn"

Frustration over the relatively small number of investigations and prosecutions carried out to date by the ICC and national-level courts has prompted a growing number of groups and individuals – mainly journalists, human rights activists, and NGOs – to emphasize documenting war crimes and crimes against humanity with an eye to public attention and future prosecutions [*Doc. 12, p. 134*]. This impulse – which some observers have referred to as the "investigative turn" in international law and human rights advocacy – has also been inspired by the fact that ongoing wars, such as the

Syrian civil war and the war between the Russian Federation and Ukraine, make formal investigations and prosecutions by the ICC extremely difficult, if not impossible. Exemplary in this regard is the **Commission for International Justice and Accountability** (CIJA). Established after the outbreak of the Syrian civil war in 2011, CIJA was created to act as a "proto-Office of the Prosecutor" (a reference to the ICC's office of the same name) by collecting evidence of war crimes and crimes against humanity in that conflict. CIJA's founder has proposed that the organization's work should serve as model for other conflicts (Burgis-Kasthala, 2020).

Another important example of this kind of work is provided by **Bellingcat,** an independent collective of private citizens established in 2014. Bellingcat's researchers use open-source resources to investigate a range of international crimes, including drug trafficking, money laundering, the proliferation of weapons of mass destruction, war crimes, and crimes against humanity. Like other NGOs, Bellingcat has worked with the ICC and the UN, and the former has increasingly incorporated open-source evidence in recent cases. Its first major success was the discovery of crucial details about the downing in July 2014 of a Malaysian Airlines passenger jet over eastern Ukraine by a rocket fired from within Russia. In 2020, researchers substantiated reports by the implementing body of the 1997 Chemical Weapons Convention that the Syrian government was responsible for three chemical weapons attacks (two involving the use of sarin gas, the other involving chlorine) in the

*Figure 10.1* Officials in Bucha, Ukraine, collect the remains of civilians killed by Russian forces, April 2022.

northern Syrian town of Al-Lataminah in March 2017, including an attack on a hospital. In the spring of 2022, researchers analyzed official and unofficial video footage to call into question the veracity of Russian Federation claims that its forces had not been responsible for the massacre of civilians in the town of Bucha (Dubberley *et al.*, 2020; Higgins, 2021).

NGOs like CIJA and Bellingcat differ somewhat from long established organizations that seek to ameliorate suffering in conflict zones (like the ICRC) or those devoted primarily to monitoring human rights around the world and advocating for victims of abuses (**Amnesty International** or Human Rights Watch). Certainly, CIJA and Bellingcat engage in the latter to some extent, and like human rights NGOs, they collaborate with the ICC and UN. CIJA has also provided information it collected in Syria for lawsuits and trials in the United States, the Netherlands, and Germany related to the civil war. But they are primarily collectors of evidence, a task greatly facilitated by the Internet, social media, the ubiquity of smart phones capable of taking relatively high quality photos and video, new software and apps, and the relative ease (pre-COVID) of international travel. Above all, the work of these organizations has depended upon the willingness of Syrians and others to risk their lives to document the crimes committed around or against them. The long-term effectiveness of these groups' work remains to be seen. And even some broadly sympathetic to the objective of recording war-related atrocities have raised numerous questions about the reliability of the material being collected and, not least, its admissibility in future trials (McDermott *et al.*, 2021).

# Part III

# Documents

## Document 1

### *General orders, No. 100, instructions for the government of armies of the United States in the field [the "Lieber Code"], 1863*

*In the midst of the U.S. Civil War, the War Department approved the adoption of a code of conduct for the armies of the United States, which in practice meant the Union, or northern, armies. The code's principal author was Francis J. Lieber (1798/1800–1872), an immigrant from Prussia and a legal scholar who taught at Columbia College (now Columbia University). It was the first codification of the laws of war in modern history and exerted a powerful influence on the Hague Conventions and codes of conduct for other armed forces. Comprised of 157 sections, the code dealt with a wide range of legal issues related to the specific features of the Civil War but with clear implications for armed conflicts in general: notably military necessity, rules for occupying enemy territory, the treatment of prisoners of war, civilians, and property, enslaved people, partisans and rebels, and armistices.*

General Orders, No. 100
War Department, Adjutant General's Office
Washington, April 24, 1863

The following "Instructions for the Government of Armies of the United States in the Field," prepared by Francis Lieber, LL.D., and revised by a Board of Officers, of which Maj. Gen. E.A. Hitchcock is president, having been approved by the President of the United States, he commands that they be published for the information of all concerned.

By order of the Secretary of War: E.D. Townsend, Assistant Adjutant-General.

. . .

14. Military necessity, as understood by modern civilized nations, consists in the necessity of those measures which are indispensable for securing the ends of the war, and which are lawful according to the modern law and usages of war.
15. Military necessity admits of all direct destruction of life or limb of armed enemies, and of other persons whose destruction is incidentally unavoidable in the armed contests of the war; it allows of the capturing of every armed enemy, and every enemy of importance to the hostile government, or of peculiar danger to the captor; it allows of all destruction of property, and obstruction of the ways and channels of traffic, travel, or communication, and of all withholding of sustenance or means of life from the enemy; of the appropriation of whatever an enemy's country affords necessary for the subsistence and safety of the army, and of such deception as does not involve the breaking of good

faith either positively pledged, regarding agreements entered into during the war, or supposed by the modern law of war to exist. Men who take up arms against one another in public war do not cease on this account to be moral beings, responsible to one another, and to God.

16. Military necessity does not admit of cruelty, that is, the infliction of suffering for the sake of suffering or for revenge, nor of maiming or wounding except in fight, nor of torture to extort confessions. It does not admit of the use of poison in any way, nor of the wanton devastation of a district. It admits of deception, but disclaims acts of perfidy; and, in general, military necessity does not include any act of hostility which makes the return to peace unnecessarily difficult.
17. War is not carried on by arms alone. It is lawful to starve the hostile belligerent, armed or unarmed, so that it leads to the speedier subjection of the enemy

. . .

42. Slavery, complicating and confounding the ideas of property, (that is of a thing,) and of personality, (that is of humanity,) exists according to municipal law or local law only. The law of nature and nations has never acknowledged it. The digest of the Roman law enacts the early dictum of the pagan jurist, that "so far as the law of nature is concerned, all men are equal." Fugitives escaping from a country in which they were slaves, villains, or serfs, into another country, have, for centuries past, been held free and acknowledged free by judicial decisions of European countries, even though the municipal law of the country in which the slave had taken refuge acknowledged slavery within its own dominions.
43. Therefore, in a war between the United States and a belligerent which admits of slavery, if a person held in bondage by that belligerent be captured by or come as a fugitive under the protection of the military forces of the United States, such person is immediately entitled to the rights and privileges of a freeman. To return such person into slavery would amount to enslaving a free person, and neither the United States nor any officer under their authority can enslave any human being. Moreover, a person so made free by the law of war is under the shield of the law of nations, and the former owner or State can have, by the law of postliminy, no belligerent lien or claim of service.
44. All wanton violence committed against persons in the invaded country, all destruction of property not commanded by the authorized officer, all robbery, all pillage or sacking, even after taking a place by main force, all rape, wounding, maiming, or killing of such inhabitants, are prohibited under the penalty of death, or such other severe punishment as may seem adequate for the gravity of the offense. A soldier, officer or private, in the act of committing such violence, and disobeying a

superior ordering him to abstain from it, may be lawfully killed on the spot by such superior.

. . .

49. A prisoner of war is a public enemy armed or attached to the hostile army for active aid, who has fallen into the hands of the captor, either fighting or wounded, on the field or in the hospital, by individual surrender or by capitulation. All soldiers, of whatever species of arms; all men who belong to the rising en masse of the hostile country; all those who are attached to the army for its efficiency and promote directly the object of the war, except such as are hereinafter provided for; all disabled men or officers on the field or elsewhere, if captured; all enemies who have thrown away their arms and ask for quarter, are prisoners of war, and as such exposed to the inconveniences as well as entitled to the privileges of a prisoner of war.

. . .

67. The law of nations allows every sovereign government to make war upon another sovereign state, and, therefore, admits of no rules or laws different from those of regular warfare, regarding the treatment of prisoners of war, although they may belong to the army of a government which the captor may consider as a wanton and unjust assailant.
68. Modern wars are not internecine wars, in which the killing of the enemy is the object. The destruction of the enemy in modern war and, indeed, modern war itself, are means to obtain that object of the belligerent which lies beyond the war. Unnecessary or revengeful destruction of life is not lawful.

. . .

81. Partisans are soldiers armed and wearing the uniform of their army, but belonging to a corps which acts detached from the main body for the purpose of making inroads into the territory occupied by the enemy. If captured, they are entitled to all the privileges of the prisoner of war.
82. Men, or squads of men, who commit hostilities, whether by fighting, or inroads for destruction or plunder, or by raids of any kind, without commission, without being part and portion of the organized hostile army, and without sharing continuously in the war, but who do so with intermitting returns to their homes and avocations, or with the occasional assumption of the semblance of peaceful pursuits, divesting themselves of the character or appearance of soldiers – such men, or squads of men, are not public enemies, and therefore, if captured, are not entitled to the privileges of prisoners of war, but shall be treated summarily as highway robbers or pirates.

Source: U.S. Library of Congress, https://tile.loc.gov/storage-services/service/ll/llmlp/Instructions-gov-armies/Instructions-gov-armies.pdf

## Document 2

### *The Hague Conventions (1899 and 1907)*

*The First Hague Peace Conference was convened in 1899 to revise the unratified declaration issued by the Conference of Brussels in 1874. Adopted and ratified by 50 state parties, the Convention with Respect to the Laws and Customs of War on Land was the first international agreement aimed at regulating the conduct of warfare. It was revised, albeit in only very minor ways, at the Second International Peace Conference (also held in The Hague) in 1907. Both conventions dealt mainly with the treatment of prisoners of war, armistices, and military occupations.*

Convention (II) with Respect to the Laws and Customs of War on Land and its annex: Regulations concerning the Laws and Customs of War on Land. The Hague, 29 July 1899

Preamble

Considering that, while seeking means to preserve peace and prevent armed conflicts among nations, it is likewise necessary to have regard to cases where an appeal to arms may be caused by events which their solicitude could not avert;

Animated by the desire to serve, even in this extreme hypothesis, the interests of humanity and the ever increasing requirements of civilization;

Thinking it important, with this object, to revise the laws and general customs of war, either with the view of defining them more precisely or of laying down certain limits for the purpose of modifying their severity as far as possible;

Inspired by these views which are enjoined at the present day, as they were twenty-five years ago at the time of the Brussels Conference in 1874, by a wise and generous foresight;

Have, in this spirit, adopted a great number of provisions, the object of which is to define and govern the usages of war on land.

In view of the High Contracting Parties, these provisions, the wording of which has been inspired by the desire to diminish the evils of war so far as military necessities permit, are destined to serve as general rules of conduct for belligerents in their relations with each other and with populations.

. . .

Until a more complete code of the laws of war is issued, the High Contracting Parties think it right to declare that in cases not included in the Regulations adopted by them, populations and belligerents remain under the protection and empire of the principles of international law, as they result from the usages established between civilized nations, from the laws of humanity, and the requirements of the public conscience;

. . .

Art. 4. Prisoners of war are in the power of the hostile Government, but not in that of the individuals or corps who captured them. They must be humanely treated. All their personal belongings, except arms, horses, and military papers remain their property.

. . .

Art. 23. Besides the prohibitions provided by special Conventions, it is especially prohibited

(a) To employ poison or poisoned arms;
(b) To kill or wound treacherously individuals belonging to the hostile nation or army;
(c) To kill or wound an enemy who, having laid down arms, or having no longer means of defence, has surrendered at discretion;
(d) To declare that no quarter will be given;
(e) To employ arms, projectiles, or material of a nature to cause superfluous injury;
(f) To make improper use of a flag of truce, the national flag or military ensigns and uniform of the enemy, as well as the distinctive badges of the Geneva Convention;
(g) To destroy or seize the enemy's property, unless such destruction or seizure be imperatively demanded by the necessities of war.

*(to the above 7 prohibited actions, the 1907 convention added the following: "To declare abolished, suspended, or inadmissible in a court of law the rights and actions of the nationals of the hostile party. A belligerent is likewise forbidden to compel the nationals of the hostile party to take part in the operations of war directed against their own country, even if they were in the belligerent's service before the commencement of the war.")*

. . .

Art. 27. In sieges and bombardments all necessary steps should be taken to spare as far as possible edifices devoted to religion, art, science, and charity, hospitals, and places where the sick and wounded are collected, provided they are not used at the same time for military purposes. The besieged should indicate these buildings or places by some particular and visible signs, which should previously be notified to the assailants.

. . .

Art. 46. Family honours and rights, individual lives and private property, as well as religious convictions and liberty, must be respected. Private property cannot be confiscated.

. . .

Convention (IV) respecting the Laws and Customs of War on Land and its annex: Regulations concerning the Laws and Customs of War on Land. The Hague, 18 October 1907

. . .

Article 1. The laws, rights, and duties of war apply not only to armies but also to militia and volunteer corps fulfilling the following conditions:

1. To be commanded by a person responsible for his subordinates;
2. To have a fixed distinctive emblem recognizable at a distance;
3. To carry arms openly; and
4. To conduct their operations in accordance with the laws and customs of war.

In countries where militia or volunteer corps constitute the army, or form part of it, they are included under the denomination "army."

. . .

Art. 54. Submarine cables connecting an occupied territory with a neutral territory shall not be seized or destroyed except in the case of absolute necessity. They must likewise be restored and compensation fixed when peace is made.

Source: https://ihl-databases.icrc.org/applic/ihl/ihl-search.nsf/content.xsp

## Document 3

### *Fighting colonial wars*

*In an influential 1896 book* Small Wars, *the British officer Charles Callwell offered a handbook for states waging colonial wars. Callwell was a veteran of British wars in Afghanistan and South Africa. He intended his book to serve as a guide for what he called disciplined soldiers facing – in his words – "savages and semi-civilized races" who refused to engage with regular armed forces on the open field. For Callwell, small wars were fought for three reasons: to conquer territory, to put down rebellions, or to retaliate for atrocities committed against imperial forces or settlers. He knew that they would often be long wars and that clear-cut victories would be elusive. He also understood that the rules of war that applied in so-called regular wars between civilized states did not apply in small wars.*

Guerilla warfare is what the regular armies always have to dread, and when this is directed by a leader with a genius for war, an effective campaign becomes well-nigh impossible. The guerilla has ever been a thorn in the side of the organized force. It was so in the Peninsular war, where the Spanish partisans proved a formidable foe to the French invaders. Fra Diavolo and his brigand bands were almost a match for the veterans of Massena in Calabria. The Cossacks, masters of this method of conducting operations, contributed almost more towards bringing about the terrible disasters which befell the Grand Army on its retreat from Moscow than the rigours of a Russian winter, or the combinations of the able commanders of the pursuing armies. The Turks, before the last Russian intervention in the Balkans, found the Montenegrins far more difficult to subdue than the organized

Servian armies. Therefore it is that the art of combating this method of conducting operations deserves especial attention when small wars are in question; and experience, moreover, proves that even when there have been at the outset armies in the field to beat, the campaign often drifts on in desultory fashion long after these have been overthrown.

. . .

The guerilla mode of war must in fact be met by an abnormal system of strategy and tactics. The great principle which forms the basis of the art of war remains – the combination of initiative with energy; but this is applied in a special form. The utmost vigour and decision must be displayed in harassing the enemy and in giving him no rest; the hostile bands may elude the regular detachments, but their villages and flocks remain. The theatre of war must be sub-divided into sections, each to be dealt with by a given force or by a given aggregate of separate detachments. Defensive posts must be established where supplies can be collected, whither raided cattle can be brought, and which form independent bases. To each such base must be attached one or more mobile, self-contained columns, organized to be ready to move out at a moment's notice, and equipped so as to penetrate to any part of the district told off to it and to return, certain of supplies for the task.

. . .

When operations are being carried out against guerillas scattered over great tracts of country, it has sometimes been found very useful to send out raiding parties, consisting generally of mounted men, to carry off the enemy's flocks and herds or to destroy encampments and villages. As already mentioned, the Russians have put this method of warfare in force in Central Asia, and the French made large use of it in some of their Algerian campaigns.

. . .

In the **Indian Mutiny** [1857], a campaign for the suppression of a rebellion when the most drastic measures were justified by the events at its outset, guerilla warfare was not a feature, except in the Central Provinces and in some few localities after the rebel armies had been overthrown. The nature of the campaign was such that the insurgents were so roughly handled in the field that the country was practically pacified on the battlefield.

But in South Africa in 1851–52, in 1877, and again in 1896, rigorous treatment was meted out to the enemy in crushing out disaffection, and with good results; the Kaffir villages and Matabili kraals were burnt, their crops destroyed, their cattle carried off. The French in Algeria, regardless of the maxim, "Les reprêsailles sont toujours inutiles" [retaliation is always unnecessary] dealt very severely with the smouldering disaffection of the conquered territory for years after Abd el Kader's power was gone, and their procedure succeeded. Uncivilized races attribute leniency to timidity. A system adapted to La Vendée is out of place among fanatics and savages, who must be thoroughly brought to book and cowed or they will rise again.

Source: Charles Caldwell, *Small Wars: Their Principles and Practice*, Lincoln, NE: University of Nebraska Press, 1996.

## Document 4

### *An American architect of the International Military Tribunal (IMT) defends the Nuremberg trials, 1947*

*While the IMT represented a landmark in international law and would influence the creation of future tribunals, notably those for the former Yugoslavia and Rwanda and then the International Criminal Court, the tribunal had many critics in and outside Germany. Former US Secretary of War Henry L. Stimson, a principal architect of the IMT, defended the court in an article published in the influential American journal* Foreign Affairs *in January 1947. In the segment below, Stimson focuses on the accusations that the entire enterprise was illegitimate because it represented the imposition of* "ex post facto" *law and that the defendants were not given a fair trial.*

Able lawyers and honest men have cried out that this aggressive war was not a crime. They have argued that the Nuremberg defendants were not properly forewarned when they made war that what they did was criminal.

Now in one sense the concept of *ex post facto* law is a strange one to apply here, because this concept relates to a state of mind on the part of the defendants that in this case was wholly absent. That concept is based on the assumption that if the defendant had known that the proposed act was criminal he would have refrained from committing it. Nothing in the attitude of the Nazi leaders corresponds to this assumption; their minds were wholly untroubled by the questions of guilt or innocence. Not in their aggression only but in their whole philosophy, they excluded the very concept of law. They deliberately put themselves below such a concept. To international law – as to the law of Germany – they paid only such respect as they found politic, and in the end they had smashed its every rule. Their attitude toward aggressive war was exactly like their attitude toward murder – both were useful instruments in a great design. It is therefore impossible to get any light on the validity of this charge of aggressive war by inspecting the Nazi mind. We must study rather the minds of the rest of the world[.]

. . .

[T]he Second World War brought it home to us that our repugnance to aggressive war was incomplete without a judgment of its leaders. What we had called a crime demanded punishment; we must bring our law in balance with the universal moral judgment of mankind. The wickedness of aggression must be punished by a trial and judgment. This is what has been done at Nuremberg.

Now this is a new judicial process, but it is not *ex post facto* law. It is the enforcement of a moral judgment which dates back a generation. It is a growth in the application of law that any student of our common law should recognize as natural and proper, for it is in just this manner that the common law grew up.

. . .

With the judgment of Nuremberg we at last reach to the very core of international strife, and we set a penalty not merely for war crimes, but for the very act of war itself, except in self-defense. If a man will argue that this is bad law, untrue to our ideals, I will listen. But I feel only pity for the casuist who would dismiss the Nazi leaders because 'they were not warned it was a crime.' They were warned, and they sneered contempt. Our shame is that their contempt was so nearly justified, not that we have in the end made good our warning.

. . .

Next after its assertion of the criminality of aggressive war, the triumph of Nuremberg rests in the manner and degree to which it has discharged with honor the true functions of a legal instrument. The crimes charged were punishable as we have seen – so clearly punishable that the only important suggested alternative to a trial was summary execution of the accused. It is in its pursuit of a different course that the Nuremberg Tribunal has demonstrated at once the dignity and value of the law, and students of law everywhere will find inspiration and enlightenment in close study of its work. In its skillful development of a procedure satisfying every traditional and material safeguard of the varying legal forms of the prosecuting nations, it represents a signal success in the field of international negotiation, and in its rigid fidelity to the fundamental principles of fair play it has insured the lasting value of it work.

In their insistence on fairness to the defendants, the Charter and the Tribunal leaned over backwards. Each defendant was allowed to testify for himself, a right denied by Continental law. At the conclusion of the trial, each defendant was allowed to address the Tribunal, at great length, a right denied by Anglo-American law. The difference between Continental and Anglo-American law was thus adjusted by allowing to the defendant his rights under both. Counsel for the defendants were leading German lawyers and professors from the German universities, some of them ardent and unrepentant Nazis. Counsel were paid, fed, sheltered, and transported at the expense of the Allies, and were furnished offices and secretarial help. The defense had full access to all documents. Every attempt was made to produce desired witnesses when the Tribunal believed they had any relevant evidence to offer. In the summation of the trial the defense had 20 days and the prosecution three, and the defense case as a whole occupied considerably more time than the prosecution.

Source: Henry L. Stimson, "The Nuremberg Trial: Landmark in Law," *Foreign Affairs*, January 1947, 179–189.

## Document 5

### *An American diplomat denounces war crimes trials in occupied Japan, 1948*

*In March 1948, the American diplomat George F. Kennan visited occupied Japan and prepared a long report for the US State Department's Policy Planning Staff (which he then directed). Kennan's sharp criticisms of the war crimes trial program reflected the views of numerous military and civilian officials at a time when the Cold War was compelling them to focus on creating a new architecture of global security arrangements, an orientation that required focusing on the future rather than the past.*

In accordance with the Potsdam Declaration, an FEC [Far Eastern Commission] policy decision was reached in April 1946, empowering SCAP [Supreme Command for the Allied Powers] to appoint special international military courts representative of any two or more of the FEC member countries to try: those who planned and waged a war of aggression or a war in violation of international treaties, etc. (Category "A"); those who violated the laws and customs of war (Category "B"); those responsible for inhumane acts against civilian population (Category "C").

The only indictment so far made of Category "A" war criminals was filed with the International Military Tribunal for the Far East on April29, 1946 against 28 persons. The International Prosecution Section of SCAP finished the presentation of evidence on January 24, 1947 and the defense began its presentation of evidence on February 24, 1947, expecting to rest its case in May, 1948. The trial will then have been in process more than two years. Of the 28 persons brought to trial, two have died natural deaths and one has been declared insane.

Although the aforementioned FEC policy decision implies otherwise, Category "B" and "C" criminals found in Japan are being prosecuted by the Legal Section of SCAP Headquarters before Eighth Army Military Commissions in Yokohama. As of March 18 1948, 237 cases involving 583 persons were completed. Remaining on trial were ten cases involving 80 persons. The number of cases awaiting trial, in which charges and specifications have already been filed, was 54 involving 165 persons.

Countenancing as they have the parade of thousands of witnesses, the examination of hundreds of thousands of documents, the exhaustive hearing of all evidence and counter-evidence by both the prosecution and the defense, the War Crimes Trials have been hailed as the ultimate in international justice. There is no gainsaying the fact that the trials have been *procedurally* thoroughly correct, according to our concepts of justice, and that at no time in history have conquerors conferred upon the vanquished such elaborate opportunities for the public defense and for vindication of their military acts.

Nevertheless, there is no question in my mind but what these trials were profoundly misconceived from the start and are working increasing injury to the Allied cause in Japan. The reasons are several.

1. There is really no law on which such judicial procedure can be founded. There is a law of common humanity which proscribes acts of inhumanity against captives or other helpless persons in wartime. The Class "B" trials rest on that law. But there is no crime of an international nature involved in the services which an individual renders to his own state as a public servant. The state, as such, stands responsible for its own policies; the vicissitudes of peace or war are its trial. And in the case of Japan, the judgment is now being enacted through the disaster which has befallen the entire country in consequence of the loss of the war. This is not to say that the victor does not have the right to punish individual leaders of the defeated nation. But the punishment should take place as an act of war, not of justice; and it should not be surrounded with the hocus-pocus of a judicial procedure which belies its real nature.
2. It is a rule with peoples, as with individuals, that punishment, if it is to have any exemplary effect, must be swift and incisive and must follow immediately on the heels of the offense. A delayed and long-protracted punishment (and what else are these interminable trials?) loses its effect on both the victim and the public. The Japanese public has long since ceased to feel any reactions toward the trials other than one of sympathy for these fellow Japanese who are forced to sit through these endless and humiliating ordeals which have so little to do with anything that anyone in Japan can understand. It would have been much better received and understood if we had shot these people out of hand at the time of the surrender.

    The persons conducting the prosecution and defense are, for the most part, not fitted for this task. These are political trials. The medium in which these people are working is politics, and international politics at that – not law. Only persons deeply versed in the history and practice of international relations could be at home in this medium. Legal experience at home is of itself no qualification whatsoever for this work. Yet that appears to have been the only criterion by which these people were chosen.

4. The spectacle of American lawyers defending the policies of past Japanese Governments, in order to improve the defense of their clients, is absolutely preposterous in its impact on the Japanese. It undermines the whole effect of the trials. It carries the clear implication that Americans themselves are insincere in their feelings about the origin of the war, that those feelings arise from professional, or other ulterior motives, and not from inner conviction. What other impression can the Japanese obtain? And if he is finally forced to the conclusion that the rightness or

wrongness of Japan's policies prior to the war was not a matter of conviction among the Americans but a moot legal point, on which Americans themselves are divided and which could be settled only by two years of abstruse judicial procedure, then he can only ask himself the question: where was the two-year judicial procedure by which it was decided that US statesmen were right *before* they undertook to oppose Japanese policies in east Asia during the nineteen-thirties?

Source: Conversation between General of the Army MacArthur and Mr. George F. Kennan, March 5, 1948, *Foreign Relations of the United States, 1948, The Far East and Australasia*, vol. 6, 717–19.

## Document 6

### *Defining "genocide"*

*Raphael Lemkin defines "genocide" (1944 and 1946)*

"Generally speaking, genocide does not necessarily mean the immediate destruction of a nation, except when accomplished by mass killings of all members of a nation. It is intended rather to signify a coordinated plan of different actions aiming at the destruction of essential foundations of the life of national groups, with the aim of annihilating the groups themselves. The objectives of such a plan would be the disintegration of the political and social institutions, of culture, language, national feelings, religion, and the economic existence of national groups, and the destruction of the personal security, liberty, health, dignity, and even the lives of the individuals belonging to such groups."

When Lemkin proposed a treaty against genocide to the United Nations in 1945, he defined it as follows:

"The crime of genocide should be recognized therein as a conspiracy to exterminate national, religious or racial groups. The overt acts of such a conspiracy may consist of attacks against life, liberty or property of members of such groups merely because of their affiliation with such groups. The formulation of the crime may be as follows: Whoever, while participating in a conspiracy to destroy a national, racial or religious group, undertakes an attack against life, liberty or property of members of such groups is guilty of the crime of genocide."

Source: Raphael Lemkin, "Genocide," *The American Scholar*, vol. 15, no. 2, spring 1946: 227–230.

The definition of "genocide" in the Genocide Convention (9 December 1948)

**Convention on the Prevention and Punishment of the Crime of Genocide**

Article I

The Contracting Parties confirm that genocide, whether committed in time of peace or in time of war, is a crime under international law which they undertake to prevent and to punish.

Article II

In the present Convention, Genocide means any of the following acts committed with intent to destroy, in whole or in part, a national, ethnical, racial or religious group, as such:

(a) Killing members of the group;
(b) Causing serious bodily or mental harm to members of the group;
(c) Deliberately inflicting on the group conditions of life calculated to bring about its physical destruction in whole or in part;
(d) Imposing measures intended to prevent births within a group;
(e) Forcibly transferring children of the group to another group.

Article III

The following acts shall be punishable:

1. (a) Genocide;
2. (b) Conspiracy to commit genocide;
3. (c) Direct and public incitement to commit genocide;
4. (d) Attempt to commit genocide;
5. (e) Complicity in genocide.

Article IV

Persons committing genocide or any of the other acts enumerated in article III shall be punished, whether they are constitutionally responsible rulers, public officials or private individuals.

Source: www.un.org

## Document 7

### *The International Criminal Tribunal for the Former Yugoslavia (ICTY) indicts Radovan Karadzic and Ratko Mladic, 1995*

*In November 1995, the ICTY charged Radovan Karadzic (b. 1945) and Ratko Mladic (b. 1943) with genocide, crimes against humanity, and violations of the laws or customs of war in connection with the massacre of Bosnian Muslims in and around Srebrenica in Bosnia Herzegovina the previous July. Karadzic was at that time President of Republika Srpska and Supreme Commander of its armed forces. He went into hiding in 1997 and was arrested near Belgrade by Serb authorities in July 2008. In 2016 the ICTY found him guilty of 10 of 11 charges (genocide, crimes against humanity, and violations of the laws or customs of war), including genocide against the residents of Srebrenica and sentenced him to 40 years in prison. Two years later a UN tribunal increased the sentence to life. Mladic was Commander of the Main Staff of the Army of Republika Srpska, Bosnia and Herzegovina. He evaded capture until May 2011, when he was arrested by Serb authorities in a small town north of Belgrade. Like Karadic, he was extradited to The Hague and charged by the ICTY of genocide, crimes against humanity, and violations of the laws or customs of war. The tribunal found him guilty of the 10 of the 11 charges against him and sentenced him to life in prison. The following document is a portion of the ICTY's July 1995 indictment against both men and highlights the charges related to the Srebrenica massacres.*

THE PROSECUTOR OF THE TRIBUNAL AGAINST RADOVAN KARADZIC, RATKO MLADIC
INDICTMENT

Richard J. Goldstone, Prosecutor of the International Criminal Tribunal for the former Yugoslavia, pursuant to his authority under Article 18 of the Statute of the International Criminal Tribunal for the former Yugoslavia ("The Statute of the Tribunal"), charges RATKO MLADIC and RADOVAN KARADZIC with GENOCIDE, CRIMES AGAINST HUMANITY and VIOLATIONS OF THE LAWS OR CUSTOMS OF WAR, as set forth below:

"SAFE AREA" OF SREBRENICA

1. After war erupted in the Republic of Bosnia and Herzegovina, Bosnian Serb military forces occupied Bosnian Muslim villages in the eastern part of the country, resulting in an exodus of Bosnian Muslims to enclaves in Gorazde, Zepa, Tuzla, and Srebrenica. All of the events referred to in this indictment took place in the Republic of Bosnia and Herzegovina.
2. On 16 April 1993, the Security Council of the United Nations, acting pursuant to Chapter VII of its Charter, adopted resolution 819, in which it demanded that all parties to the conflict in the Republic of Bosnia and Herzegovina treat Srebrenica and its surroundings as a safe area which should be free from any armed attack or any other hostile act. Resolution 819 was reaffirmed by Resolution 824 on 6 May 1993 and by Resolution 836 on 4 June 1993.
3. Before the attack by Bosnian Serb forces, as described in this indictment, the estimated Bosnian Muslim population in the safe area of Srebrenica, was approximately 60,000. ATTACK ON THE SAFE AREA OF SREBRENICA
4. On or about 6 July 1995, the Bosnian Serb army shelled Srebrenica and attacked United Nations observation posts that were manned by Dutch soldiers and located in the safe area. The attack on the Srebrenica safe area by the Bosnian Serb army continued through 11 July 1995, when the first units of the attacking Bosnian Serb forces entered Srebrenica.

5. The Bosnian Muslim men, women and children who remained in Srebrenica after the beginning of the Bosnian Serb attack took two courses of action. Several thousand women, children and some mostly elderly men fled to the UN compound in Potocari, located within the safe area of Srebrenica, where they sought the protection of the Dutch battalion responsible for the compound. They remained at the compound from 11 July 1995 until 13 July 1995, when they were all evacuated by buses and trucks under the control of and operated by Bosnian Serb military personnel.
6. A second group of approximately 15,000 Bosnian Muslim men, with some women and children, gathered at Susnjari during the evening hours of 11 July 1995 and fled, in a huge column, through the woods towards Tuzla. Approximately one-third of this group consisted of armed Bosnian military personnel and armed civilians. The rest were unarmed civilians.

. . .

GENERAL ALLEGATIONS

41. At all times relevant to this indictment, a state of armed conflict and partial occupation existed in the Republic of Bosnia and Herzegovina in the territory of the former Yugoslavia.
42. In each paragraph charging genocide, a crime recognised by Article 4 of the Statute of the Tribunal, the alleged acts or omissions were committed with the intent to destroy, in whole or in part, a national, ethnical, or religious group, as such.
43. In each paragraph charging crimes against humanity, crimes recognised by Article 5 of the Statute of the Tribunal, the alleged acts or omissions were part of a widespread or systematic or large-scale attack directed against a civilian population.
44. RATKO MLADIC and RADOVAN KARADZIC are individually responsible for the crimes alleged against them in this indictment pursuant to Article 7(1) of the Tribunal Statute. Individual criminal responsibility includes committing, planning, instigating, ordering or otherwise aiding and abetting in the planning, preparation or execution of any crimes referred to in Articles 2 to 5 of the Tribunal Statute.
45. RATKO MLADIC and RADOVAN KARADZIC are also, or alternatively, criminally responsible as commanders for the acts of their subordinates pursuant to Article 7(3) of the Tribunal Statute. Command criminal responsibility is the responsibility of a superior officer for the acts of his subordinate if he knew or had reason to know that his subordinate was about to commit such acts or had done so and the superior failed to take the necessary and reasonable measures to prevent such acts or to punish the perpetrators thereof.

46. The general allegations contained in paragraphs 41 through 45 are realleged and incorporated into each of the charges set forth below.

CHARGES COUNTS 1–2 (GENOCIDE) (CRIME AGAINST HUMANITY)

47. Between about 12 July 1995 and 13 July 1995, Bosnian Serb military personnel, under the command and control of RATKO MLADIC and RADOVAN KARADZIC, arrived in Potocari where thousands of Muslim men, women and children had sought refuge in and around the UN military compound. Bosnian Serb military personnel, under the command and control of RATKO MLADIC and RADOVAN KARADZIC, summarily executed many Bosnian Muslim refugees who remained in Potocari.
48. Between about 13 July 1995 and 22 July 1995, Bosnian Serb military personnel, under the command and control of RATKO MLADIC and RADOVAN KARADZIC, summarily executed many Bosnian Muslim men who fled to the woods and were later captured or surrendered.
49. Thousands of Bosnian Muslim men, who fled Srebrenica and who surrendered or had been captured, were transported from various assembly locations in and around Srebrenica to a main assembly point at a school complex near Karakaj.
50. On or about 14 July 1995, Bosnian Serb military personnel, under the command and control of RATKO MLADIC and RADOVAN KARADZIC, transported thousands of Muslim men from this school complex to two locations a short distance away. At these locations, Bosnian Serb soldiers, with the knowledge of RATKO MLADIC, summarily executed these Bosnian Muslim detainees and buried them in mass graves.
51. RATKO MLADIC and RADOVAN KARADZIC, between about 6 July 1995 and 22 July 1995, individually and in concert with others, planned, instigated, ordered or otherwise aided and abetted in the planning, preparation or execution of the following crimes:

    a) summary executions of Bosnian Muslim men and women in and around Potocari on 12 July 1995 and 13 July 1995,
    b) summary executions, which occurred between 13 July 1995 and 22 July 1995, of Bosnian Muslims who were hors de combat because of injury, surrender or capture after fleeing into the woods towards Tuzla,
    c) summary executions of Bosnian Muslim men, which occurred on or about 14 July 1995 at mass execution sites in and around Karakaj.

By their acts and omissions in relation to the events described in paragraphs 13, 14, 20.1–20.7, 23, 26 and 28, RATKO MLADIC and RADOVAN KARADZIC committed: Count 1: GENOCIDE as recognised by Article 4(2)(a) (killing members of the group) of the Statute of the Tribunal. Count 2: A CRIME AGAINST HUMANITY as recognised by Article 5(b) (extermination) of the Statute of the Tribunal.

Source: www.icty.org/en/case/karadzic/#ind

## Document 8

### *African and international NGOs urge African states parties to the International Criminal Court to continue supporting the court, 2017*

Foreign Ministers, African States Parties to the International Criminal Court (ICC), November 20, 2017

Dear Minister:

We, the undersigned African and international non-governmental organizations, write to express our appreciation to African ICC states parties, many of which strongly affirmed support to the International Criminal Court during a challenging period over the past year.

. . .

The creation of the ICC in 1998 represented a profound, unprecedented shift in the fight against impunity, the securing of which African states played a crucial role. . .. The African Union in 2014 expanded the authority of the African Court of Justice and Human Rights to include serious crimes under international law, but it is a long way off from making it operational. In addition, immunity for sitting heads of state or government and other senior state officials under the African Court's new authority runs counter to at least two core principles of international law recognized in the Rome Statute: the irrelevance of official capacity before the court and the principle of equality of all before the law. We believe the most effective route to enhance the ICC's reach and practice is through strong support and meaningful engagement. Seeking universal ratification of the Rome Statute, and its incorporation into domestic legal systems, will foster the delivery of justice for serious crimes under international law at the national level, with the ICC as the essential backstop to guard against impunity.

When Burundi, Gambia, and South Africa announced their intentions to become the first states to withdraw from the court in October and November 2016, 16 African governments spoke out from their capitals, as well as in New York, Addis Ababa, and The Hague against withdrawals from the Rome Statute of the ICC and to reaffirm their support for the court. . . . In February, the new Gambian government decided to reverse plans for ICC withdrawal, and in March, South Africa abandoned domestic legislation to leave the ICC.

Only Burundi has moved forward on withdrawal, which went into effect October 27 . . ..

Going forward, robust support from African and other ICC states parties may be more important than ever. On October 26, ICC Prosecutor Fatou Bensouda announced that her office was seeking authorization from the judges to open an investigation into alleged crimes committed in Afghanistan since 2003. If authorized, the investigation could provide a long overdue path to justice, but may also potentially lead to new backlash against the ICC. Accordingly, during the December 4 to 14 Assembly of States Parties session, we respectfully request your government to:

Send high-level representatives to participate in the session's general debate to signal your government's continued backing for the ICC as the crucial court of last resort.

Highlight in interventions throughout the session how your government cooperates with the ICC, including by adopting domestic implementing legislation for the Rome Statute; the need for the court to take additional steps to have impact with the communities most affected by the crimes; and the importance of the court having sufficient resources to implement its mandate.

Raise areas where improvements are needed to support the effective exercise of the ICC's mandate, while also expressing full support for the ICC's judicial and prosecutorial independence.

Support the ICC having adequate resources to fulfill its mandate . . .

Support the election of the most highly qualified candidates to fill the six judicial vacancies.

Use the plenary session on the twentieth anniversary of the Rome Statute to identify steps your government will take to demonstrate its support for the court around the anniversary.

. . .

Continue to expressly support the work and mandate of the ICC in high-level bilateral and multilateral meetings.

Convene ministerial conferences on the Rome Statute and the ICC nationally and subregionally.

Implement the Rome Statute domestically, if not yet done, and promote greater cooperation with the court by concluding cooperation agreements.

. . .

Revisit the request for the ICC to establish a Liaison Office at the headquarters of the African Union in Addis Ababa, which would help improve communication and understanding between the ICC and the AU.

Propose that the AU drop its call for the Rome Statute to be amended to include immunity for sitting leaders. Such immunity should also be removed from the proposed expansion of the African Court of Justice and Human Rights.

Request that the ICC withdrawal strategy, adopted with reservations by African ICC states parties in January 2017, be suspended. African ICC states parties played an important role in supporting justice for victims over the past year.

We stand ready to support your government in further advancing the cause of justice for serious crimes under international law and appreciate your consideration of this letter.

Source: www.hrw.org/news/2017/11/20/letter-foreign-ministers-african-states-parties-international-criminal-court

## Document 9

### *An African NGO reports on female perpetrators of genocide in Rwanda, 1995*

*In 1995 the NGO African Rights published a detailed account of the many ways in which Hutu girls and women participated in the genocide of Tutsis and moderate Hutus. Based on hundreds of interviews, the report revealed that Hutu women were involved at every level of the genocide: high-level officials in the Hutu Power government, local administrators, homemakers, nuns, nurses, journalists, and teachers and elementary school pupils. The passages below report the experiences of a woman who encouraged men to kill by singing with other women and of a local administrator.*

Very often, groups of women ululated their men into the "action" that would result in the death of thousands of innocent men, women and children, many of them their own neighbors.

Zakia Uwamugira, forty-two, comes from the cellule of Gisenyi, commune Rubavu in the region of Gisenyi. She fled with her husband and six children to Goma in early July 1994. Her husband died of cholera in Goma. She returned to Rwanda on 28 July with her children. She said that her own mother was Tutsi and that she had not been able to save her. At the time of the interview in late January, she was imprisoned in Gisenyi. She had been arrested in September, accused of killing a man and a woman who were her neighbors, encouraging the interahamwe to kill and for some activities she undertook while in the refugee camp to Muyange. She denies the charges of murder and having been involved in political activities in Zaire. But she readily admits encouraging the interahamwe through songs.

'I am accused of being there when people were killed and singing. I admit I did this. I was there when people were being killed. Many people. I joined the *animation* just as I would join any other choir. I did not have any idea that such encouragement would result in a genocide. But I came back from Goma because I did not think I had done anything wrong. I went to Goma because I thought maybe people would think I was an accomplice of the former regime. But then I decided to come back because I realized I had not done anything that was wrong.'

Asked how she could regard singing alongside armed people on their way to mass murder as 'joining a choir,' she kept insisting that 'she had not done anything wrong.' Asked if she stopped participating once she understood that this was a killing machine and not a choir, Zakia was unable to give a clear response.

. . .

Rose Karushara, fifty-three, was a councilor in the sector of Kimisagara, commune Nyarugenge in Kigali. She lived in the cellule of Kimuhoza in

Kimisagara. Karushara is originally from the commune of Bwarkira in Kibuye. She used to sell beer before she was put in charge of Kimuhoza cellule. She was then appointed as councilor of Kimisagara by the (mayor), Francois Karera, who was a close ally.

Rose Karushara took an extremely active role in the genocide, wearing military uniform throughout. A tall and physically strong woman, she used to beat up the refugees herself before handing them over to interahamwe for the final kill. She distributed firearms to the assassins and was seen frequently at the roadblocks in her sector, deciding on the spot whether the refugees should be killed or allowed to live. She held meetings with the militia at a place called Ntaraga in Kimisagara. The plans that led to various massacres were drawn up in Ntaraga. The distribution of weapons to the interahamwe in Kimisagara was carried out at her house. Many of the people massacred in her sector, both residents and refugees, were thrown into the Nyabarongo river, or their bodies were dumped in a mass grave situated around the hides and skins factory known as SODEPARAL. Others were killed in front of her house while she watched.

Like a lot of extremists in positions of authority, Karushara used her power to enrich herself. Regarded as exceptionally corrupt, she began her threats against Tutsis immediately after the war began in October 1990. Knowing her susceptibility to money, many of the Tutsi men in Kimisagara were forced to buy her off.

. . .

One of the most detailed testimonies against Karushara comes from Callixte Rwamunyana who lived in Nyamabuye in cellule Kimisagara. He is forty and has worked for the hides and skins factory, SODEPARAL, since 1986.

. . .

As I was a Hutu and wasn't at all threatened, I knew a lot of things about Karushara and other criminals. She launched attacks in the different neighborhoods of Kigali town and even in other prefectures. . .. She took a lot of interahamwe, the most violent, and named the place she was going to 'work,' a term meaning to kill Tutsis . . .. She often went to the border between her sector and the commune of Butamwa. [Here, there were] a lot of Tutsis from Kibungo and Kigali who wanted to flee toward Gitarama. Karushara and her allies killed a lot of people. At least five thousand people were killed, all thrown into the Nyabarongo river under orders from Karushara. The Tutsis were thrown into the Nyabarongo river as paper is thrown into the dustbin. I know several places where Karushara and her interahamwe threw Tutsi corpses here in Kimisagara. I am ready to show all these mass graves."

Source: African Rights, *Rwanda: Not So Innocent: When Women Become Killers*, London: African Rights, 1995.

## Document 10

### *A proposed definition of ecocide as a violation of international law, 2021*

*In 2020, the NGO Stop Ecocide International, established in 2017, convened an independent panel of experts and charged it with writing a definition of "ecocide" as an international crime with the objective of seeking an amendment to the Rome Statute of the International Criminal Court.*

Independent Expert Panel for the Legal Definition of Ecocide, Commentary and Core Text, June 2021

It is widely recognised that humanity stands at a crossroads. The scientific evidence points to the conclusion that the emission of greenhouse gases and the destruction of ecosystems at current rates will have catastrophic consequences for our common environment. Along with political, diplomatic and economic initiatives, international law has a role to play in transforming our relationship with the natural world, shifting that relationship from one of harm to one of harmony. Despite significant progress, the inadequacies of current global environmental governance are widely acknowledged. National and international laws are in place to contribute to the protection of the natural systems upon which our well-being depends, yet it is apparent that such laws are inadequate and more is needed.

. . .

It is the hope of the Panel that the proposed definition might serve as the basis of consideration for an amendment to the Rome Statute of the International Criminal Court (ICC).

. . .

The inclusion of ecocide in the Rome Statute would add a new crime to international criminal law. This would be the first to be adopted since 1945. It would build on the existing crime of severe damage to the environment during armed conflict, whilst reflecting the fact that today, most severe environmental damage occurs during times of peace, a situation that currently falls outside the jurisdiction of the ICC. This definition of ecocide offers the States Parties to the Rome Statute the opportunity to meet current challenges.

Proceeding to agree a crime of ecocide could contribute to a change of consciousness, in support of a new direction, one that enhances the protection of the environment and supports a more collaborative and effective legal framework for our common future on a shared planet. It offers a new and practical legal tool.

The work has been inspired by earlier efforts, in 1945, to forge definitions of new international crimes, including 'genocide' and 'crimes against humanity'. Ecocide draws from both terms, in form and substance.

Taken with these two crimes, and with war crimes and the crime of aggression, we hope that ecocide might take its place as the fifth international crime.

. . .

Ecocide

1. For the purpose of this Statute, "ecocide" means unlawful or wanton acts committed with knowledge that there is a substantial likelihood of severe and either widespread or long-term damage to the environment being caused by those acts.

. . .

The structure of the proposed definition is drawn from Article 7 of the Rome Statute, Crimes Against Humanity: the first paragraph sets out the crime, and the second paragraph defines a number of its core elements.

A number of aspects of the proposed definition are drawn from the existing provision of the Rome Statute concerning damage to the natural environment . . .

These include:

(i) use of the terms 'widespread', 'long-term' and 'severe' to describe the prohibited damage;
(ii) a proportionality test ('clearly excessive in relation to the concrete and direct overall military advantage anticipated'); and
(iii) the use of endangerment liability, rather than a requirement for materialization of harm.

The new crime proposed here draws its essential elements from language that is already familiar, having been included in existing international law agreements. However, as proposed, the scope *ratione materiae* of the new crime of ecocide would develop the existing law by extending the protection of the environment by international criminal law beyond times of armed conflict to times of peace (it might be said that the exercise follows on developments in 1945, when certain prohibitions as war crimes were extended into what would become the prohibitions at all times of genocide and crimes against humanity).

. . .

'Environment' "Environment" means the earth, its biosphere, cryosphere, lithosphere, hydrosphere and atmosphere, as well as outer space.

The Panel recognises that defining the 'environment' (or 'natural environment'), has proved to be challenging for international law. To date, there is no single agreed definition of these terms. Available definitions vary with regard to their scope, content, and approach. One possible approach was to leave the term 'environment' undefined, as the International Law Commission has done in the topic 'Protection of the environment in relation to Armed Conflicts.' One benefit of this approach is that, as human understanding of the environment changes, the evolution in knowledge could be taken into account for the purposes of this crime.

. . .

Endangerment Culpability for the crime of ecocide attaches to the creation of a dangerous situation, rather than to a particular outcome. It is the commission of acts with knowledge of the substantial likelihood that they will cause severe and either widespread or long-term damage that is criminalised. The crime of ecocide is thus formulated as a crime of endangerment rather than of material result.

Source: www.stopecocide.earth

## Document 11

### *The president of Microsoft argues for the necessity of a "digital Geneva Convention," 2017*

*In February 2017, Brad Smith, the president and vice-chair of Microsoft, addressed the RSA Conference, an annual meeting of cybersecurity professionals, and called for the creation of a "digital Geneva Convention" to address the growing threats of cyberattacks and cyberterrorism to individuals and states.*

Let's face it, cyberspace is the new battlefield. The world of potential war has migrated from land to sea to air and now cyberspace.

But cyberspace is a different kind of space. Not only can we not find it in the physical world, but cyberspace is us. For all of us in this room, it is us. Cyberspace is owned and operated by the private sector. It is private property, whether it's submarine cables or datacenters or servers or laptops or smartphones. It is a different kind of battlefield than the world has seen before.

. . .

For over two-thirds of a century, the world's governments have been committed to protecting civilians in times of war. But when it comes to cyberattacks, nation-state hacking has evolved into attacks on civilians in times of peace.

This is not the world that the Internet's inventors envisioned a quarter of a century ago, but it is the world that we inhabit today.

. . .

We need to recognize that the time has come for us to come together as an industry around the world to call on the world's governments. We need to call on the world's governments to come together. They came together in 1949 in Geneva, Switzerland, and that is what led to the recognition that they needed the Fourth Geneva Convention to protect civilians in times of war.

Now is the time for us to call on governments to protect civilians on the Internet in times of peace. And there is progress on which we can build.

. . .

What we need now is a Digital Geneva Convention. We need a convention that will call on the world's governments to pledge that they will not engage in cyberattacks on the private sector, that they will not target civilian infrastructure, whether it's of the electrical or the economic or the political variety.

We need governments to pledge that, instead, they will work with the private sector to respond to vulnerabilities, that they will not stockpile vulnerabilities, and they will take additional measures.

And, perhaps as much as anything else, we need governments to take a page out of the 1949 Geneva Convention and other instruments that have followed. What the world needs is a new independent organization, a bit like the International Atomic Energy Agency that has addressed nuclear nonproliferation for decades.

. . .

If you look back at what happened in 1949, the world's governments realized that they could not protect civilians in times of war without a private organization – the International Committee of the Red Cross. 12 While we don't have the same kind of organization, we have within these walls many people from many organizations. And as a global technology sector, we need to come together as the ICRC did in 1949. We need to sign our own pledge in conjunction with the world's states.

We need to pledge that we will protect customers, that we will focus on defense. We need to be concrete in showing and pledging how we will collaborate with each other to respond to attacks. That we will provide patches to all customers everywhere, regardless of the attacks that they face. That we will do our part to address the world's needs.

. . . [E]ven in an age of rising nationalism, we as a global technology sector need to become a trusted and neutral Digital Switzerland.

Source: https://blogs.microsoft.com/on-the-issues/2017/02/14/need-digital-geneva-convention/

## Document 12

### *A Russian-American journalist reports on war crimes committed by the armed forces of the Russian Federation in Ukraine, August 2022*

*In the summer of 2022, about six months after the Russian invasion of Ukraine, the Russian-American journalist Masha Gessen reported on war crimes allegedly committed by Russian forces in the western suburbs of the nation's capital of Kyiv. Their report was published in* The New Yorker *magazine in August.*

On February 27th [2022], Russian troops entered Bucha, and were quickly ambushed by Ukrainian forces. Artillery fire – and, some said, Molotov cocktails thrown by residents – destroyed about a hundred Russian vehicles, including about a dozen on Vokzalna Street. The soldiers burned alive in their tanks as missiles and molten armor flew through the air, striking roofs and shattering windows. Ludmila and Valeriy hid in the cellar. After a few days, the explosions quieted, and Ludmila ventured out to inspect the smoldering Russian tanks. On March 3rd, a group of Ukrainian soldiers raised the country's flag in front of city hall. Ludmila thought the war was over.

That day, the Russians returned – a column of tanks surrounded by paratroopers on foot. A group of nine local men who were staffing a checkpoint on Yablunska Street took refuge in a nearby house. Only some of them had officially enlisted with Territorial Defense, an all-volunteer force within the Ukrainian military, and it's unclear how many of them were armed. The next day, they were captured by Russian soldiers, led to a small courtyard beside an office building on Yablunska – secluded just enough not to be visible from a nearby parking lot – and lined up in a row. The soldiers released one of the men, who had agreed to switch sides, and told the rest of them to kneel, with their hands behind their backs. Then they shot them.

. . .

The Russian forces occupied Bucha and Irpin for a month. Most of the dead lay wherever the killings had occurred. A resident of Yablunska Street told me that, when he stepped out of his yard on March 8th, he saw a road strewn with bodies and heard music. It was coming from cell phones ringing in the pockets of the dead.

. . .

Russian troops withdrew from Bucha on March 31st. Within days, as journalists gained access to the area, the town's name became synonymous with Russian war crimes. According to Roman Avramenko, the executive director of Truth Hounds, a Ukrainian N.G.O. that documents war crimes, Russian troops have perpetrated similar atrocities, on a comparable scale, in nearly every place that his organization has visited.

. . .

Alexander Cherkasov, the former head of the Memorial Human Rights Center, a Russian organization that since the early nineties has documented human-rights violations in conflict zones – and which was shut down by the Kremlin, in the spring – said that the atrocities in Ukraine had direct parallels to those in Chechnya and Syria.

. . .

In theory, international bodies have the authority to prosecute war crimes wherever and whenever they occur. But Russia has not meaningfully had to account for atrocities committed during earlier conflicts. In Syria, Russian troops fought on the side of the government. Chechnya is legally a part of Russia. In neither case would senior officials be prosecuted domestically, and Russia, as a permanent member of the United Nations Security Council, could veto any attempt by the U.N. to launch a tribunal. Russia also has not ratified the Rome Statute, which gives the International Criminal Court, in The Hague, jurisdiction over its signatory states.

Until recently, Russia was under the jurisdiction of the European Court of Human Rights, but, in March, it announced that it was leaving the Council of Europe, which empowers the court. In 2005, the E.C.H.R. ruled, in a case brought by Memorial, that Russian troops had knowingly bombed a civilian convoy in Chechnya in 1999. The E.C.H.R., which has the power only to order governments to pay monetary damages, imposed fines totalling about seventy thousand Euros. But even such minor interventions were rare. "Between three and five thousand people disappeared in Chechnya during the second war," Cherkasov said. "There is a total of four court decisions, making for an impunity rate of 99.9 per cent." In Ukraine, Russia is using not only the same tactics as in past conflicts but, in many cases, the same people: a number of senior officers commanding the war in Ukraine fought in Chechnya.

Parts of Ukraine have been under occupation since 2014, when Russia annexed Crimea and began a war in the Donbas region. Occupying authorities have employed forced conscription, kidnappings, detentions, and torture. But international legal bodies have been slow to get involved, and Ukraine has made little progress prosecuting crimes from the earlier phase of the war.

. . .

What justice . . . can a war-crimes trial offer if it's neither a suitable penalty for the criminal nor compensation for the victim? [Oleksandra] Matviichuk, of the Center for Civil Liberties, suggested that war-crime trials might facilitate a more just end to the war itself. "The Russian regime is trying to win this war by causing intolerable suffering to civilians," Matviichuk said. "Our duty is to keep reminding the world of the brutality and the scale of these crimes."

Source: Masha Gessen, "The Prosecution of Russian War Crimes in Ukraine," *The New Yorker*, 1 August, 2022.

# Glossary

**Accession:** When a state agrees to become party to a treaty (one that is ratified by other states and usually already in effect). Accession carries with it the same legal status as ratification.

**African Union (AU):** Established in 2002 in South Africa, the African Union is a non-governing organization of African states currently comprising 55 members. It replaced the Organization of African Unity (1963–99) and works for greater unity among African states and to represent and defend rights and economic interests of member states and the continent as a whole. It also promotes conflict resolution and the protection of human rights.

**Agreement and Charter for the Prosecution and Punishment of Major War Criminals of the European Axis ("London Agreement," 1945):** Having already decided to investigate and prosecute war crimes and those responsible for committing them, the United States, the United Kingdom, USSR, and Free French governments drew up a charter for an international tribunal to try "major criminals" who alleged offenses were not limited to particular locations. Signed by the four allied states on 8 August 1945 and then by 20 other states, the charter formed the legal and organizational bases for the International Military Tribunals in Nuremberg and Tokyo.

**Allied Control Council Law No. 10 (1945):** In December 1945, the four power Allied Control Council in occupied Germany passed a law that authorized officials in each of the four occupation zones to arrest and try suspected war criminals in their respective zones.

**Amnesty International (est. 1961):** Founded in London by the British lawyer Peter Benenson, Amnesty International became one of the world's most visible and influential human rights NGOs. Initially focused on securing the release of political prisoners around the world, the organization advocates for the protection of human rights broadly defined.

**Armenian genocide (1915–23):** The mass murder of Armenians perpetrated by Turkish nationalists (the Young Turks) between 1915 and 1923 with the objective of establishing an ethnically "pure" nation state in Anatolia. In a series of premeditated attacks that continued until

1923, around 1.3 million Armenians out of a prewar population of about two million were killed or perished as a result of deportations and deprivations. The widely publicized atrocities resulted in the first time states (Russia, France, and Britain) that used the term "crimes against humanity" to describe the actions of another state. The term "genocide" was applied retrospectively. Successive Turkish governments to the present day deny that genocide ever took place.

**Bellingcat:** An independent collective of private citizens established in 2014, Bellingcat's researchers use open-source resources to investigate international crimes such as drug trafficking, money laundering, the proliferation of weapons of mass destruction, war crimes, and crimes against humanity. Like other NGOs, Bellingcat has worked with the ICC and the UN.

**Cambodian genocide (1975–9):** During the rule of the communist Khmer Rouge regime in Cambodia (1975–9, formally Democratic Kampuchea), around 1.7 million people were killed (amounting to about 21 percent of the country's population). In addition to targeting supposed class enemies, the regime also persecuted the country's Vietnamese ethnic minority and the minority population of Cham Muslims. In 2018, Cambodian and international judges of the Extraordinary Chambers in the Courts of Cambodia (ECCC) found two former high-ranking regime officials guilty of genocide and other international crimes. The Khmer Rouge's leader, Pol Pot, died in 1998.

**Central Office of State Judicial Administrations for the Investigation of National Socialist Crimes (est. 1958):** The West German government created the Central Office to serve as a clearing house for investigating war crimes committed during World War II. Based in the southwestern town of Ludwigsburg, the agency was granted the authority to investigate crimes and provide names to regional prosecutors. Of the nearly 120,000 investigations undertaken by the agency, 5,000 were eventually tried.

**Collaboration:** The terms "collaboration" and "collaborator" were first used early in World War II to characterize states, parties, and individuals who allied themselves by choice or necessity with Nazi Germany, fascist Italy, and/or Imperial Japan. Collaboration was particularly important in the Holocaust, which could not have taken place the way it did without the complicity of hundreds of thousands of non-Jewish Europeans. The brutal nature of Axis rule and the destructiveness of the war changed the meaning of collaboration, and in the postwar period, many saw collaborators as traitors. In the war's immediate aftermath, being identified as a collaborator could get one summarily executed or subjected to ritualized public degradation. Extensive purges and trials of suspected collaborators accompanied this wave of violent score settling.

**Command responsibility:** The principle in customary international humanitarian law that a military commander and/or other superior officers may be held responsible for war crimes committed by those under their command if they were aware of or could have had reason to know that their subordinates were about to commit a crime or were committing a crime and did not take measures to prevent or punish those responsible.

**Commission for International Justice and Accountability (CIJA, est. 2012):** An NGO that investigates war crimes and crimes against humanity. CIJA is the most prominent NGO representing a broader move toward collecting evidence of international crimes with an eye to future prosecutions. The Syrian civil war was the initial focus of its work, and currently CIJA works with the ICC and law enforcement agencies around the world on other cases and violations of international law.

**Concentration camps:** The first concentration camps were established during the colonial wars of the late 19th century in Cuba, South Africa, and the Philippines. They were designed to temporarily separate rebels from the general population. The first camps created to hold political prisoners were created by Vladimir Lenin and Leon Trotsky in the summer of 1918 (the basis of what became the Gulag). Fascist Italy also constructed camps, though it was the Nazi regime that built the most extensive system in the 1930s and during World War II. Historians estimate that the Nazis built over 40,000 concentration camps, sub- and satellite camps, "ghettos" for Jews, and death camps. Former camp personnel would become a significant target of postwar investigations and trials and have continued in Germany to the present day.

**Convention for the Amelioration of the Condition of the Wounded in Armies in the Field (Geneva Convention, 1864):** Representatives of 16 states met in Geneva in August 1864 and signed the first of what would be four Geneva Conventions. The provisions of the 1864 convention sought to ensure the humane treatment of wounded and sick soldiers and protection for civilians providing treatment. It also established a red cross as the identifying symbol of civilians covered by the convention's terms. Within three years, all major European and many other states had ratified the convention. It was updated in July 1929, and its provisions were incorporated into the 1949 Geneva Convention.

**Convention on the Prevention and Punishment of the Crime of Genocide (Genocide Convention (1948):** Passed by the UN General Assembly in December 1948, the convention defines genocide as "any of the following acts committed with intent to destroy, in whole or in part, a national, ethnical, racial or religious group, as such: (a) Killing members of the group; (b) Causing serious bodily or mental harm to members of the group; (c) Deliberately inflicting on the group conditions of life calculated to bring about its physical destruction in whole or in part; (d) Imposing measures intended to prevent births within a group; (e) Forcibly transferring children of the group to another group" (Convention on the Prevention and Punishment of the Crime of Genocide, 1948). A conspiracy to commit it, incitement, an attempt to carry it out, and complicity were also considered punishable acts. A formal charge of genocide must prove intent to be considered a violation of the convention. Investigating and prosecuting alleged instances of genocide was left up to individual states. Representatives of 14 states signed the convention in 1948 and 1949, though in some cases did not ratify the treaty for years. As of 2019, a total of 153 states (including Palestine, a non-state member of the UN) have acceded to the convention.

**Courts Martial:** A court convened by a given military to its own personnel for violating military law. The first courts martial appeared in Britain in the 16th century.

**Crimes against humanity:** The first known use of the term to describe the actions of a state against civilians was in 1915 in a joint statement by Russia, France, and Britain in response to widely publicized massacres of Armenians by Turkish forces. The term was used to categorize one of the three main crimes prosecuted by the post-World War II international military tribunals and was incorporated by the ICTY and ICTR. The 1998 Rome Statute provided the most detailed definition to date, and the category is one of four crimes prosecutable by the ICC. The statute defined crimes against humanity as one or more of the following acts knowingly committed as part of a systematic attack on a civilian population: murder, extermination, enslavement, deportation or forcible transfer, unlawful imprisonment, torture, rape and other sexual crimes, persecution on political, racial, ethnic, religious, cultural, or gender grounds, enforced disappearances, apartheid, and unspecified inhumane acts causing great physical or mental suffering.

**Crimes against peace:** Also known as the crime of aggression. A category of international crime involving the preparation and initiation of a war of aggression (as opposed to a war of self-defense). One of the three main crimes prosecuted by the post-World War II international military tribunals and currently one of the four crimes prosecutable by the ICC.

**Customary international law:** A body of legal principles and rules that may not be written or codified in conventions, conduct codes, or treaties. The term applies when states act consistently and when actions are undertaken with the understanding that they conform to international law (*opinio juris*).

**Cyberwar:** Distinct from "cybercrime," "cyberwar" involves the use of computers and computer networks as offensive or defensive weapons. A "cyberattack" is any form of cyberwar that can be expected to produce injuries to persons or result in their deaths and/or damage or destroy physical objects (including attacks on vital cyber infrastructures). Cyberattacks are not by themselves violations of the laws of war: how the rules of war may or may not apply depends on how the particular weapon is used.

**Darfur genocide (2003 to the present):** Following a rebellion by non-Arab groups in the Darfur region of western Sudan in 2003, the Sudanese government counter-attacked, relying heavily on Arab militias ("Janja-weed") to terrorize the population in the region. The resulting civil war has displaced around two million people and resulted in the deaths of several hundred thousands, mostly civilians. In 2008, the ICC accused the president, Omar al-Bashir of responsibility for war crimes, crimes against humanity, and genocide (Sudan is not a party to the treaty that created the ICC), and issued an arrest warrant for him in 2009 for war crimes and crimes against humanity only. A charge of genocide was issued in 2010. The ICC suspended the investigation in 2014 due to the UN Security Council's failure to compel Bashir to surrender himself. In 2019, Bashir was ousted in a coup d'etat staged by the military. He was convicted by Sudanese courts on multiple counts unrelated to the genocide in Darfur.

**Declaration Renouncing the Use, In Time of War, of Certain Explosive Projectiles (1868):** Also known as the St. Petersburg Declaration. In response to a particularly destructive new type of bullet (one that exploded upon contact with hard or soft objects), Tsar Alexander II (1818–81) convened an international conference in 1868 in St. Petersburg. The resulting declaration was signed by representatives of 14 European states and the Ottoman Empire, who pledged that their respective armies would not use explosive bullets of a certain size. The declaration was the first international agreement to ban the use of a particular weapon for humanitarian reasons. While the focus was on a single type of projectile, the declaration's expression of a principal may have been its most important legacy: namely, that there were limits to what actions can be taken by the belligerents in a war and that it was "contrary to the laws of humanity" to deploy weapons that caused excessive suffering.

**Declaration Respecting Maritime Law (1856):** The declaration abolished privateering and included provisions to protect the property of neutral states and proclaimed that in order to be binding, blockades had to be implemented effectively. Representatives of 56 states, federations, and principalities ratified or at least agreed to abide by its provisions, thus making the declaration the first multilateral treaty in history aimed at regulating the conduct of war.

**Denazification:** The policy of eliminating the influence of former Nazis and National Socialism from Germany society through the automatic arrests, prosecutions, and employment bans of individual Germans. Denazification was implemented by all four allied states in the occupation years (1945–9) and carried over into the early years of the two German states. Denazification courts were authorized by allies to charge Germans in one of five categories: "major offenders," "offenders," "lesser offenders," "followers," and "exonerated." Between 1945 and 1949, the courts handled over 3.6 million cases and convicted 1,667 as major offenders, 23,000 as offenders, 150,425 as lesser offenders, over one million as followers, and the rest either exonerated or not charged.

**Digital Geneva Convention:** A 2017 proposal by the President and Chief Legal Officer of Microsoft for a revision to the Geneva Convention to include protections for civilians and non-combatants against cyberattacks and cyberwarfare.

**East Timor genocide (1975–99):** In 1975, Indonesian government forces invaded East Timor (Timor-Leste), then a colony of Portugal. About one-fifth of the population perished during the ensuing occupation, which ended in 1999. The territory achieved full independence in 2002.

**Ecocide:** The intentional destruction of the physical environment in both war and peacetime conditions defined as an international crime. First articulated in 1970 by antiwar activists in response to the US military's extensive use of an herbicide and defoliant chemical in the Vietnam War. With reference to Vietnam, the Swedish Prime Minister Olof Palme (1927–86) became the first head of state to propose the idea of ecocide as an international crime at the 1972 UN Conference on the Human Environment. By the first decade of the 21st century, the UN had debated making ecocide a violation of international law and ten states have criminalized ecocide. The strongest support for adding ecocide to the four core crimes prosecuted by the ICC has come from NGOs and a handful of small island nations faced with destruction as a result of rising sea levels.

**Ethnic cleansing:** The attempt by state or sub-state actors to create a "pure" geographic region by forcibly removing those who do not belong to the desired ethnic, racial, cultural, or religious group(s). Broadly defined, instances of ethnic cleansing can be traced as far back as the 9th century BCE, but the term only became widely used in the course of the civil wars in the former Yugoslavia in the 1990s. While there is no universally acknowledged legal definition of ethnic cleansing, the practice is now established within international criminal law.

**Extraordinary Chambers in the Courts of Cambodia (ECCC, 2001 to the present):** An *ad hoc* international court convened to try senior leaders and other culpable individuals for violations of Cambodian law, international humanitarian law and custom, and international conventions recognized by Cambodia committed in the 1975–9 period of Khmer Rouge rule. The court held its first trial until 2007 and indicted only five suspects and convicted three. A disagreement over further prosecutions between the French judge and his Cambodian counterparts, who believed that more trials would have a destabilizing effect on the country, combined with the fact that many perpetrators have died effectively ensured that no more cases will be brought before the ECCC.

**Extraordinary State Commission for Ascertaining and Investigating Atrocities Perpetrated by the German Fascist Invaders and Their Accomplices (1942–44):** A Soviet commission created to gather evidence for what would be the first war crimes trials of World War II. In 1943 and 1944, Soviet military courts then tried thousands of suspects, and the vast majority of them were Soviet citizens accused of collaboration. A smaller number of trials were public and publicized widely. These were show trials in which guilty verdicts were a foregone conclusion. The commission also supplied evidence it had collected to the IMT in Nuremberg.

**Frankfurt Auschwitz Trials (1963–5):** Initiated by Fritz Bauer (1903–68), a state prosecutor and Jewish German Holocaust survivor, a West German court prosecuted 22 former mid-ranking SS officers and capos who had served in Auschwitz. The accused had been living openly in West Germany but had remained unprosecuted. They were not charged with committing war crimes or crimes against humanity but with violating German law. Eighteen were convicted, with six sentenced to life terms and the others receiving sentences ranging from five to 14 years. Though the trial received extensive coverage by the West German and foreign press, much public opinion in the FRG was indifferent and even hostile to the proceedings.

**Gacaca courts (2001–12):** While some of the highest-ranking individuals responsible for organizing the 1994 Rwandan genocide were tried by the ICTR, the vast majority of perpetrators were living freely and openly in Rwanda or neighboring states. The established system of courts in Rwanda was unable to handle the huge number of cases, with only 1,292 suspects tried by 1998. The Gacaca initiative thus aimed at bringing as many foot soldiers of the genocide to justice as possible. Around 12,000 local courts were created, each comprising a panel of judges – who were not required to be trained in the law – drawn from the local community. The courts ultimately presided over nearly two million cases, tried around one million people, and achieved a conviction range of 86 percent. The convicted were sentenced to prison terms or to terms of manual labor.

**Genocide:** A portmanteau combining the Greek prefix "genos" (race or tribe) and the Latin suffix "cide" (killing), the term genocide was first proposed by the Polish-born lawyer Raphael Lemkin (1900–59) in his 1944 book *Axis Rule in Occupied Europe*. Lemkin defined genocide as "a coordinated plan of different actions aiming at the destruction of essential foundations of the life of national groups, with the aim of annihilating the groups themselves." For Lemkin, genocide was a premeditated act and not simply a description of the outcome of an armed conflict. Lemkin then worked to establish genocide as a crime in international law. Though unable to get it included by name as a charge in the indictments of the Nuremberg or Tokyo IMTs, its essence was incorporated into count 3 (war crimes) of the Nuremberg IMT. Lemkin then worked to get the new United Nations to adopt a resolution on genocide. The Genocide Convention was approved by the General Assembly in December 1948.

**Guantanamo Bay:** The US military base in Cuba selected by the US government as a detention center and host site of military commissions to try suspected terrorists. Beset by multiple legal challenges regarding jurisdiction, the legality of the courts, and the treatment of detainees, only eight commissions were conducted to completion from 2002 to 2020, with no case completed since 2014.

**Hague Convention (Convention II with Respect to the Laws and Customs of War on Land and its annex:** Regulations concerning the Laws and Customs of War on Land, 1899): Initiated by Tsar Nicholas II (1868–1918) to contain accelerating arms race and defuse rising international tensions 100 delegates representing 28 nations convened in The Hague from May to July 1899 to consider disarmament, revisit the 1864 Geneva Convention, and otherwise explore ways to resolve international disputes peacefully. While little progress was made on containing the arms race, delegates from 23 states ratified what was the first codification in the form of an international treaty of the laws of war on land and sea. The convention defined belligerents, dealt extensively with the status of prisoners of war and sick and wounded soldiers, and set limits on the "means of injuring the enemy," the status of spies, truces, capitulations, and armistices, and occupations.

**Herero-Nama War (1904–8):** The first genocide of the 20th century. Between 1884 and 1890, Imperial Germany took control of what it called German Southwest Africa (today Namibia). Expanding German settlements provoked conflict with the Indigenous and pastoral Herero people over scare resources in the largely desert environment. Fighting erupted in January 1904 and spread rapidly. The German government demanded the violent suppression of rebelling Hereros. German forces drove Herero fighters and non-combatants retreated into the desert, where thousands would perish. Colonial troops also executed those who were captured or had surrendered and prevented the Herero from exiting the desert. They also erected concentration camps in larger towns. As the Herero rebellion was suppressed in the fall of 1904, the Nama people in the southern part of the colony mobilized and struck at the Germans. They, too, were rounded up and imprisoned in camps, where mortality rates reached 80 percent. Historians estimate that around 80,000 Herero and Nama perished between 1904 and 1908, amounting to 75 percent of the Herero population and perhaps half of the Nama.

**Holocaust (genocide of European Jews):** A German-initiated and German-led pan-European attack on European Jews that was aided by hundreds of thousands of non-German collaborators. Intent on removing Jews from Germany and Europe entirely, the Nazi regime first planned to relocate them to the island of Madagascar. When that plan proved impossible, removal to the interior of the Soviet Union was contemplated, a plan that had to be scrapped when the Germans failed to defeat the Red Army in Russia. Ultimately, the regime settled upon mass executions and killings in purpose-built camps (death camps) in Poland. An estimated five million to six million Jews were killed or allowed to die, amounting to over half of Europe's 1933 Jewish population of 9.5 million.

**Human Rights Watch (est. 1978 as Helsinki Watch):** An influential international NGO based in New York monitors human rights around the world to ensure adherence to the provisions of the Universal Declaration of Human Rights. It also investigates and exposes violations of international humanitarian law.

**Humanitarian intervention:** Military and non-military actions taken by states, coalitions of states, or international organizations (intergovernmental or NGO) in response to widespread human suffering within the borders of a particular state. Such actions proliferated in the 1970s and especially the 1990s and have generated ongoing debate about violations of state sovereignty. Crimes committed by intervening actors have also become a prominent part of the debate over the legality and effectiveness of interventions.

**Indian Mutiny (1857–8):** Also known as the Sepoy Mutiny and the First War of Independence, the rebellion was fueled by elite and popular discontent over various aspects of British rule in India. It was sparked in April when Indian troops (or Sepoys) serving in the Bengal army in Meerut were punished harshly for refusing to use new British rifle cartridges they believed to have been lubricated with cow and pig fat. Their fellow soldiers attacked British officers, marched to Delhi, and restored the former Mughal emperor. The revolt spread in northern India and involved the killing of British military personnel and civilians. British forces responded against rebels and civilians with extreme harshness. Around 6,000 British subjects were killed in the 18-month-long rebellion and at least 800,000 Indians perished in the fighting and as a result of famines and disease. Following the mutiny's suppression, the British government took direct control of India and began consulting with Indians on legislative matters while instituting other minor reforms and developing infrastructure. British rule was assured for the time being, and the groundwork had been laid for a new Indian nationalism and independence movement.

**Instructions for the Government of Armies of the United States in the Field (Lieber Code, 1863):** The first codification of the rules of war for use by armies in the field. Issued by the US War Department during the Civil War, it was and remains to be known as the "Lieber Code" after its principal author, Francis J. Lieber (1798 or 1800–72), a German-born scholar. Comprising 157 articles, the code dealt with the issue of military necessity, rules for occupying enemy territory, the treatment of prisoners of war, civilians, and property, enslaved people, irregulars (or guerillas), and armistices. President Lincoln ordered the code to be included in the Union Army's General Orders, effective in 1863. Officials of the Confederacy eventually adopted it, though Confederate forces violated its provisions repeatedly. The militaries of numerous other nations adopted similar codes and their articles influenced the language of the Geneva and Hague Conventions.

**International Committee of the Red Cross (ICRC, est. 1863):** In 1862, a Swiss businessman, Henry J. Dunant (1828–1910), proposed the creation of a neutral, international organization of volunteer medical professionals dedicated to the care of wounded soldiers in wartime with the idea that belligerents would not interfere with the organization's work in the field. Dunant's proposal inspired the creation of the International Committee for Relief to the Wounded in 1863. The Swiss government then offered to host an international conference to promote the new organization's mission. Representatives of 16 states met in Geneva in August 1864 and signed the Geneva Convention for the Amelioration of the Condition of the Wounded in Armies in the Field, the first of what would be four Geneva Conventions. In 1875, the International Committee for Relief to the Wounded became the International Committee of the Red Cross. In addition to its work in wars around the world, the ICRC became one of the most important sources of the development of the laws of war and its post-World War II embodiment, international humanitarian law.

**International Court of Justice (est. 1945):** Also known as the World Court, the 15-member ICJ is based in The Hague in the Netherlands and is the main judicial body of the United Nations. It settles legal disputes submitted to it by member states and issues advisory opinions on legal matters facing UN bodies and agencies.

**International Criminal Court (2003 to the present):** Established by the Rome Statute in 1998, the Hague-based court began operating in 2003 as the first permanent international criminal court. By 2022, 137 states had signed the treaty and 123 are states parties. The ICC is an independent entity charged with investigating and prosecuting individuals accused of one or more of four international crimes: genocide, crimes against humanity, war crimes, and the crime of aggression committed in a state party's borders or by nationals of a state party. It claims jurisdiction only when a state party has not investigated its own nationals for the most serious violations (the principle of complementarity), though the UN Security Council can authorize an expansion of the ICC's jurisdiction. It does not maintain any kind of police force and relies entirely on cooperation by state parties. Widely regarded as a milestone in the evolution of international humanitarian law, the court is permanent and in terms of its purpose and structure, it promotes due process, accountability, the rule of law, fair trials, global governance, and the protection of human rights. It has upheld the Nuremberg principles and expanded the range of prosecutable war crimes and crimes against humanity. It has established what most informed observers consider to be an important track record of cases.

**International Criminal Tribunal for Rwanda (ICTR, est. 1994):** On 8 November 1994, the UN created the International Criminal Tribunal for Rwanda (ICTR) to prosecute individuals responsible for genocide and other violations of international humanitarian law committed in 1994. The court is based in Arusha, Tanzania, with offices in Kigali and an appeals court in The Hague. Since 1995, it has indicted 93 individuals and convicted 62. Those indicted included high-ranking military and political officials and numerous civilians. The ICTR was the first international court to prosecute and convict individuals responsible for committing genocide. It prosecuted former prime minister Jean Kambanda (b. 1955), making him the first head of state to be convicted on the charge of perpetrating genocide. The ICTR was the first court of its kind to recognize rape as a tool of genocide. It also held the media responsible for inciting the public to commit mass murder (Scheffer, 2011).

**International Criminal Tribunal for the Former Yugoslavia (ICTY, 1993–2017):** The widely publicized massacres, reports of mass rape, and population displacement perpetrated during the wars in the former Yugoslavia spurred the UN Security Council to authorize the creation of an international tribunal for all of the former Yugoslavia to prosecute violations of international law and to establish a lasting peace. Based in The Hague, ICTY, in the period of its mandate (1993–2017) charged 161 individuals with committing one or more of four crimes: genocide, crimes against humanity, violations of the customs of war, and grave breaches of the Geneva Conventions. Ninety were convicted and sentenced, most of them Bosnian Serbs, including several high-ranking political and military officials. The ICTY was the first of its kind since the Nuremberg and Tokyo trials and the first war crimes court created by the UN. It confirmed the main achievement of the Nuremberg IMT: that heads of state and government officials can be held accountable for their actions under international law. The tribunal set important new precedents, namely by affirming that violations of international law could be prosecuted in cases of civil war, that rape constitutes a form of torture in international humanitarian law, and that command responsibility applies to military and civilian commanders. The ICTY also served as the model for future international tribunals.

**International Humanitarian Law:** In the decades following World War II, a broad new international framework aimed at constraining war – particularly its impact on civilian non-combatants – came into existence. The foundations of this framework were the Genocide Convention of 1948 and the two Geneva Conventions of 1949 and their additional protocols. The former made the deliberate attempt to eliminate entire groups of people a violation of international law while the latter emphasized regulating the conduct of war among combatants, including important new provisions for protecting non-combatants. These agreements, which greatly expanded upon the Geneva and Hague Conventions of the late 19th and early 20th centuries, and the body of international law that emerged from it comprise what has become known as international humanitarian law (IHL). A complementary development was the emergence in the 1970s of international human rights activism and law, which aims to institute protections of a universal set of rights for all people in all circumstances.

**International Military Tribunal at Nuremberg (1945–6):** The international court established by the wartime allies and 20 other states to try the surviving leaders of the Nazi Party. The accused were charged with one or more of four counts: conspiracy (or "common plan") to participate in crimes against peace (or crimes of aggression), war crimes (the killing of combatants and civilians for no military purpose), and crimes against humanity (atrocities committed against civilians). Nineteen of 22 defendants were convicted, with 12 receiving death sentences. The IMT was a landmark in the evolution of international law and a model for future international tribunals. For the first time, individuals who violated international laws were held accountable, with neither the sovereignty of states nor claims of acting on superior orders accepted as viable defenses. In December 1946, the UN General Assembly affirmed provisions of the IMT's charter as principles of international law.

**International Military Tribunal for the Far East (Tokyo) (1946–8):** The international court created to try Japan's principal political and military leaders. The tribunal created three categories: "Class A" war criminals to be charged with planning and committing crimes against peace and "Class B" and "C" for lower-ranking officials charged with committing war crimes and crimes against humanity. Individual defendants would also be accused of committing war crimes and crimes against humanity as part of a wider conspiracy to wage wars of territorial conquest. The 28 defendants included former high-ranking government officials and military officers. All defendants were found guilty, with seven former leaders convicted and sentenced to death. Emperor Hirohito was not tried as he was protected by American officials who saw him as playing an essential role in Japan's recovery, a move that made a mockery of the principal of holding individuals – including national leaders – accountable for committing war crimes.

**Institute of International Law (est. 1873):** A Swiss-based organization of jurists co-founded by Johann Caspar Bluntschli and Gustave Moynier, the Institute drew up the Manual of the Laws and Customs of War at Oxford in 1880 which, along with the Lieber Code, would form the basis for the two Hague Conventions in 1899 and 1907. In 1904, the institute was awarded the Nobel Prize for Peace. Since then, the Geneva-based institution has become the most influential non-governmental body of lawyers devoted to the development of international law.

**Investigative Team to Promote Accountability for Crimes Committed by Da'esh/ISIL (UNITAD) (2017 to the present):** Prompted by the 2014 ISIL attack on Yazidi communities in northern Iraq, a UN Security Council resolution created UNITAD to collect evidence in Iraq of war crimes, crimes against humanity, and crimes that may constitute genocide-committed ISIL. It also works to counter ISIL propaganda disseminated to attract new members.

***ius ad bellum:*** The right to wage war.

***ius in bellum*:** The just conduct of warfare.

**League of Nations (1920–46):** The first international organization comprised representatives of states devoted to maintaining peace. It was founded in January 1920 by the Paris Peace Conference and pursued disarmament, collective security, and the peaceful resolution of disputes between nations. Its effectiveness was undercut by the unwillingness of the United States to join, the absence of any enforcement mechanisms, and the requirement of unanimous consent. The League also reinforced (and even participated in the expansion of) the existing system of European-dominated empires. Though formally disbanded in 1946, it had effectively ceased to function by 1939. Its successor organization, the United Nations, sought to remedy many of the League's most glaring weaknesses.

**Lethal Autonomous Weapons (LAWs):** Weapons systems that use artificial intelligence to operate without direct human control. A number of states have already developed such weapons and even deployed them in conflict zones. As only individuals are held accountable for ordering, abetting, or committing war crimes and crimes against humanity, the central legal question when it comes to LAWs is who would be prosecuted should such a weapon violate the laws of war.

**Leipzig trials (1921):** Shortly after World War I, British, French, and Belgium officials drew up a list of 862 suspects to be handed over by the German government for trial by an envisioned international tribunal, a list that included Germany's most prominent military leaders and a former Chancellor. Suspects were to be charged with responsibility for atrocities committed against civilians in Belgium and France, crimes against prisoners of war, and the deportation of civilians for forced labor. But the allies dropped the extradition demand in the face of strong German resistance and settled for trials held in Leipzig, Germany, by the country's supreme court. The ensuing trials were a farce. The court put 12 individuals from the original on trial and convicted six. In these and other cases investigated but not tried, the Reichsgericht downplayed or ignored reliable evidence. Having decided to hand responsibility over to the Reichsgericht, British, French, and Belgian officials attending the proceedings could do little more than walk out in protest and (in the case of the latter two) hold trials of suspects *in absentia* in their respective countries. The memory of this failure bolstered the determination of the allies in World War II to create an international tribunal.

**London Agreement (1945):** In June 1945, the allies met in London to prepare for the agreed-upon international tribunal for major war criminals. After two months of negotiations, they produced the court's charter: the Agreement and Charter for the Prosecution and Punishment of Major War Criminals of the European Axis. The accused could be charged with one or more of four counts. The first was conspiracy (or "common plan") to participate in the remaining three: crimes against peace (or crimes of aggression), war crimes (the killing of combatants and civilians for no military purpose), and crimes against humanity (another new category to account for atrocities committed against civilians). The four Allied governments would each appoint a judge and an alternate, with the four judges selecting a president (they would choose the British jurist Sir Geoffrey Lawrence). Decisions would be made by majority vote of the judges, and there was no possibility of appeal. The agreement also defined the rights of the accused to a fair trial. The location for the tribunal was selected: the city of Nuremberg, chosen for its symbolic significance – it had been the site of annual Nazi Party rallies and its name was associated with a series of race laws that formed much of the legal basis for the regime's persecution of Germany's Jews – and because the city's court building was intact.

**Manual of the Laws and Customs of War at Oxford (1880):** Produced by the Institute for International Law, the manual was to serve as a handbook on the laws of war for national governments. Comprising 86 articles and informed by the Lieber Code and the 1864 Geneva Convention, the manual would then inform the language of the two Hague Conventions (1899 and 1907).

**Military commissions:** Also known as military courts or tribunals. A military commission conducts proceedings, usually during and shortly after hostilities, against enemy combatants and sometimes civilians accused of violating the laws and customs of war. The tradition of political and military authorities convening special courts to try soldiers for violating codes of conduct dates back to the Middle Ages. But it was not until the mid-19th century that the first formal military commission was convened by the US Army during the US war with Mexico (1846–8). It was during the Civil War, however, that military commissions were used on a significant scale: nearly 3,500 military commissions were convened. Less well-known were the hundreds of cases in which Native Americans were tried in the 1860s and 1870s during multiple wars on the western frontier. Military commissions were again convened in significant numbers by the United States and other states after World War II and virtually disappeared until the aftermath of the 11 September 2001 terrorist attacks on the United States, when commissions were convened at the US military base at Guantanamo Bay in Cuba.

**Montreux Document (2008):** A non-binding re-affirmation of international laws as they relate to the operations of private military companies signed by representatives of 17 states and since joined by 41 more and NATO, the EU, and the Organization for Security and Co-operation in Europe.

**Moscow declaration (1943):** During a conference held in Moscow in October 1943, the American, British, Soviet foreign, and Chinese foreign ministers declared their determination to create an international organization to succeed the League of Nations, agreed that postwar Italy and Austria be independent states, and that accused German war criminals would be sent to the countries in which crimes had been committed. But they withheld for themselves the authority to pursue those whose crimes were not restricted to particular locations.

**Non-Governmental Organizations (NGOs):** Sub-state and often transnational organizations formed to advocate for particular causes or in some cases provide direct forms of assistance. NGOs have played an important role in exposing war crimes and other atrocities, advising states and international bodies, and amassing evidence for legal proceedings.

***Nullum crimen sine lege*:** No crime without a law. The basis for the accusation that post-World War II International Military Tribunals and other courts imposed the law *ex post facto*.

**Pact of Paris ("Kellogg-Briand pact," 1928):** Along with the creation of the League of Nations, the Pact of Paris represented the highpoint of the post-World War I international movement to prevent war. Signed by representatives of 44 nations on 27 August 1928, the terms of the treaty did not "outlaw war." Wars of self-defense, for instance, were considered legitimate. Rather, the signatories pledged that their governments henceforth renounced war as an instrument of national policy. There was no provision for holding individuals accountable for starting a war or committing war crimes.

**Permanent Court of International Justice (PCIJ, 1922–46):** The predecessor of the International Court of Justice, the League of Nations Covenant, created the Permanent Court of International Justice to arbitrate relatively minor disputes between states. The PCIJ handled 29 cases and delivered 29 non-binding opinions between 1922 and 1940.

**Privateering:** When states, through "letters of marquee," authorize private ships to conduct military operations at sea, mainly the seizure of merchant shipping.

**Private Military Companies (PMCs, also known as private security companies):** The first PMCs were formed during World War II, but regional conflicts in Africa and the Middle East combined with the end of the Cold War and the global movement toward the privatization of a growing number of state functions all fueled the rapid growth of the industry. Contemporary PMCs are multinational corporations that contract with governments, international organizations, and private enterprises to provide a range of security services, most often training, logistical support, the protection of personnel and properties, and varying levels of engagement in armed conflicts, with personnel recruited from state military services, especially counterinsurgency and special forces units. By 2021, hundreds of PMCs were operating in nearly every part of the world. PMCs have been used as proxies by states when those states wish to influence the course of an armed conflict or occupation but do not want to involve their own national forces. This situation is a continuation of a pattern set during the Cold War: namely, the connections between the intelligence services of major powers like the United States and the United Kingdom and mercenaries. In the post-Cold War world, the relationship between national governments and PMCs is much clearer. Moreover, eyewitnesses, UN investigators, NGOs, reporters, and foreign government sources have implicated the personnel of multiple PMCs in multiple war crimes and crimes against humanity.

**Protocol for the Prohibition of the Use in War of Asphyxiating, Poisonous or Other Gases and of Bacteriological Methods of Warfare (1925):** Usually referred to as the Geneva Protocol, the protocol was signed during a convention in Geneva dealing with the international arms trade. Signed by representatives of 38 nations in 1925 and 108 since, the protocol updated provisions regarding the use of poison gasses (by adding bacteriological weapons) established in the 1899 Hague Convention and by the Versailles and other post-World War I treaties.

**Reparations and restitution:** Reparation entails attempting to restore or repair what has been damaged in the form of compensation for damages incurred by individuals or groups of people (and their descendants) victimized in wartime or various non-war-related forms of oppression. Restitution entails the return by states or private institutions of something – usually property, assets of some kind, or artifacts of cultural significance – that had been taken by force or illegally from its rightful owner(s). The postwar German states, which ultimately paid out billions of their respective currencies to victims of the Nazis, the state of Israel, and to the international Jewish Claims Conference, were pioneers in restitution and reparations and in some ways exemplary. Since then, the right to both forms of compensation has become widely accepted by states and international bodies as important components of transitional justice, namely, the UN, the ICC, and human rights NGOs. The ICC was the first international criminal body to authorize reparations and restitution to the victims of individual perpetrators of war crimes and crimes against humanity.

**Rohingya genocide (2017 to the present):** In 2017, the government of Myanmar began a crackdown on the Muslim Rohingya ethnic minority in the coastal Rakhine State. Several hundred thousand Rohingya fled the country and an estimated 6,700 people were killed in the first wave of attacks. In 2018, UN investigators accused Myanmar's military of killings and rape with the intent to commit genocide. In 2019, the ICC opened an investigation into the attacks, and in March 2021, US President Joe Biden accused the government of Myanmar of committing genocide.

**Rome Statute (1998):** The idea of a permanent international criminal court originated with a proposal by a founder of the International Committee of the Red Cross in 1872 and taken up by jurists in the 1920s and 1930s and again shortly after World War II. The catalyst for the creation of the International Criminal Court (ICC) was a proposal in 1989 to the UN by the government of Trinidad and Tobago to create a permanent court to deal with drug trafficking and terrorism. The proposal generated nearly a decade of work by the UN and NGOs resulting in the Rome Statute in July 1998: the treaty establishing the first permanent international criminal court. The treaty was signed by representatives of 120 states. The ICC formally came into existence in 2002 after 60 nations ratified the treaty. By 2022, 137 states had signed the treaty and 123 are states parties. Thirty-five states, including the United States, the Russian Federation, and China, never became parties to the treaty.

**Special Court for Sierra Leone (2002–13):** Created by the UN and based in Freetown, the Special Court for Sierra Leone convicted eight members of three armed factions involved in that country's civil war for war crimes and violations of international humanitarian law. The highest-visibility defendant was Charles Taylor (b. 1948), the former president of Liberia, who supported a rebel faction in Sierra Leone. Taylor was charged with 11 counts related to war crimes and crimes against humanity, convicted on all counts in 2012, and sentenced to 50 years in prison. He became the first head of state to be convicted by an international tribunal.

**Srebrenica massacre (1995):** The widely publicized massacre by the Bosnia Serb Army (BSA) of at least 7,000 Bosnian Muslim (Bosniak) men and teenagers in the town of Srebrenica which was part of a supposed UN "safe haven." In response, NATO conducted a series of airstrikes on BSA positions to force Serbia to negotiate an end to the war. The massacre, along with reports of mass rape and population displacement, spurred the United Nations Security Council to authorize the creation of an international tribunal for all of the former Yugoslavia.

**Tallinn manuals (2013, 2017):** Beginning in 2009, the NATO-sponsored Cooperative Cyber Defense Centre of Excellence (CCDCOE) produced a non-binding guidebook for policymakers and lawyers regarding cyberspace and international law.

**Transitional justice:** An international movement emerging in the 1990s and involving states, NGOs, and individual actors and aimed at combining the administration of justice (or at least the investigation of alleged crimes) with public memory, memorialization, and forms of restitution in order to establish a peaceful post-conflict political and social order.

**Truth commissions:** *Ad hoc* state-sponsored institutions charged with investigating political violence, usually during the negotiated transition from some form of autocracy to a liberal democratic system or in the aftermath of war. Truth commissions are neither courts nor alternatives to courts. Their main purpose is to gather evidence – documentary and eyewitness – and make recommendations for legal action, institutional change, compensation for victims, and memorialization. While truth commissions are government-sponsored entities, their creation and work have been influenced strongly by non-governmental actors, namely, victims and victims' groups and NGOs. The first self-proclaimed truth commission was created in Uganda in 1974 but the first effective commissions were established in South America in the 1980s. Dozens of others in Latin America and Africa followed, the best known among them being the Commission of Truth and Reconciliation in South Africa (1995–2002), which was the only such commission to be empowered to grant amnesty to perpetrators of crimes who confessed openly.

**Uighur genocide (2014 to the present):** Accelerating measures by the Chinese government to suppress the Uighur ethnic minority in Xinxiang province has led the governments of the United States, the United Kingdom, Canada, and the Netherlands to accuse China of committing genocide. These measures include leaked official documentation and otherwise credible reports of mass incarceration in concentration camps, forced labor, family separations, forced sterilization of women, and the suppression of cultural and religious traditions and institutions.

**United Nations (est. 1945):** The successor to the League of Nations, the United Nations was established after World War II as a body of independent nation states, the main purpose of which is to maintain peace and coordinate the actions of members to address issues related to global security. The UN comprises six bodies: the General Assembly, the Security Council, the Economic and Social Council, the Trusteeship Council, the International Court of Justice, and the UN Secretariat.

**Universal jurisdiction:** A principal in customary international law that provides a state with jurisdiction over violations of international law even when those violations did not take place on that state's territory or when the perpetrator or victim is a national of that state.

**UN War Crimes Commission (UNWCC, 1943–8):** In January 1942, the USSR, Great Britain, the United States, and six governments in exile established the Inter-Allied Commission on the Punishment of War Crimes, which issued a demand for postwar trials of suspected war criminals. The British government proposed that a United Nations commission be established to gather evidence of atrocities. Accordingly, the United Nations Commission for the Investigation of War Crimes (renamed the United Nations War Crimes Commission) was established and based in London. It could do no more than gather evidence and was not well funded or staffed sufficiently. Josef Stalin's refusal to cooperate was another liability. Nonetheless, the commission debated legal issues related to the laws of war and war crimes, with some of its proposals incorporated into the IMT's charter. It also provided states with evidence of war crimes, eventually creating over 8,000 files on 36,810 individuals and groups. The commission's records became accessible to the public in 2019.

**Versailles Treaty (1919):** The post-World War I peace treaty between Germany and the United Kingdom, France, the United States (which never ratified the treaty), and Italy. In addition to clauses requiring changes in territory, disarmament, and reparations, the treaty included the Covenant for the League of Nations. It also included clauses demanding the extradition of the former Emperor and trials for suspected war criminals.

**Women's International War Crimes Tribunal (2000):** A coalition of women's NGOs, the Violence against Women in War Network sponsored a Women's International War Crimes Tribunal in Tokyo as a symbolic venue for giving voice to the victims of wartime sexual crimes. Sixty-four survivors from nine countries participated in the proceedings, calling attention to their experiences and to the lack of prosecution of the perpetrators in postwar trials. More generally, the tribunal heightened international visibility of the persistent problem of sexual crimes in war.

**Yazidi genocide (2014):** Massacres and other atrocities committed against the Yazidi ethnic and religious minority in northern Iraq by members of the Islamic State. Thousands of Yazidis were executed and thousands of more girls and women were raped and forced into sexual slavery. An estimated half million Yazidis fled the region. In 2014, the US government accused IS of committing genocide and conducted airstrikes against IS positions. In 2016, UN investigators also accused IS of genocide. In September 2021, a German court sentenced a German-born woman to ten years' imprisonment for doing nothing to prevent the death of a Yazidi girl whom she and her husband had enslaved. A month later, her husband – an Iraqi IS member – was sentenced to life imprisonment for the girl's murder. A second IS member was convicted in July 2022 by another German court for aiding and abetting genocide as well as of crimes against humanity and war crimes for the enslavement of a Yazidi woman.

# Guide to further reading

## General works

An invaluable introduction to the global history of war crimes is Michael Bryant's *A World History of War Crimes: From Antiquity to the Present* (London: Bloomsbury Academic, 2021). Also useful is David M. Crowe's *War Crimes, Genocide, and Justice* (Palgrave Macmillan, 2014). For the 19th century forward, Gary Solis' *The Law of Armed Conflict: International Humanitarian Law in War* (Cambridge: Cambridge University Press, 2022) is a detailed and up-to-date survey supplemented with abundant primary sources (with an emphasis on the United States). The best single study of the politics of war crimes trials is Gary Jonathan Bass' *Stay the Hand of Vengeance: The Politics of War Crimes Tribunals* (Princeton, NJ: Princeton University Press, 2002). On the hunt for war criminals, see Eric Stover, Victor Peskin, and Alexa Koenig's *Hiding in Plain Sight: The Pursuit of War Criminals From Nuremberg to the War on Terror* (Oakland, CA: University of California Press, 2016). Also useful is John C. Watkins, Jr. and John Paul Weber's *War Crimes and War Crime Trials: From Leipzig to the ICC and Beyond: Cases, Materials and Comments* (Carolina Academic Press, 2005), which covers the period from the late 19th century to 2004. Less well-known trials are the subject of Kevin Jon Heller and Gerry Simpson's edited volume *The Hidden Histories of War Crimes Trials* (NY: Oxford University Press, 2013).

Particularly important for historians and jurists alike has been the work of Theodor Meron (b. 1930), a Polish-born American jurist who served as a judge in the International Criminal Courts for the former Yugoslavia and for Rwanda. The prolific Meron's most important works relevant to the modern world are *Human Rights in International Law: Legal and Policy Issues* (Oxford: Oxford University Press, 1986), *War Crimes Law Comes of Age: Essays* (London: Clarendon Press, 1999), *The Making of International Criminal Justice: The View From the Bench: Selected Speeches* (Oxford: Oxford University Press, 2011), and *Standing Up for Justice: The Challenges of Trying Atrocity Crimes* (NY: Oxford University Press, 2021). Also important is the work of another jurist and one-time judge on the

International Court of Justice, Richard Baxter (1921–80). See *Humanizing the Laws of War: Selected Writings of Richard Baxter*, edited by Detlev Vagts, Theodor Meron, Stephen M. Schwebel, and Charles Keever (NY: Oxford University Press, 2013). Also see the writings of the Italian jurist Antonio Cassese, particularly his *International Criminal Law* (Oxford: Oxford University Press, 2005).

## The 19th century

The best introduction to the life and work of Francis J. Lieber and the influence of his code is Jon Fabian Witt's *Lincoln's Code: The Laws of War in American History* (NY: Free Press, 2013). For an assessment of the extent to which the Union Army observed the rules of war, see D.H. Dilbeck's *A More Civil War: How the Union Waged a Just War* (Chapel Hill, NC: The University of North Carolina Press, 2016). Shai Dromi's *Above the Fray: The Red Cross and the Making of the Humanitarian NGO Sector* (Chicago, IL: University of Chicago Press, 2020) provides a good introduction to the history and impact of the International Committee of the Red Cross. A concise introduction to the history of military commissions (in addition to Witt's *Lincoln's Code*) is found in Jody Prescott's "Military Commissions, Past and Future," *Military Review*, March-April 2003: pp. 42–51 and Peter Maguire's *Law and War: An American Story* (New York: Columbia University Press, 2002). For the evolution of the military commission in the United States after September 11, see Josh Bravin's *The Terror Courts: Rough Justice at Guantanamo Bay* (New Haven, CT: Yale University Press, 2013).

## Colonial wars

Scholarship on war crimes and the laws of war have tended to marginalize or ignore the colonial wars of the 19th and early 20th centuries. An influential first-hand account from the perspective of the colonizer is Charles Callwell's 1899 book *Small Wars: Their Principles and Practice* (Lincoln, NE: University of Nebraska Press, 1996). An invaluable scholarly introduction is Dierk Walter's *Colonial Violence: European Empires and the Use of Force* (NY: Oxford University Press, 2017). Also important for global context is William Mulligan, Andreas Rose, and Dominik Geppert's (eds.) *The Wars Before the Great War: Conflict and International Politics Before the Outbreak of the First World War* (Cambridge: Cambridge University Press, 2015). For North America, Bruce Vandervort's *Indian Wars of Canada, Mexico and the United States, 1812–1900* (Abingdon, Oxfordshire: Routledge, 2005) is an excellent starting point. Important comparative studies are James O. Gump's *The Dust Rose Like Smoke: The Subjugation of the Zulu and the Sioux* (University of Nebraska Press, 2016) and Edward B. Westermann's *Hitler's Ostkrieg and the Indian Wars: Comparing Genocide and Conquest* (Norman, OK: University of Oklahoma Press, 2016).

Caroline Elkins makes violence the central theme of her history of the British Empire: *Legacy of Violence: A History of the British Empire* (NY: Knopf, 2022). A good introduction to the vast literature on colonial wars in Africa is Bruce Vandervort's *Wars of Imperial Conquest in Africa, 1830–1914* (Bloomington, IN: Indiana University Press, 2009). For Germany, Shelley Baranowski's *Nazi Empire: German Colonialism and Imperialism From Bismarck to Hitler* (NY: Cambridge University Press, 2010) connects the 19th and 20th centuries without overdetermining the connections between the genocide of the Herero and Nama and the genocide of the Jews. For more context on German Southwest Africa, see Jürgen Zimmerer's *German Rule, African Subjects: State Aspirations and the Reality of Power in Colonial Namibia* (NY: Berghahn Books, 2021). For Italy's invasion of Ethiopia, see Bruce G. Strang's *Collision of Empires: Italy's Invasion of Ethiopia and Its International Impact* (Abingdon, Oxfordshire: Routledge, 2013). Also see John Gooch's "Re-conquest and Suppression: Fascist Italy's Pacification of Libya and Ethiopia, 1922–39," *The Journal of Strategic Studies*, vol. 28, no. 6, 2005: pp. 1005–1032.

The best current study of Imperial Russia's conquest of Central Asia is Alexander Morrison's *The Russian Conquest of Central Asia: A Study in Imperial Expansion, 1814–1914* (Cambridge: Cambridge University Press, 2021). On the Dutch in Indonesia, see Bart Luttikhuis and A. Dirk Moses' (eds.) *Colonial Counterinsurgency and Mass Violence: The Dutch Empire in Indonesia* (Abingdon, Oxfordshire: Routledge, 2014). For Japan, see the contributions to Ramon H. Myers and Mark R. Peattie's *The Japanese Colonial Empire, 1895–1945* (Princeton, NJ: Princeton University Press, 1987), Seiji Shirane's *Imperial Gateway: Colonial Taiwan and Japan's Expansion in South China and Southeast Asia, 1895–1945* (Ithaca, NY: Cornell University Press, 2022) and Jun Uchida's *Brokers of Empire: Japanese Settler Colonialism in Korea, 1876–1945* (Cambridge, MA: Harvard University Asia Center, 2014). Useful introductions to informal imperialism in China are Stephen Platt's *Imperial Twilight: The Opium War and the End of China's Last Golden Age* (NY: Vintage, 2019) and David Silbey's *The Boxer Rebellion and the Great Game in China: A History* (NY: Hill and Wang, 2013). Emmanuel Kreike's pathbreaking *Scorched Earth: Environmental Warfare as a Crime Against Humanity and Nature* (Princeton, NJ: Princeton University Press, 2021) deals extensively with colonial wars.

## World War I and its aftermath

On war crimes and World War I, see John Horne and Alan Kramer's *German Atrocities, 1914: A History of Denial* (New Haven, CT: Yale University Press, 2001). Also important is Isabel Hull's *A Scrap of Paper: Breaking and Making International Law During the Great War* (Ithaca, NY: Cornell University Press, 2019). The scholarly literature on the Armenian genocide is extensive. Important recent assessments are Taner Akçam's *A Shameful Act:*

*The Armenian Genocide and the Question of Turkish Responsibility* (NY: Henry Holt and Company, 2007), Raymond Kevorkian's *The Armenian Genocide: A Complete History* (London: I.B. Tauris, 2011), and Ronald Gregor Suny's *They Can Live in the Desert but Nowhere Else: A History of the Armenian Genocide* (Princeton, NJ: Princeton University Press, 2015). Also important in this context is Benny Morris and Ze'evi Dror's *The Thirty-Year Genocide: Turkey's Destruction of Its Christian Minorities, 1894–1924* (Cambridge, MA: Harvard University Press, 2019). Robert Gerwarth's *The Vanquished: Why the First World War Failed to End* (NY: Farrar, Straus and Giroux, 2016) is among a number of recent works that challenge the conventional chronologies of both world wars. The abortive attempt to try the exiled former German Kaiser is the subject of William Schabas' *The Trial of the Kaiser* (NY: Oxford University Press, 2018). Alan Kramer's "The First Wave of International War Crimes Trials: Istanbul and Leipzig," *European Review*, vol. 14, no. 4, 2006: pp. 441–455 is a useful summary of the Leipzig trials in comparison with trials of suspected Turkish war criminals. On the League of Nations, Mark Mazower's *Governing the World: The History of an Idea, 1815 to the Present* (NY: Penguin Books, 2013) provides context. On the United States and the League, see Cooper and John Milton's *Breaking the Heart of the World: Woodrow Wilson and the Fight for the League of Nations* (Cambridge: Cambridge University Press, 2010). An important reevaluation of the League vis-à-vis the world's empires is Susan Pedersen's *The Guardians: The League of Nations and the Crisis of Empire* (NY: Oxford University Press, 2017). The much-maligned Kellogg-Briand Pact of 1928 is defended in Oona Hathaway and Scott Shapiro's *The Internationalists: How a Radical Plan to Outlaw War Remade the World* (NY: Simon & Schuster, 2017).

## World War II and postwar trials

The scholarly literature on World War II is, of course, vast and growing. An important recent global history is Richard Overy's *Blood and Ruins: The Last Imperial War, 1931–1945* (NY: Viking, 2022). Regarding war crimes, Germany and Imperial Japan have been the focus of most research and writing. Baranowski's *Nazi Empire* is a good place to start. For the crimes of the regular German army (Wehrmacht), see Omer Bartov, *Germany's War and the Holocaust: Disputed Histories* (Ithaca, NY: Cornell University Press, 2013). A useful introduction to the historiography of the Holocaust is Dan Stone's edited collection *The Historiography of the Holocaust* (London: Palgrave Macmillan, 2004) and Tom Lawson's *Debates on the Holocaust* (Manchester: Manchester University Press, 2010). Important recent surveys of the Holocaust are Doris L. Bergen's *The Holocaust: A Concise History* (London: Rowman & Littlefield, 2009) and Norman Goda's *The Holocaust: Europe, the World, and the Jews, 1918–1945* (Abingdon, Oxfordshire: Routledge, 2022). István Deák's *Europe on Trial: The Story of Collaboration,*

*Resistance, and Retribution During World War II* (Abingdon, Oxfordshire: Routledge, 2013) provides a good introduction to the vexing problem of collaboration. For Japan, start with Yuki Tanaka's *Hidden Horrors: Japanese War Crimes in World War II* (Boulder, CO: Westview, 1996).

For the planning of the post-World War II trials in Europe, see Arieh J. Kochavi's *Prelude to Nuremberg: Allied War Crimes Policy and the Question of Punishment* (University of North Carolina Press, 1998), Telford D. Taylor's *The Anatomy of the Nuremberg Trials: A Personal Memoir* (NY: Knopf, 1992), Bradley D. Smith's *The American Road to Nuremberg: The Documentary Record, 1944–1945* (Stanford, CA: University of California Press, 1982), and Francine Hirsch's *Soviet Judgment at Nuremberg: A New History of International Military Tribunal After World War II* (NY: Oxford University Press, 2020). On the history of the United National War Crimes Commission, see Dan Plesch's *Human Rights After Hitler: The Lost History of Prosecuting Axis War Crimes* (Washington, DC: Georgetown University Press, 2017). Patricia Heberer and Jürgen Matthäus' edited volume *Atrocities on Trial: Historical Perspectives on the Politics of Prosecuting War Crimes* (Lincoln, NE: University of Nebraska Press, 2008) provides essential context, going back to the post-World War I Leipzig trials. For the IMT, Taylor's memoir and Hirsch's history of the Soviet contribution are essential secondary sources. Also useful is Leon Goldensohn's *The Nuremberg Interviews: An American Psychiatrist's Conversations With the Defendants and Witnesses* (NY: Vintage Books, 2005). On the fate of the convicted men in the context of the Cold War, see Norman Goda's *Tales from Spandau: Nazi War Criminals and the Cold War* (Cambridge: Cambridge University Press, 2006).

The NMT has received close attention from historians in recent years. The two best overviews are Kim Priemel and Alexa Stiller's (eds.) *Unearthing the Subsequent Nuremberg Trials: Transitional Justice, Trial Narratives, and Historiography* (Providence, RI: Berghahn Books, 2012) and Kevin Jon Heller's *The Nuremberg Military Tribunal and the Origins of International Criminal Law* (NY: Oxford University Press, 2011). Important studies of individual cases are Hilary Earl's *The Nuremberg SS-Einsatzgruppen Trial, 1945–1958: Atrocity, Law, and History* (Cambridge: Cambridge University Press, 2010) and Valerie Hebert's *Hitler's Generals on Trial: The Last War Crimes Tribunal at Nuremberg* (Lawrence, KS: University of Kansas Press, 2010).

Historians have also looked closely at trials held by the US Army in occupied Germany. See Tomaz Jardim's *The Mauthausen Trial: American Military Justice in Germany* (Cambridge, MA: Harvard University Press, 2012), Joshua Greene's *Justice at Dachau: The Trials of an American Prosecutor* (NY: Broadway Books, 2003), and Steven P. Remy's *The Malmedy Massacre: The War Crimes Trial Controversy* (Cambridge, MA: Harvard University Press, 2017). The unmaking of the outcomes of war crimes trials is another subject only recently addressed by historians. In addition to Goda's *Tales from Spandau* and Remy's *The Malmedy Massacre*, see Norbert Frei's *Adenauer's Germany and the Nazi Past: The Politics of Amnesty and Integration* (New York: Columbia University Press, 2002), Kerstin von Lingen's *Kesselring's Last Battle: War Crimes Trials and Cold War Politics, 1945–1960* (Lawrence, KS: University Press of Kansas, 2009) and Robert Hutchinson's *After Nuremberg: American Clemency for Nazi War Criminals* (New Haven, CT: Yale University Press, 2022).

On trials in Asia, a good place to start is John Dower's *Embracing Defeat: Japan in the Wake of World War II* (New York: W.W. Norton & Co., 1999). A recent reassessment of the Tokyo IMT is found in Yuki Tanaka, Tim McCormack, and Gerry Simpson's (eds.) *Beyond Victor's Justice? The Tokyo War Crimes Revisited* (Leiden, the Netherlands: Martinus Nijhoff, 2011). On the Yamashita trial, see Allan A. Ryan's *Yamashita's Ghost: War Crimes, MacArthur's Justice, and Command Accountability* (Lawrence, KS: University Press of Kansas, 2012). For trials of Japanese war criminals elsewhere in Asia, see Sandra Wilson, Robert Cribb, Beatrice Trefalt, and Dean Aszkielowicz's *Japanese War Criminals: The Politics of Justice After the Second World War* (New York: Columbia University Press, 2017). Also important is Barak Kushner's *Men to Devils, Devils to Men: Japanese War Crimes and Chinese Justice* (Cambridge, MA: Harvard University Press, 2015) and Adam Wakeling's *Stern Justice: The Forgotten Story of Australia, Japan and the Pacific War Crimes Trials* (Penguin Random House Australia, 2019).

On national trials of war criminals and collaborators in Europe, a good starting point is István Deák, Jan Gross, and Tony Judt's (eds.) *The Politics of Retribution in Europe: World War II and Its Aftermath* (Princeton, NJ: Princeton University Press, 2000). More recent scholarship is presented in Vesna Drapac and Gareth Pritchard's *Resistance and Collaboration in Hitler's Europe* (London: Palgrave Macmillan, 2017) and Götz Aly's *Europe Against the Jews, 1880–1945* (NY: Metropolitan Books, 2020). On trials in postwar Hungary, see Ildikó Barna and Andrea Pető's *Political Justice in Budapest After World War II* (Budapest: Central European University Press, 2015). Gabriel Finder and Laura Jockusch's edited volume *Jewish Honor Courts: Revenge, Retribution, and Reconciliation in Europe and Israel After the Holocaust* (Detroit: Wayne State University Press, 2015) confronts the history and legacies of Jewish honor courts. Recent research has shed much light on trials of Germans and collaborators in Poland and the Soviet Union. On the former, see Gabriel Finder and Alexander V. Prusin's *Justice Behind the Iron Curtain: Nazis on Trial in Communist Poland* (University of Toronto Press, 2018). On the latter, see Alexander Prusin's "Fascist Criminals to the Gallows!": The Holocaust and Soviet War Crimes Trials, December 1945–February 1946, *Holocaust and Genocide Studies*, vol. 17, no. 1, 2003: pp. 1–30.

For Germany, an important recent overview of the memory of the Nazi past in the three postwar Germanys, including the history of war crimes trials, is Mary Fulbrook's *Reckonings: Legacies of Nazi Persecution and the Quest for Justice* (NY: Oxford University Press, 2018). Also valuable on the question of postwar justice is Annette Weinke's *Law, History, and*

*Justice: Debating German State Crimes in the Long Twentieth Century* (Providence, RI: Berghahn Books, 2018). For a survey of denazification, see Frederick Taylor's *Exorcising Hitler: The Occupation and Denazification of Germany* (London: Bloomsbury Press, 2011). Norman Naimark's *The Russians in Germany: A History of the Soviet Zone of Occupation, 1945–1949* (Cambridge, MA: The Belknap Press of Harvard University Press, 1995) remains the essential starting point for the Soviet zone. On trials in the Federal Republic, see Devin O. Pendas's *The Frankfurt Auschwitz Trial, 1963–1965: Genocide, History, and the Limits of the Law* (Cambridge: Cambridge University Press, 2010). The best account of the case of John Demjanjuk is Lawrence Douglas' *The Right Wrong Man: John Demjanjuk and the Last Great Nazi War Crimes Trial* (Princeton, NJ: Princeton University Press, 2018). For the Eichmann trial in Jerusalem, Hannah Arendt's *Eichmann in Jerusalem: A Report on the Banality of Evil* (NY: Penguin Classics, 2006) remains valuable, but should be read with Deborah Lipstadt's *The Eichmann Trial* (NY: Schocken, 2011). Two trials in France have attracted close attention from historians. One was the 1953 trial in Bordeaux of the surviving perpetrators of the 1944 massacre at Oradour-sur-Glane, analyzed by Sarah Farmer in *Martyred Village: Commemorating the 1944 Massacre at Oradour-sur-Glane* (Berkeley, CA: University of California Press, 2000). The other is the 1987 trial of Klaus Barbie. See Richard J. Golsan in *Justice in Lyon: Klaus Barbie and France's First Trial for Crimes Against Humanity* (Toronto: University of Toronto Press, 2022).

## The postwar world: Genocide and human rights

There is an enormous body of scholarship on the concept of genocide and its relevance to international law. The essential starting point is Raphael Lemkin's 1944 *Axis Rule in Occupied Europe: Laws of Occupation, Analysis of Government, Proposals for Redress* (Clark, NJ: The Lawbook Exchange, Ltd., 2005). Lemkin's work and legacy has also undergone a critical reevaluation in recent years. See the special issue of *The Journal of Genocide Research*, vol. 7, no. 4, December 2005. A critique of Lemkin and the entire concept of genocide is in A. Dirk Moses's *The Problems of Genocide: Permanent Security and the Language of Transgression* (Cambridge: Cambridge University Press, 2021). Important general histories of genocide are Ben Kiernan's *Blood and Soil: A World History of Genocide and Extermination From Sparta to Darfur* (New Haven, CT: Yale University Press, 2009), Norman Naimark's *Genocide: A World History* (NY: Oxford University Press, 2016), and Eric D. Weitz's *A Century of Genocide: Utopias of Race and Nation* (Princeton, NJ: Princeton University Press, 2015). On the linkages between imperialism, colonialism, and genocide, see A. Dirk Moses' *Empire, Colony, Genocide: Conquest, Occupation, and Subaltern Resistance in World History* (Providence, RI: Berghahn Books, 2009). On the relationship between the United States and postwar genocides, see

Samantha Power's *A Problem From Hell: America and the Age of Genocide* (NY: Basic Books, 2002). For an attempt to link climate change to genocide, see Alex Alvarez's *Unstable Ground: Climate Change, Conflict, and Genocide* (London: Rowman & Littlefield, 2021).

## The postwar world: Third world wars

The continuation of armed conflicts after the defeat of Nazi Germany and Imperial Japan in 1945, mainly in Asia, has attracted close attention from historians. Two essential recent books are Paul Thomas Chamberlin's *The Cold War's Killing Fields: Rethinking the Long Peace* (NY: Harper, 2018) and Ronald Spector's *A Continent Erupts: Decolonization, Civil War, and Massacre in Postwar Asia, 1945–1955* (New York: W.W. Norton & Co., 2022). Also useful are Michael Burleigh's *Small Wars, Faraway Places* (NY: Viking, 2013) and Christopher Bayly and Tim Harper's *Forgotten Wars: Freedom and Revolution in Southeast Asia* (Cambridge, MA: The Belknap Press of Harvard University Press, 2010). A superb history of the Cold War in the "Third World" is Odd Arne Westad's *The Global Cold War: Third World Interventions and the Making of Our Times* (Cambridge: Cambridge University Press, 2011).

The wars in the former Yugoslavia and the Rwandan genocide generated an enormous amount of commentary and analysis. On Yugoslavia in historical context, Misha Glenny's *The Balkans, 1804–2012: Nationalism, War and the Great Powers* (London: Granta Books, 2017) is the best place to start. Also invaluable is Tim Judah's *The Serbs: History, Myth and the Destruction of Yugoslavia* (New Haven, CT: Yale University Press, 1997). On Rwanda, start with the books of Gérard Prunier's *Africa's World War: Congo, the Rwandan Genocide, and the Making of a Continental Catastrophe* (NY: Oxford University Press, 2011) and *The Rwanda Crisis: History of a Genocide* (New York: Columbia University Press, 1997). Also valuable are Mahmood Mamdani's *When Victims Become Killers: Colonialism, Nativism, and the Genocide in Rwanda* (Princeton, NJ: Princeton University Press, 2002) and Philip Gourevitch's *We Wish to Inform You That Tomorrow We Will Be Killed With Our Families: Stories From Rwanda* (NY: Picador, 1999). On the ICTY, see Pierre Hazan's *Justice in a Time of War: The True Story Behind the International Criminal Tribunal for the Former Yugoslavia* (Texas A&M University Press, 2004). For the ICTR, see David Scheffer's *All the Missing Souls: A Personal History of the War Crimes Tribunals* (Princeton, NJ: Princeton University Press, 2011) and Thierry Cruvellier's *Court of Remorse: Inside the International Criminal Tribunal for Rwanda* (Madison, WI: University of Wisconsin Press, 2010).

On other instances of genocide and their aftermaths in Africa and Asia, see Gérard Prunier's *Darfur: The Ambiguous Genocide* (Ithaca, NY: Cornell University Press, 2007), Linus Nnabuike's *The International Criminal Court and Peace Processes: Côte d'Ivoire, Kenya and Uganda* (London: Palgrave

Macmillan, 2019), Oumar Ba's *States of Justice: The Politics of the International Criminal Court* (Cambridge: Cambridge University Press, 2022), and Richard Gaskins' *The Congo Trials in the International Criminal Court* (Cambridge: Cambridge University Press, 2022). For East Timor, see Ben Kiernan's *Genocide and Resistance in Southeast Asia: Documentation, Denial, and Justice in Cambodia and East Timor* (Abingdon, Oxfordshire: Routledge, 2007). There is a large literature on the Cambodian genocide. Ben Kiernan's *The Pol Pot Regime: Race, Power, and Genocide in Cambodia Under the Khmer Rouge, 1975–79* (New Haven, CT: Yale University Press, 2008) and the collection of essays and sources edited by Paul R. Bartrop's *Cambodian Genocide: The Essential Reference Guide* (Santa Barbara, CA: ABC-CLIO, 2022).

The origins and early history of the ICC are covered in Scheffer's *All the Lost Souls*, William Schabas' *An Introduction to the International Criminal Court* (Cambridge: Cambridge University Press, 2020), and David Bosco's *Rough Justice: The International Criminal Court in a World of Power Politics* (NY: Oxford University Press, 2014). A valuable collection of essays, including ICC officials, is Viviane E. Dittrich and Alexander Heinze's (eds.) *The Past, Present and Future of the International Criminal Court* (Florence: Torkel Opsahl Academic Epublisher, 2021). An assessment of the controversy surrounding the ICC and African states is in Kamari Maxine Clarke's *Affective Justice: The International Criminal Court and the Pan-Africanist Pushback* (Durham, NC: Duke University Press, 2019). Also see the books of Gaskins, Malu, and Ba cited earlier. On the prosecution of sexual crimes, see Rosemary Grey's *Prosecuting Sexual and Gender-Based Crimes at the International Criminal Court* (Cambridge: Cambridge University Press, 2020).

The postwar evolution of the laws of war and international law is connected closely to human rights politics, law, and activism. For historical context, see Micheline R. Ishay's *The History of Human Rights: From Ancient Times to the Globalization Era* (Berkeley, CA: University of California Press, 2008), Lynn Hunt's *Inventing Human Rights: A History* (New York: W.W. Norton & Co., 2008), and Eric D. Weitz's *A World Divided: The Global Struggle for Human Rights in the Age of Nation-States* (Princeton, NJ: Princeton University Press, 2019). For the postwar period, see Samuel Moyn's *The Last Utopia: Human Rights in History* (Cambridge, MA: The Belknap Press of Harvard University Press, 2010), *Human Rights and the Uses of History* (London: Verso Books, 2014), and *Christian Human Rights* (Philadelphia, PA: University of Pennsylvania Press, 2015). For the history of NGOs, see Thomas Davies' *NGOs: A New History of Transnational Civil Society* (NY: Oxford University Press, 2014). For a close look at operations of Amnesty International, see Stephen Hopgood's *Keepers of the Flame: Understanding Amnesty International* (Ithaca, NY: Cornell University Press, 2006). On humanitarian interventions, see Norbert Frei, Daniel Stahl, and Annette Weinke's (eds.) *Human Rights and Humanitarian*

*Intervention: Legitimizing the Use of Force Since the 1970s* (Göttingen: Wallstein Verlag GmbH, 2017).

## Women and war crimes

Important introductions to the problems of war, gender, and sexual crimes are Carol Cohn's (ed.) *Women and Wars: Contested Histories, Uncertain Futures* (Cambridge: Polity, 2012), Victoria Sanford, Katarina Stefatos, Cecilia M. Salvi's (eds.) *Gender Violence in Peace and War: States of Complicity* (New Brunswick, NJ: Rutgers University Press, 2016), Elissa Bemporad and Joyce W. Warren's (eds.) *Women and Genocide: Survivors, Victims, Perpetrators* (Bloomington, IN: Indiana University Press, 2018), and Dagmar Herzog's (ed.) *Brutality and Desire: War and Sexuality in Europe's Twentieth Century* (London: Palgrave Macmillan, 2008). Also see the work of Grey, cited earlier, along with Chiseche Salome Mibenge's *Sex and International Tribunals: The Erasure of Gender From the War Narrative* (Philadelphia, PA: University of Pennsylvania Press, 2013) and Sara Sharratt's *Gender, Shame and Sexual Violence: The Voices of Witnesses and Court Members at War Crimes Tribunals* (Abingdon, Oxfordshire: Routledge, 2011). There are very few studies of women as perpetrators. In addition to the relevant contributions to Bemporad and Warren's volume, two valuable studies are Wendy Lower's *Hitler's Furies: German Women in the Nazi Killing Fields* (Boston, MA: Mariner Books, 2013) and Izabela Steflja and Jessica Trisko Darden's *Women as War Criminals: Gender, Agency, and Justice* (Stanford, CA: Stanford University Press, 2020). Also see the material collected by the NGO African Rights in *Rwanda: Not So Innocent: When Women Become Killers* (London: African Rights, 1995).

## Private military companies, drones, cyberwar, and ecocide

On the history of mercenaries, see William Urban's *Medieval Mercenaries: The Business of War* (Barnsley: Frontline Books, 2015), Janice E. Thomson's *Mercenaries, Pirates, and Sovereigns* (Princeton, NJ: Princeton University Press, 1996), Sarah Percy's *Mercenaries: The History of a Norm in International Relations* (NY: Oxford University Press, 2007), and Tony Geraghty's *Soldiers of Fortune: A History of the Mercenary in Modern Warfare* (Pegasus Books, 2009). For an important case study of a proto private military company and alleged war crimes committed by its members, see Phil Miller's *Keenie Meenie: The British Mercenaries Who Got Away With War Crimes* (London: Pluto Press, 2020). There is now a substantial body of writing on private military companies. A good place to start is Simon Chesterman and Chia Lehnardt's edited volume *From Mercenaries to Market: The Rise and Regulation of Private Military Companies* (Oxford: Oxford University Press, 2007). Particularly important is the work of P.W. Singer's *Corporate Warriors: The Rise of the Privatized Military Industry* (Ithaca,

NY: Cornell University Press, 2007) and Sean McFate's *The Modern Mercenary: Private Armies and What They Mean for World Order* (NY: Oxford University Press, 2017). A compact, more up-to-date overview is provided by McFate in *Mercenaries and War: Understanding Private Armies Today* (Washington, DC: National Defense University Press, 2019). On Blackwater, see Jeremy Scahill's *Blackwater: The Rise of the World's Most Powerful Mercenary Army* (NY: Bold Type Books, 2007).

On the issue of drones, useful basic information is found in Gary Solis' *The Law of Armed Conflict* (cited earlier). Also see P.W. Singer's *Wired for War: The Robotics Revolution and Conflict in the 21st Century* (NY: Penguin Books, 2009), Benjamin Wittes and Gabriella Blum's *The Future of Violence: Robots and Germs, Hackers and Drones* (NY: Basic Books, 2015), and Peter L. Bergen and Daniel Rothenberg's (eds.) *Drone Wars: Transforming Conflict, Law, and Policy* (NY: Cambridge University Press, 2015). A compact, highly critical assessment of the use of drones in war is Grégoire Chamayou's *Drone Theory* (NY: Penguin, 2015). On cyberwar, see Ahmed Al-Rawi's *Cyberwar in the Middle East* (New Brunswick, NJ: Rutgers University Press, 2021), John Arquilla's *Bitskrieg: The New Challenge of Cyberwarfare* (Cambridge: Polity, 2021), Joel Brenner's *America the Vulnerable: Inside the New Threat Matrix of Digital Espionage, Crime, and Warfare* (NY: Penguin, 2011), Fred Kaplan's *Dark Territory: The Secret History of Cyber War* (NY: Simon and Schuster, 2017), Andy Greenberg's *Sandworm: A New Era of Cyberwar and the Hunt for the Kremlin's Most Dangerous Hackers* (NY: Anchor, 2020), and P.W. Singer's *Likewar: The Weaponization of Social Media* (Boston, MA: Mariner Books, 2019).

On environmental warfare and ecocide, Emmanuel Kreike's *Scorched Earth* (cited earlier) is of singular importance. A few scholars of the Holocaust have started to investigate the environmental dimensions of the genocide. See the forum in *The Journal of Genocide Research*, vol. 24, no. 3, 2022. Also see the special issue of *Journal of Genocide Research* on the genocide-ecocide nexus (vol. 23, no. 2, 2021). On ecocide and international law, see Polly Higgins' *Eradicating Ecocide: Laws and Governance to Prevent the Destruction of Our Planet* (London: Shepheard-Walwyn Ltd., 2010), Pamela McElwee's "The Origins of Ecocide: Revisiting the Ho Chi Minh Trail in the Vietnam War," *Arcadia*, no. 20, spring 2020, Lauren J. Eichler's "Ecocide Is Genocide: Decolonizing the Definition of Genocide," *Genocide Studies and Prevention: An International Journal*, vol. 14, no. 2, 2020: pp. 104–121, and Anya Gauger *et al.'s The Ecocide Project: "Ecocide Is the missing 5th Crime Against Peace"* (London: Human Rights Consortium, 2012).

## Memory, transitional justice, and the investigative turn

Martha Minow's *Between Vengeance and Forgiveness: Facing History After Genocide and Mass Violence* (Boston: Beacon Press, 1999) is a good place to start to consider problems of memory after mass violence. A provocative counterpoint is David Rieff's *In Praise of Forgetting: Historical Memory and Its Ironies* (New Haven, CT: Yale University Press, 2016). For the paradigmatic case of Germany, essential sources on the politics of memory are Frei's *Adenauer's Germany* and Fulbrook's *Reckonings*, cited earlier, and Jeffrey Herf's *Divided Memory: The Nazi Past in the Two Germanys* (Cambridge, MA: Harvard University Press, 1997), Robert G. Moeller's *War Stories: The Search for a Usable Past in the Federal Republic of Germany* (Berkeley, CA: University of California Press, 2001), Susan Neiman's *Learning From the Germans: Race and the Memory of Evil* (NY: Farrar, Straus and Giroux, 2019), Omer Bartov's *Germany's War and the Holocaust: Disputed Histories* (Ithaca, NY: Cornell University Press, 2013), and Judith M. Hughes' *The Perversion of Holocaust Memory: Writing and Rewriting the Past After 1989* (London: Bloomsbury Academic, 2022). On the controversy in Poland over the question of Polish collaboration in the Holocaust, see Anna Bikont's *The Crime and the Silence: Confronting the Massacre of Jews in Wartime Jedwabne* (NY: Farrar, Straus and Giroux, 2015). A good introduction to the memory of the Armenian genocide is Thomas de Waal's *Great Catastrophe: Armenians and Turks in the Shadow of Genocide* (NY: Oxford University Press, 2015). On the memory of "comfort women," see Sarah C. Soh's *The Comfort Women: Sexual Violence and Postcolonial Memory in Korea and Japan* (Chicago, IL: University of Chicago Press, 2009). On memory in post-genocide Cambodia, see Craig Etcheson's *After the Killing Fields: Lessons From the Cambodian Genocide* (Lubbock, TX: Texas Tech University Press, 2005).

For recent assessments of transitional justice, see Hakeem O. Yusuf and Hugo van der Merwe's (eds.) *Transitional Justice: Theories, Mechanisms and Debates* (Abingdon, Oxfordshire: Routledge, 2021), Olivera Simić's (ed.) *An Introduction to Transitional Justice* (Abingdon, Oxfordshire: Routledge, 2021), and Mia Kent and Melissa Demian's (eds.) *Transitional Justice in Law, History and Anthropology* (Abingdon, Oxfordshire: Routledge, 2019). For an introduction to truth commissions, see Onur Bakiner's *Truth Commissions: Memory, Power, and Legitimacy* (Philadelphia, PA: University of Pennsylvania Press, 2016), Alison Bisset's *Truth Commissions and Criminal* Courts (Cambridge: Cambridge University Press, 2012), and Priscilla B. Hayner's *Unspeakable Truths: Transitional Justice and the Challenge of Truth Commissions* (Abingdon, Oxfordshire: Routledge, 2010). A critical recent assessment of the Gacaca court system in Rwanda is found in Anuradha Chakravarty's *Investing in Authoritarian Rule: Punishment and Patronage in Rwanda's Gacaca Courts for Genocide Crimes* (Cambridge: Cambridge University Press, 2015). Important recent studies of the return of stolen cultural artifacts are Jeremy Sarkin-Hughes' *Colonial Genocide and Reparations Claims in the 21st Century: The Socio-legal Context of Claims Under International Law by the Herero against Germany for Genocide in Namibia, 1904–1908* (Westport, CT: Praeger Security International, 2009)

Dan Hicks' *The Brutish Museums: The Benin Bronzes, Colonial Violence and Cultural Restitution* (London: Pluto, 2020), and Barnaby Phillips' *Loot: Britain and the Benin Bronzes* (London: Oneworld Publications, 2021).

On the "investigative turn" in war crimes and crimes against humanity investigations, see Alexa Koenig, Emma Irving, Yvonne McDermott, and Daragh Murray's "New Technologies and the Investigation of International Crimes," *Journal of International Criminal Justice*, vol. 19, 2021: pp. 1–7 and Michelle Burgis-Kasthala's "Entrepreneurial Justice: Syria, the Commission for International Justice and Accountability and the Renewal of International Criminal Justice," *The European Journal of International Law*, vol. 30, no. 4, 2020: pp. 1165–1185. Also useful are the contributions to John Lannon and Edward F. Halpin's (eds.) *Human Rights and Information and Communications Technologies: Trends and Consequences of Use* (Hershey, PA: Information Science Reference, 2013). For an assessment of the Commission for International Justice and Accountability (CIJA), see Melinda Rankin's "The Future of International Criminal Evidence in New Wars? The Evolution of the Commission for International Justice and Accountability (CIJA)," *Journal of Genocide Research*, vol. 20, no. 3: pp. 392–411. But also see the objections raised by Alexa Koenig, Yvonne McDermott, and Daragh Murray in "Open Source Information's Blind Spot: Human and Machine Bias in International Criminal Investigations," in *Journal of International Criminal Justice*, vol. 19, 2021: pp. 85–105 and Sarah Zarmsky's "Why Seeing Should Not Always Be Believing: Considerations Regarding the Use of Digital Reconstruction Technology in International Law," *Journal of International Criminal Justice*, vol. 19, 2021: pp. 213–225. For an introduction to Bellingcat written by its founder, see Eliot Higgins' *We Are Bellingcat: Global Crime, Online Sleuths, and the Bold Future of News* (London: Bloomsbury, 2021).

# Bibliography

www.amnesty.org (Amnesty International)
www.avalon.law.yale.edu (The Avalon Project: Documents in Law, History and Diplomacy)
www.bellingcat.com
www.cijaonline.org (Commission for International Justice and Accountability)
www.ecocidelaw.com
www.genocidewatch.com
www.hrw.org (Human Rights Watch)
www.icc-cpi.int (International Criminal Court)
www.icrc.org (International Committee of the Red Cross)
https://imtfe.law.virginia.edu/ (The International Military Tribunal for the Far East Digital Collection)
www.msf.org (Medecins sans Frontiers/Doctors Without Borders)
www.un.org (United Nations)
www.ushmm.org (United States Holocaust Memorial Museum)
www.unitad.un.org/ (Investigative Team to Promote Accountability for Crimes Committed by Da'esh/ISIL [UNITAD])
www.sierraleonetrc.org/ (Sierra Leone Truth and Reconciliation Commission)

Akçam, Taner, *A Shameful Act: The Armenian Genocide and the Question of Turkish Responsibility*, New York: Henry Holt and Company, 2007.
African Rights, *Rwanda: Not So Innocent: When Women Become Killers*, London: African Rights, 1995.
Ageli, Stella, 'Private Military Companies (PMCs) and International Criminal Law: Are PMCs the New Perpetrators of International Crimes?' *Amsterdam Law Forum*, vol. 8, no. 1, 2016: 28–47.
Alexander, Edward, *A Crime of Vengeance: An Armenian Struggle for Justice*, New York: Free Press, 1991.
Al-Rawi, Ahmed, *Cyberwar in the Middle East*, New Brunswick, NJ: Rutgers University Press, 2021.
Alvarez, Alex, *Unstable Ground: Climate Change, Conflict, and Genocide*, London: Rowman & Littlefield, 2021.
Alvarez, Alex, Hirsch, Herb, Markusen, Eric, and Totten, Samuel, eds., 'Special Issue on Darfur,' *Genocide Studies and Prevention*, vol. 1, no. 1, 2006.
Aly, Götz, *Europe Against the Jews, 1880–1945*, New York: Metropolitan Books, 2020.

Angell, Norman, *The Great Illusion*, New York: Cosimo Classics, 2010 (originally published in 1910).
Arendt, Hannah, *Eichmann in Jerusalem: A Report on the Banality of Evil*, New York: Penguin Classics, 2006.
Arquilla, John, *Bitskrieg: The New Challenge of Cyberwarfare*, Cambridge: Polity, 2021.
Bakiner, Onur, *Truth Commissions: Memory, Power, and Legitimacy*, Philadelphia, PA: University of Pennsylvania Press, 2016.
Baranowski, Shelley, *Nazi Empire: German Colonialism and Imperialism From Bismarck to Hitler*, Cambridge: Cambridge University Press, 2010.
Barkan, Elazar, *The Guilt of Nations – Restitution and Negotiating Historical Injustice*, New York: Norton, 2000.
Bartov, Omer, *Germany's War and the Holocaust: Disputed Histories*, Ithaca, NY: Cornell University Press, 2013.
Bass, Gary, *Stay the Hand of Vengeance: The Politics of War Crimes Tribunals*, Princeton, NJ: Princeton University Press, 2001.
Battini, M., *The Missing Italian Nuremberg: Cultural Amnesia and Postwar Politics*, London: Palgrave Macmillan, 2007.
Baxter, Richard, *Humanizing the Laws of War: Selected Writings of Richard Baxter*, New York: Oxford University Press, 2013.
Bergen, Doris L., *The Holocaust: A Concise History*, London: Rowman & Littlefield, 2009.
Bergen, Peter L., and Rothenberg, Daniel, eds., *Drone Wars: Transforming Conflict, Law, and Policy*, New York: Cambridge University Press, 2015.
Bisset, Alison, *Truth Commissions and Criminal Courts*, Cambridge: Cambridge University Press, 2012.
Bloxham, Donald, *The Great Game of Genocide: Imperialism, Nationalism, and the Destruction of the Ottoman Armenians*, New York: Oxford University Press, 2007.
Boister, Neil, and Cryer, Robert, *The Tokyo International Military Tribunal: A Reappraisal*, New York: Oxford University Press, 2008.
Borch, Fred L., *Military Trials of War Criminals in the Netherlands East Indies 1946–1949*, New York: Oxford University Press, 2017.
Brahm, Eric, 'Uncovering the Truth: Examining Truth Commission Success and Impact,' *International Studies Perspectives*, vol. 8, no. 1, 2007: 16–35.
Bravin, Josh, *The Terror Courts: Rough Justice at Guantanamo Bay*, New Haven, CT: Yale University Press, 2013.
Bryant, Michael, *A World History of War Crimes: From Antiquity to the Present*, London: Bloomsbury Academic, 2021.
Burgis-Kasthala, Michelle, 'Entrepreneurial Justice: Syria, the Commission for International Justice and Accountability and the Renewal of International Criminal Justice,' *The European Journal of International Law*, vol. 30, no. 4, 2020: 1165–1185.
Burleigh, Michael, *Small Wars, Faraway Places*, New York: Viking, 2013.
Callwell, Charles, *Small Wars: Their Principles and Practice*, Lincoln, NE: University of Nebraska Press, 1899/1996.
Chakravarty, Anuradha, *Investing in Authoritarian Rule: Punishment and Patronage in Rwanda's Gacaca Courts for Genocide Crimes*, Cambridge: Cambridge University Press, 2015.

Chamberlin, Paul Thomas, *The Cold War's Killing Fields: Rethinking the Long Peace*, New York: Harper, 2018.

Chinkin, Christine M., 'Women's International Tribunal on Japanese Military Sexual Slavery,' *The American Journal of International Law*, vol. 95, no. 2, 2001: 335–331.

Clarke, Kamari Maxine, *Affective Justice: The International Criminal Court and the Pan-Africanist Pushback*, Durham, NC: Duke University Press, 2019.

Clarke, Richard A., and Knake, Robert K., *The Fifth Domain: Defending Our Country, Our Companies, and Ourselves in the Age of Cyber Threats*, New York: Penguin Press, 2019.

Cooper, John Milton, *Breaking the Heart of the World: Woodrow Wilson and the Fight for the League of Nations*, Cambridge: Cambridge University Press, 2010.

Crowe, David M., *War Crimes, Genocide, and Justice*, London: Palgrave Macmillan, 2014.

Cruvellier, Thierry, *Court of Remorse: Inside the International Criminal Tribunal for Rwanda*, Madison, WI: University of Wisconsin Press, 2010.

Deak, Istvan, *Europe on Trial: The Story of Collaboration, Resistance, and Retribution During World War II*, Abingdon, Oxfordshire: Routledge, 2013.

Deak, Istvan, Gross, Jan, and Judt, Tony, eds., *The Politics of Retribution in Europe: World War II and Its Aftermath*, Princeton, NJ: Princeton University Press, 2000.

Derderian, Katherine, 'Common Fate, Different Experience: Gender-Specific Aspects of the Armenian Genocide, 1915–1917,' *Holocaust and Genocide Studies*, vol. 19, no. 1, Spring 2005: 1–25.

Dilbeck, D. H., *A More Civil War: How the Union Waged a Just War*, Chapel Hill, NC: The University of North Carolina Press, 2016.

Dojcinovic, Predrag, ed., *Propaganda, War Crimes Trials and International Law: From Speakers' Corner to War Crimes*, Abingdon, Oxfordshire: Routledge, 2012.

Douglas, Lawrence, *The Right Wrong Man: John Demjanjuk and the Last Great Nazi War Crimes Trial*, Princeton, NJ: Princeton University Press, 2018.

Dower, John, *Embracing Defeat: Japan in the Wake of World War II*, New York: W.W. Norton & Co., 1999.

Dower, John, *The Violent American Century: War and Terror Since World War II*, Chicago, IL: Haymarket Books, 2017.

Drapac, Vesna, and Pritchard, Gareth, *Resistance and Collaboration in Hitler's Europe*, London: Palgrave Macmillan, 2017.

Droege, Cordula, 'Get Off My Cloud: Cyber Warfare, International Humanitarian Law, and the Protection of Civilians,' *International Review of the Red Cross*, vol. 94, no. 886, 2012: 533–578.

Dromi, Shai, *Above the Fray: The Red Cross and the Making of the Humanitarian NGO Sector*, Chicago, IL: University of Chicago Press, 2020.

Dubberley, Sam, Koenig, Alexa, and Murray, Daragh, eds., *Digital Witness: Using Open Source Information for Human Rights Investigation, Documentation, and Accountability*, Oxford: Oxford University Press, 2020.

Earl, Hilary, *The Nuremberg SS-Einsatzgruppen Trial, 1945–1958: Atrocity, Law, and History*, Cambridge: Cambridge University Press, 2010.

Eichler, Lauren J., 'Ecocide Is Genocide: Decolonizing the Definition of Genocide,' *Genocide Studies and Prevention: An International Journal*, vol. 14, no. 2, 2020: 104–121.

Elkins, Caroline, *Imperial Reckoning: The Untold Story of Britain's Gulag in Kenya*, New York: Holt Paperbacks, 2005.

Elkins, Caroline, *Legacy of Violence: A History of the British Empire*, New York: Knopf, 2022.

Farmer, Sarah, *Martyred Village: Commemorating the 1944 Massacre at Oradour-sur-Glane*, Berkeley, CA: University of California Press, 2000.

Ferstman, C., and Goetz, Mariana, eds., *Reparations for Victims of Genocide, War Crimes and Crimes Against Humanity: Systems in Place and Systems in the Making*, Leiden: Brill, 2020.

Finder, Gabriel N., and Jokusch, Laura, eds., *Jewish Honor Courts: Revenge, Retribution, and Reconciliation in Europe and Israel After the Holocaust*, Detroit, MI: Wayne State University Press, 2015.

Finder, Gabriel N., and Prusin, Alexander V., *Justice Behind the Iron Curtain: Nazis on Trial in Communist Poland*, Toronto: University of Toronto Press, 2018.

Finkelman, Paul, 'Francis Lieber and the Modern Law of War,' *University of Chicago Law Review*, vol. 80, no. 4, Fall 2013: 2071–2132.

Frei, Norbert, *Adenauer's Germany and the Nazi Past: The Politics of Amnesty and Integration*, New York: Columbia University Press, 2002.

Frei, Norbert, Stahl, Daniel, and Weinke, Annette, eds., *Human Rights and Humanitarian Intervention: Legitimizing the Use of Force since the 1970s*, Göttingen: Wallstein Verlag GmbH, 2017.

Fulbrook, Mary, *Reckonings: Legacies of Nazi Persecution and the Quest for Justice*, New York: Oxford University Press, 2018.

Geraghty, Mark Anthony, 'Gacaca, Genocide, Genocide Ideology: The Violent Aftermaths of Transitional Justice in the New Rwanda,' *Comparative Studies in Society and History*, vol. 62, no. 3, 2020: 588–618.

Geraghty, Tony, *Soldiers of Fortune: A History of the Mercenary in Modern Warfare*, New York, NY: Pegasus Books, 2009.

Gauger, Anya, et al., *The Ecocide Project: 'Ecocide Is the Missing 5th Crime Against Peace'*, London: Human Rights Consortium, 2012.

Gaunt, David, *Massacres, Resistance, Protectors: Muslim-Christian Relations in Eastern Anatolia During World War I*, Piscataway, NJ: Gorgias Press, 2006.

Gerwarth, Robert, *The Vanquished: Why the First World War Failed to End*, New York: Farrar, Straus and Giroux, 2016.

Glenny, Misha, *The Balkans, 1804–2012: Nationalism, War and the Great Powers*, London: Granta Books, 2017.

Goda, Norman J. W., *Tales From Spandau: Nazi War Criminals and the Cold War*, Cambridge: Cambridge University Press, 2006.

Goda, Norman J. W., *The Holocaust: Europe, the World, and the Jews, 1918–1945*, Abingdon, Oxfordshire: Routledge, 2022.

Goldensohn, Leon, *The Nuremberg Interviews: An American Psychiatrist's Conversations With the Defendants and Witnesses*, New York: Vintage Books, 2005.

Golsan, Richard J., *Justice in Lyon: Klaus Barbie and France's First Trial for Crimes Against Humanity*, Toronto: University of Toronto Press, 2022.

Gooch, John, 'Re-conquest and Suppression: Fascist Italy's Pacification of Libya and Ethiopia, 1922–39,' *The Journal of Strategic Studies*, vol. 28, no. 6, 2005: 1005–1032.

Greenberg, Andy, *Sandworm: A New Era of Cyberwar and the Hunt for the Kremlin's Most Dangerous Hackers*, New York: Anchor, 2020.

Greenberg, Andy, 'The Untold Story of NotPetya, the Most Devastating Cyberattack in History,' *Wired*, 22 August 2018.

Greene, Joshua, *Justice at Dachau: The Trials of an American Prosecutor*, New York: Broadway Books, 2003.

Gump, James O., *The Dust Rose Like Smoke: The Subjugation of the Zulu and the Sioux*, Lincoln, NE: University of Nebraska Press, 2016.

Gunneflo, Markus, *Targeted Killings: A Legal and Political History*, Cambridge: Cambridge University Press, 2016.

Hathaway, Oona, and Shapiro, Scott, *The Internationalists: How a Radical Plan to Outlaw War Remade the World*, New York: Simon & Schuster, 2017.

Hayner, Priscilla B., *Unspeakable Truths: Transitional Justice and the Challenge of Truth Commissions*, Abingdon, Oxfordshire: Routledge, 2009.

Hazan, Pierre, *Justice in a Time of War: The True Story Behind the International Criminal Tribunal for the Former Yugoslavia*, College Station, TX: Texas A&M University Press, 2004.

Heberer, Patricia, 'The American Military Commission Trials of 1945,' in Stoltzfus, Nathan, and Friedlander, Henry, eds., *Nazi Crimes and the Law*, Washington, DC: German Historical Institute, 2008: 43–62.

Heberer, Patricia, and Matthäus, Jürgen, eds., *Atrocities on Trial: Historical Perspectives on the Politics of Prosecuting War Crimes*, Lincoln, NE: University of Nebraska Press, 2008.

Hebert, Valerie, *Hitler's Generals on Trial: The Last War Crimes Tribunal at Nuremberg*, Lawrence, KS: University of Kansas Press, 2010.

Heller, Kevin Jon, *The Nuremberg Military Tribunal and the Origins of International Criminal Law*, New York: Oxford University Press, 2011.

Heller, Kevin Jon, and Simpson, Gerry, eds., *The Hidden Histories of War Crimes Trials*, New York: Oxford University Press, 2013.

Henry, Nicola, 'Memory of an Injustice: The "Comfort Women" and the Legacy of the Tokyo Trial,' *Asian Studies Review*, vol. 37, no. 3, 2013: 362–380.

Herf, Jeffrey, *Divided Memory: The Nazi Past in the Two Germanys*, Cambridge, MA: Harvard University Press, 1997.

Herf, Jeffrey, *Undeclared Wars With Israel: East Germany and the West German Far Left, 1967–1989*, Cambridge: Cambridge University Press, 2016.

Hicks, Dan, *The Brutish Museums: The Benin Bronzes, Colonial Violence and Cultural Restitution*, London: Pluto, 2020.

Hicks, George L., *The Comfort Women: Japan's Brutal Regime of Enforced Prostitution in the Second World War*, New York: W.W. Norton & Co., 1995.

Higgins, Eliot, *We Are Bellingcat: Global Crime, Online Sleuths, and the Bold Future of News*, London: Bloomsbury, 2021.

Higgins, Polly, *Eradicating Ecocide: Laws and Governance to Prevent the Destruction of Our Planet*, London: Shepheard-Walwyn Ltd, 2010.

Hirsch, Francine, *Soviet Judgment at Nuremberg: A New History of International Military Tribunal After World War II*, New York: Oxford University Press, 2020.

Holbrooke, Richard, *To End a War: The Conflict in Yugoslavia-America's Inside Story-Negotiating With Milosevic*, New York: Modern Library, 1999.

Horne, John, and Kramer, Alan, *German Atrocities, 1914: A History of Denial*, New Haven, CT: Yale University Press, 2001.

Howard, Douglas A., *A History of the Ottoman Empire*, Cambridge: Cambridge University Press, 2017.

Hughes, Judith M., *The Perversion of Holocaust Memory: Writing and Rewriting the Past After 1989*, London: Bloomsbury Academic, 2022.

Hull, Isabel, *Absolute Destruction: Military Culture and the Practices of War in Imperial Germany*, Ithaca, NY: Cornell University Press, 2006.

Hull, Isabel, *A Scrap of Paper: Breaking and Making International Law During the Great War*, Ithaca, NY: Cornell University Press, 2019.

Hunt, Lynn, *Inventing Human Rights: A History*, New York: W.W. Norton & Co., 2008.

Hutchinson, Robert, *After Nuremberg: American Clemency for Nazi War Criminals*, New Haven, CT: Yale University Press, 2022.

International Committee of the Red Cross, *The Montreux Document on the Pertinent International Legal Obligations and Good Practices by States related to Operations of Private Military and Security Companies During Armed Conflict*, Geneva: International Committee of the Red Cross, 2009.

Jalloh, Charles C., and Ilias Bantekas, eds., *The International Criminal Court and Africa*, New York: Oxford University Press, 2017.

James, Lawrence, *The Savage Wars. British Campaigns in Africa, 1870–1920*, New York: St. Martins, 1985.

Jardim, Tomaz, *The Mauthausen Trial: American Military Justice in Germany*, Cambridge, MA: Harvard University Press, 2012.

Judah, Tim, *The Serbs: History, Myth and the Destruction of Yugoslavia*, New Haven, CT: Yale University Press, 1997.

Judt, Tony, *Postwar: A History of Europe Since 1945*, New York: Penguin Press, 2005.

Kennedy, David, *Of Law and War*, Princeton, NJ: Princeton University Press, 2006.

Kevorkian, Raymond, *The Armenian Genocide: A Complete History*, London: I.B. Tauris, 2011.

Kiernan, Ben, *Genocide and Resistance in Southeast Asia: Documentation, Denial, and Justice in Cambodia and East Timor*, Abingdon, Oxfordshire: Routledge, 2007.

Kiernan, Ben, *Blood and Soil: A World History of Genocide and Extermination From Sparta to Darfur*, New Haven, CT: Yale University Press, 2009.

Kittrie, Orde F., *Lawfare: Law as a Weapon of War*, New York: Oxford University Press, 2016.

Knop, Karen, and Riles, Annelise, 'Space, Time, and Historical Injustice: A Feminist Conflict-of-Laws Approach to the Comfort Women Agreement,' *Cornell Law Review*, vol. 102, no. 4, 2017: 853–928.

Kochavi, Arieh J., *Prelude to Nuremberg: Allied War Crimes Policy and the Question of Punishment*, Chapel Hill, NC: University of North Carolina Press, 1998.

Koenig, Alexa, Irving, Emma, McDermott, Yvonne, and Murray, Daragh, 'New Technologies and the Investigation of International Crimes,' *Journal of International Criminal Justice*, vol. 19, 2021: 1–7.

Kössler, Reinhart, *Namibia and Germany: Negotiating the Past*, Windhoek, Namibia: University of Namibia, 2015.

Kramer, Alan, 'The First Wave of International War Crimes Trials: Istanbul and Leipzig,' *European Review*, vol. 14, no. 4, 2006: 441–455.

Kreike, Emmanuel, 'Genocide in the Kampongs? Dutch nineteenth century colonial warfare in Aceh, Sumatra,' *Journal of Genocide Research*, vol. 14, nos. 3–4, 2012: 297–315.

Kreike, Emmanuel, *Scorched Earth: Environmental Warfare as a Crime Against Humanity and Nature*, Princeton, NJ: Princeton University Press, 2021.

Kushner, Barak, *The Dismantling of Japan's Empire in East Asia: Deimperialization, Postwar Legitimation and Imperial Afterlife*, Abingdon, Oxfordshire: Routledge, 2018.

Kushner, Barak, *Men to Devils, Devils to Men: Japanese War Crimes and Chinese Justice*, Cambridge, MA: Harvard University Press, 2015.

Lamb, Christina, *Our Bodies, Their Battlefields: War Through the Lives of Women*, New York: Scribner, 2020.

Lannon, John, and Halpin, Edward F., eds., *Human Rights and Information and Communications Technologies: Trends and Consequences of Use*, Hershey, PA: Information Science Reference, 2013.

Large, Stephen, 'Far East War Crimes Trials,' in Dear, I. C. B., ed., *The Oxford Companion to World War II*, New York: Oxford University Press, 1995: 347–51.

Lawson, Tom, *Debates on the Holocaust*, Manchester: Manchester University Press, 2010.

Lemkin, Raphael, 'Genocide,' *The American Scholar*, vol. 15, no. 2, Spring 1946: 227–230.

Lemkin, Raphael, *Axis Rule in Occupied Europe: Laws of Occupation, Analysis of Government, Proposals for Redress*, Clark, NJ: The Lawbook Exchange, Ltd., 1944/2005.

Lewis, Michael W., ed., *The War on Terror and the Laws of War*, Oxford: Oxford University Press, 2009.

Lipstadt, Deborah E., *The Eichmann Trial*, New York: Schocken, 2011.

Lowe, Keith, *Savage Continent: Europe in the Aftermath of World War II*, New York, NY: St. Martin's, 2012.

Lower, Wendy, *Hitler's Furies: German Women in the Nazi Killing Fields*, Boston, MA: Mariner Books, 2013.

Luttikhuis, Bart, and Moses, A. Dirk, eds., *Colonial Counterinsurgency and Mass Violence: The Dutch Empire in Indonesia*, Abingdon, Oxfordshire: Routledge, 2014.

Maguire, Peter, *Law and War: An American Story*, New York: Columbia University Press, 2002.

Maguire, Peter, *Facing Death in Cambodia*, New York: Columbia University Press, 2005.

Malu, Linus Nnabuike, *The International Criminal Court and Peace Processes: Côte d'Ivoire, Kenya and Uganda*, London: Palgrave Macmillan, 2019.

Malu, Linus Nnabuike, *Transitional Justice in West Africa*, Abingdon, Oxfordshire: Routledge, 2022.

Mamdani, Mahmood, *When Victims Become Killers: Colonialism, Nativism, and the Genocide in Rwanda*, Princeton, NJ: Princeton University Press, 2020.

May, Larry, and Forcehimes, Andrew, eds., *Morality, Jus Post Bellum, and International Law*, Cambridge: Cambridge University Press, 2012.

Mazower, Mark, *Governing the World: The History of an Idea, 1815 to the Present*, New York: Penguin Books, 2013.

McDermott, Yvonne, Koenig, Alexa, and Murray, Daragh, 'Open Source Information's Blind Spot: Human and Machine Bias in International Criminal Investigations,' *Journal of International Criminal Justice*, vol. 19, 2021: 85–105.

McElwee, Pamela. 'The Origins of Ecocide: Revisiting the Ho Chi Minh Trail in the Vietnam War,' *Arcadia*, no. 20, Spring 2020.

McFate, Sean, *The Modern Mercenary: Private Armies and What They Mean for World Order*, New York: Oxford University Press, 2017.

McFate, Sean, *Mercenaries and War: Understanding Private Armies Today*, Washington, DC: National Defense University Press, 2019.

Meron, Theodor, *Human Rights in International Law: Legal and Policy Issues*, Oxford: Oxford University Press, 1986.

Meron, Thedor, *War Crimes Law Comes of Age: Essays*, London: Clarendon Press, 1999.

Meron, Theodor, *The Making of International Criminal Justice: The View From the Bench: Selected Speeches*, Oxford: Oxford University Press, 2011.

Meron, Theodor, *Standing Up for Justice: The Challenges of Trying Atrocity Crimes*, New York: Oxford University Press, 2021.

Mettraux, Geunael, ed., *Perspectives on the Nuremberg Trial*, New York: Oxford University Press, 2008.

Michael Howard, George J. Andreopoulos, and Mark R. Shulman, eds., *The Laws of War. Constraints on Warfare in the Western World*, New Haven, CT: Yale University Press, 1994.

Miller, Phil, *Keenie Meenie: The British Mercenaries Who Got Away With War Crimes*, London: Pluto Press, 2020.

Moeller, Robert G., *War Stories: The Search for a Usable Past in the Federal Republic of Germany*, Berkeley, CA: University of California Press, 2001.

Morris, Benny, and Dror, Ze'evi, *The Thirty-Year Genocide: Turkey's Destruction of Its Christian Minorities, 1894–1924*, Cambridge, MA: Harvard University Press, 2019.

Morrison, Alexander, *The Russian Conquest of Central Asia: A Study in Imperial Expansion, 1814–1914*, Cambridge: Cambridge University Press, 2021.

Moses, A. Dirk, *Empire, Colony, Genocide: Conquest, Occupation, and Subaltern Resistance in World History*, Providence, RI: Berghahn Books, 2009.

Moses, A. Dirk, *The Problems of Genocide: Permanent Security and the Language of Transgression*, Cambridge: Cambridge University Press, 2021.

Moyn, Samuel, *The Last Utopia: Human Rights in History*, Cambridge, MA: The Belknap Press of Harvard University Press, 2012.

Muehlhaeuser, Regina, 'Reframing Sexual Violence as a Weapon and Strategy of War: The Case of the German Wehrmacht During the War and Genocide in the Soviet Union, 1941–1944,' *Journal of the History of Sexuality*, vol. 26, no. 3, 2017: 366–401.

Muehlhaeuser, Regina, and Spengler, Jessica, *Sex and the Nazi Soldier: Violent, Commercial and Consensual Encounters During the War in the Soviet Union, 1941–45*, Edinburgh: Edinburgh University Press, 2022.

Mulligan, William, Rose, Andreas, and Geppert, Dominik, eds., *The Wars Before the Great War: Conflict and International Politics Before the Outbreak of the First World War*, Cambridge: Cambridge University Press, 2015.

Murphy, John F., *The United States and the Rule of Law in International Affairs*, Cambridge: Cambridge University Press, 2004.

Myers, R. H., and Peattie, M. R., eds., *The Japanese Colonial Empire, 1895–1945*, Princeton, NJ: Princeton University Press, 1987.

Naimark, Norman, *The Russians in Germany: A History of the Soviet Zone of Occupation, 1945–1949*, Cambridge, MA: The Belknap Press of Harvard University Press, 1995.

Naimark, Norman, *Genocide: A New History*, New York: Oxford University Press, 2016.

Neff, Stephen C., *War and the Law of Nations: A General History*, Cambridge: Cambridge University Press, 2008.

Neier, Aryeh, *War Crimes: Brutality, Genocide, Terror and the Struggle for Justice*, New York: Times Books, 1998.

Neiman, Susan, *Learning From the Germans: Race and the Memory of Evil*, New York: Farrar, Straus and Giroux, 2019.

Osiel, M., *Mass Atrocity, Collective Memory and the Law*, New Brunswick, NJ/London: Transaction Publishers, 2000.

O'Toole, Fintan, 'Our Hypocrisy on War Crimes,' *New York Review of Books*, 26 May 2022.

Overy, Richard, *Blood and Ruins: The Last Imperial War, 1931–1945*, New York: Viking, 2022.

Pedersen, Susan, *The Guardians: The League of Nations and the Crisis of Empire*, New York: Oxford University Press, 2017.

Peers, Douglas M., *India Under Colonial Rule: 1700–1885*, Abingdon, Oxfordshire: Routledge, 2013.

Pendas, Devin O., 'Seeking Justice, Finding Law: Nazi Trials in Postwar Europe,' *The Journal of Modern History*, vol. 81, 2008: 347–368.

Pendas, Devin O., *The Frankfurt Auschwitz Trial, 1963–1965: Genocide, History, and the Limits of the Law*, New York, NY: Cambridge University Press, 2010.

Percy, Sarah, *Mercenaries: The History of a Norm in International Relations*, New York, NY: Oxford University Press, 2007.

Peto, Andrea, and Barna, Ildiko, *Political Justice in Budapest After World War II*, Budapest: Central European University Press, 2015.

Phillips, Barnaby, *Loot: Britain and the Benin Bronzes*, London: Oneworld, 2021.

Platt, Stephen R., *Imperial Twilight: The Opium War and the End of China's Last Golden Age*, New York: Vintage, 2019.

Plesch, Dan, *Human Rights After Hitler: The Lost History of Prosecuting Axis War Crimes*, Washington, DC: Georgetown University Press, 2017.

Power, Samantha, *"A Problem From Hell": America and the Age of Genocide*, New York: Basic Books, 2002.

Prescott, Jody, 'Military Commissions, Past and Future,' *Military Review*, March–April 2003: 42–51.

Priemel, Kim, and Stiller, Alexa, eds., *Unearthing the Subsequent Nuremberg Trials: Transitional Justice, Trial Narratives, and Historiography*, Providence, RI: Berghahn Books, 2012.

Prusin, Alexander V., ' "Fascist Criminals to the Gallows!": The Holocaust and Soviet War Crimes Trials, December 1945-February 1946,' *Holocaust and Genocide Studies*, vol. 17, no. 1, 2003: 1–30.

Quinn, Frederick, *The French Overseas Empire*, Westport, CT: Praeger, 2001.

Rabinovich, Itamar, and Valensi, Carmit, *Syrian Requiem: The Civil War and Its Aftermath*, Princeton, NJ: Princeton University Press, 2021.

Rankin, Melinda, 'The Future of International Criminal Evidence in New Wars? The Evolution of the Commission for International Justice and Accountability (CIJA),' *Journal of Genocide Research*, vol. 20, no. 3, 2018: 392–411.

Remy, Steven P., *The Malmedy Massacre: The War Crimes Trial Controversy*, Cambridge, MA: Harvard University Press, 2017.

Rieff, David, *In Praise of Forgetting: Historical Memory and Its Ironies*, New Haven, CT: Yale University Press, 2016.

Roberts, Mary Louise, *What Soldiers Do: Sex and the American GI in World War II France*, Chicago, IL: University of Chicago Press, 2013.

Roht-Arrazia, Naomi, *The Pinochet Effect: Transnational Justice in the Age of Human Rights*, Philadelphia, PA: University of Pennsylvania Press, 2005.

Ryan, Allan A., *Yamashita's Ghost: War Crimes, MacArthur's Justice, and Command Accountability*, Lawrence, KS: University Press of Kansas, 2012.

Sakamoto, Rumi, 'The Women's International War Crimes Tribunal on Japan's Military Sexual Slavery: A Legal and Feminist Approach to the 'Comfort Women' Issue,' *New Zealand Journal of Asian Studies*, vol. 3, no. 1, 2001: 49–58.

Sarat, Austin, Douglas, Lawrence, and Umphrey, Martha Merrill, eds., *Law and War*, Stanford, CA: Stanford University Press, 2014.

Sarkin-Hughes, Jeremy, *Colonial Genocide and Reparations Claims in the 21st Century: The Socio-legal Context of Claims Under International Law by the Herero Against Germany for Genocide in Namibia, 1904–1908*, Westport, CT: Praeger Security International, 2009.

Scahill, Jeremy, *Blackwater: The Rise of the World's Most Powerful Mercenary Army*, New York, NY: Bold Type Books, 2007.

Schabas, William, *The Trial of the Kaiser*, New York: Oxford University Press, 2018.

Schabas, William, *An Introduction to the International Criminal Court*, Cambridge: Cambridge University Press, 2020.

Scheffer, David, *All the Missing Souls: A Personal History of the War Crimes Tribunals*, Princeton, NJ: Princeton University Press, 2011.

Shirane, Seiji, *Imperial Gateway: Colonial Taiwan and Japan's Expansion in South China and Southeast Asia, 1895–1945*, Ithaca, NY: Cornell University Press, 2022.

Silbey, David, *The Boxer Rebellion and the Great Game in China: A History*, New York: Hill and Wang, 2013.

Singer, P. W., *Corporate Warriors: The Rise of the Privatized Military Industry*, Ithaca, NY: Cornell University Press, 2007.

Smeulers, Alette, 'Female Perpetrators: Ordinary or Extra-Ordinary Woman?' *International Criminal Law Review*, vol. 15, 2015: 207–253.

Smith, Bradley D., *The American Road to Nuremberg: The Documentary Record, 1944–1945*, Stanford, CA: University of California Press, 1982.

Soh, C. Sarah, *The Comfort Women: Sexual Violence and Postcolonial Memory in Korea and Japan*, Chicago, IL: University of Chicago Press, 2009.

Solis, Gary D., *The Law of Armed Conflict: International Humanitarian Law in War*, Cambridge: Cambridge University Press, 2022.

Spector, Ronald, *A Continent Erupts: Decolonization, Civil War, and Massacre in Postwar Asia, 1945–1955*, New York: W. W. Norton & Co., 2022.

Steflja, Izabela, and Darden, Jessica Trisko, *Women as War Criminals: Gender, Agency, and Justice*, Stanford, CA: Stanford University Press, 2020.

Stover, Eric, Peskin, Victor, and Koenig, Alexa, *Hiding in Plain Sight: The Pursuit of War Criminals From Nuremberg to the War on Terror*, Oakland, CA: University of California Press, 2016.

Stone, Dan, *The Historiography of the Holocaust*, London: Palgrave Macmillan, 2004.

Strachan, Hew, *The First World War*, New York: Penguin Books, 2005.

Strang, G. Bruce, *Collision of Empires: Italy's Invasion of Ethiopia and Its International Impact*, Abingdon, Oxfordshire: Routledge, 2013.

Suny, Ronald Gregor, *They Can Live in the Desert but Nowhere Else: A History of the Armenian Genocide*, Princeton, NJ: Princeton University Press, 2015.

Tanaka, Yuki, *Hidden Horrors: Japanese War Crimes in World War II*, Boulder, CO: Westview, 1996.

Tanaka, Yuki, McCormack, Tim, and Simpson, Gerry, eds., *Beyond Victor's Justice? The Tokyo War Crimes Revisited*, Leiden, Netherlands: Martinus Nijhoff, 2011.
Taylor, Frederick, *Exorcising Hitler: The Occupation and Denazification of Germany*, London: Bloomsbury Press, 2011.
Taylor, Telford D., *The Anatomy of the Nuremberg Trials: A Personal Memoir*, New York: Knopf, 1992.
Thomson, Janice E., *Mercenaries, Pirates, and Sovereigns*, Princeton, NJ: Princeton University Press, 1996.
Uchida, Jun, *Brokers of Empire: Japanese Settler Colonialism in Korea, 1876–1945*, Cambridge, MA: Harvard University Asia Center, 2014.
United Nations General Assembly, Resolution 260 A (III) of 9 December 1948, "Convention on the Prevention and Punishment of the Crime of Genocide".
United Nations General Assembly, Security Council, Report of the Secretary General, *Prioritizing Prevention and Strengthening Response: Women and the Responsibility to Protect*, 2020.
United Nations War Crimes Commission (UNWCC), *History of the United Nations War Crimes Commission and the Development of the Laws of War*, London: United Nations War Crimes Commission, 1948.
Urban, William, *Medieval Mercenaries: The Business of War*, Barnsley: Frontline Books, 2015.
Vagts, Detlev, Meron, Theodor, Schwebel, Stephen M., and Keever, Charles, eds., *Humanizing the Laws of War: Selected Writings of Richard Baxter*, New York: Oxford University Press, 2013.
Vandervort, Bruce, *Indian Wars of Canada, Mexico and the United States, 1812–1900*, Abingdon, Oxfordshire: Routledge, 2005.
Vandervort, Bruce, *Wars of Imperial Conquest in Africa, 1830—1914*, Bloomington, IN: Indiana University Press, 2009.
Von Lingen, Kerstin, *Kesselring's Last Battle: War Crimes Trials and Cold War Politics, 1945–1960*, Lawrence, KS: University Press of Kansas, 2009.
Wakeling, A., *Stern Justice: The Forgotten Story of Australia, Japan and the Pacific War Crimes Trials*, Sydney: Penguin Random House Australia, 2019.
Walter, Dierk, *Colonial Violence: European Empires and the Use of Force*, New York: Oxford University Press, 2017.
Watkins, John C., and Weber, John Paul, *War Crimes and War Crime Trials: From Leipzig to the ICC and Beyond: Cases, Materials and Comments*, Durham, NC: Carolina Academic Press, 2005.
Weinke, Annette, Law, *History, and Justice: Debating German State Crimes in the Long Twentieth Century*, Providence, RI: Berghahn Books, 2018.
Wesseling, H. L., *The European Colonial Empires: 1815–1919*, Abingdon, Oxfordshire: Routledge, 2004.
Westad, Odd Arne, *The Global Cold War: Third World Interventions and the Making of Our Times*, Cambridge: Cambridge University Press, 2011.
Westermann, Edward B., *Hitler's Ostkrieg and the Indian Wars: Comparing Genocide and Conquest*, Norman, OK: University of Oklahoma Press, 2016.
Willis, James F., *Prologue to Nuremberg: The Politics and Diplomacy of Punishing War Criminals of the First World War*, Westport, CT/London: Greenwood Press, 1982.
Wilson, Sandra, Cribb, Robert, Trefalt, Beatrice, and Aszkielowicz, *Japanese War Criminals: The Politics of Justice After the Second World War*, New York: Columbia University Press, 2017.

Witt, John Fabian, *Lincoln's Code: The Laws of War in American History*, New York: Free Press, 2013.

Wittes, Benjamin, *Law and the Long War: The Future of Justice in the Age of Terror*, New York: Penguin, 2008.

Wittes, Benjamin, and Blum, Gabriella, *The Future of Violence: Robots and Germs, Hackers and Drones*, New York: Basic Books, 2015.

Zaalberg, Thijs Brocades, and Luttikhuis, Bart, eds., *Empire's Violent End: Comparing Dutch, British, and French Wars of Decolonization, 1945–1962*, Ithaca, NY: Cornell University Press, 2022.

Zarmsky, Sara, 'Why Seeing Should Not Always Be Believing: Considerations Regarding the Use of Digital Reconstruction Technology in International Law,' *Journal of International Criminal Justice*, vol. 19, 2021: 213–225.

Zimmerer, Jürgen, *German Rule, African Subjects: State Aspirations and the Reality of Power in Colonial Namibia*, Providence, RI: Berghahn Books, 2021.

# Index

For Product Safety Concerns and Information please contact our EU representative GPSR@taylorandfrancis.com
Taylor & Francis Verlag GmbH, Kaufingerstraße 24, 80331 München, Germany

www.ingramcontent.com/pod-product-compliance
Ingram Content Group UK Ltd.
Pitfield, Milton Keynes, MK11 3LW, UK
UKHW020005200926
475702UK00015B/2483
* 9 7 8 0 3 6 7 6 3 2 9 2 2 *